The global politics of power, justice and death

This exciting new text adopts a challenging question-led approach to the major issues facing global society today, in order to investigate the nature and complexity of global change. Among other things it looks at the future of the state, the environment, the international political economy, war and global rivalries, and the role of international law and the UN in the post-Cold War world.

The book devises a readily comprehensible 'Change Map', which both incorporates a wide range of the fundamental concepts of international relations theory and suggests a number of new concepts capable of assisting the investigation of global change. This new framework is deployed to look closely at real world issues in order to isolate the crucial factors which determine whether or not mass hunger, for example, or environmental abuse, can be eliminated.

Students of International Relations and International Politics will find this a stimulating and provocative introduction to a fascinating subject.

Peter J. Anderson is a Senior Lecturer in European and International Studies, University of Central Lancashire.

The global politics of power, justice and death

An introduction to international relations

Peter J. Anderson

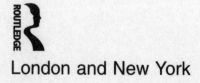

London and New York

First published 1996
by Routledge
11 New Fetter Lane, London EC4P 4EE

Simultaneously published in the USA and Canada
by Routledge
29 West 35th Street, New York, NY 10001

Routledge is an International Thomson Publishing company

Typeset in Bembo and Helvetica by
Keystroke, Jacaranda Lodge, Wolverhampton
Printed and bound in Great Britain by
Clays Ltd, St Ives PLC

British Library Cataloguing in Publication Data
A catalogue record for this book is available from the British Library

Library of Congress Cataloguing in Publication Data
A catalogue record for this book has been requested

ISBN 0–415–10945–0 (hbk)

ISBN 0–415–10946–9 (pbk)

This book is dedicated with thanks to my parents,
Mary and Thomas Anderson,
to my godchildren, David Anderson and Elizabeth Ford,
and to the memory of Olga Néokle.

Contents

4 The second challenge:
the threats to the state from scientific, technological
and cultural aspects of global interfusion   **72**

5 Global environmental problems   **82**

6 The political economy of death:
what causes global poverty?   **108**

Preface

This is a text which is designed to be readily accessible to new students of international relations. However those readers who are not greatly familiar with the history of global politics during the twentieth century might find it useful to read this book in conjunction with such texts as Peter Calvocoressi's *World Politics Since 1945* and Paul Kennedy's rather more advanced *The Rise and Fall of the Great Powers*, full details of which are provided in the bibliography at the end.

Acknowledgements

The author wishes to acknowledge the financial assistance provided by the Research Committee of the University of Central Lancashire and the Department of Politics and European Studies of the same, without which this project could not have been completed on time. Thanks are due also to Alastair Thomas, Terry Hopton, Alex Thompson and Frands Pedersen of the University of Central Lancashire for helpful comments on sections of the draft, and to Routledge for its encouragement of the project throughout. Acknowledgement is made also of the substantial contribution made to Chapter 12 by Steven Wheatley of the University of Central Lancashire. All of the legal sections of that chapter were written by him.

List of extracts

Chapter 1

A game beyond chess:
explaining the Global Change Map

Introduction

International politics can be seen as a special kind of game, one that frequently is deadly in its consequences. The key players *generally* are relatively few in number, but on *some* issues it is possible for entire populations to have a role to play. Sometimes that role can be very direct and influential, as in the case of the referendums held in France, Denmark and Ireland during 1992 on the question of whether or not to implement the Treaty on European Union (or the later referendums held within several new applicants to the EU on the question of whether or not they should join). In some circumstances, as in the case of nuclear war, that role can be simply to die.

The most commonly used analogy that has been drawn is between global politics and the game of chess. This is a poor image to use, because it suggests that strategy and calculation are all-important. The reality is that chance also plays a substantial role, and an awareness of that fact has to be built into any attempt to understand the complexities of international relations.

This is a book which is centred around the theme of change in global politics. It adopts a question-led approach to analyse what are widely accepted to be some of the major issues facing global society today. In some cases it examines the causes of past changes which have affected the evolution of those issues or set the agenda which presently surrounds them, and in others it assesses how likely it is that substantial further changes – for good or for ill – will affect those issues during the foreseeable future. In order to do this, it devises and applies a readily comprehensible 'Change Map'. This isolates the crucial factors which determine whether or not the appalling phenomenon of mass hunger, for example, or the dangers from continuing environmental abuse, can be eliminated. Several chapters attempt to determine some of the key ways in which a selection of those factors would have to interrelate in order for remedial change to have a chance of occurring. This means that, to some extent, the book shows what the solutions to some worrying global problems might be. What it can not do of course is guarantee that those solutions will be produced in the real world. Among other things, as implied above, any 'change equation' is complicated by the omnipresent element of chance, and that in itself can always make nonsense of even the most well-reasoned of predictions in international relations. As will be seen from the diagram, in recognition of this fact, chance is built into the heart of the Change Map.

It is important to emphasise that it is not claimed that the map offered here is the only useful way in which change in global politics can be conceptualised. There has been a long and varied debate as to how such a task might best be performed with no overall consensus emerging to resolve the matter. A number of interesting entry-level texts on that debate exist, such as Charles Kegley and Eugene Witkopf's *World Politics: Trend and Transformation* (New York, St Martin's Press, 1993). An example of a rather more sophisticated analysis is set out in Anthony McGrew and Paul Lewis *et al.'s Global Politics* (Cambridge, Polity Press, 1992). In addition, Charles Hermann has produced some extremely interesting thoughts on change at the foreign policy level ('Changing Course: When Governments Choose to Redirect Foreign Policy', *International Studies Quarterly*, 1990, vol. 34, no. 2, pp. 3–21).

The intention here is not to engage directly in the cut and thrust of the debate as such, although small skirmishes will be entered into with regard to such matters as globalisation, but rather simply to put forward for consideration a framework for thinking about global change which this author believes to be easy to use and highly effective. The primary intention is to provide a worthwhile addition to the frameworks available within the literature, rather than to try and resolve the apparently irresolvable in the form of the great debate itself, and to do so in a manner which is comprehensible to and stimulating for those who are new to the subject.

Inevitably, the framework used here has to simplify the 'real world' to an extent in order to make analysis of it manageable. Business, technical and cultural elites, for example, are split into many more subdivisions elsewhere in the literature than are used in this study. But it is the contention of this book that the simplifications that have been employed are capable of combining manageability with effective analysis of global politics. The chapters which follow will be the evidence which enables the reader to decide whether or not this is a fair judgement.

The degree to which global and regional change is possible is affected by any of the factors shown below, either in isolation or (most often) interaction:

The outcome of **competition** *between the holders of any of the differing views listed below* [1] *that occurs,* **via power and influence,** *at one or more of the following: the intra-state, transnational,*[2] *transgovernmental* [3] *and intergovernmental levels.*

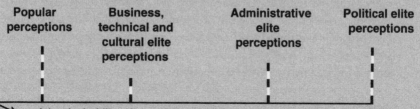

| Popular perceptions | Business, technical and cultural elite perceptions | Administrative elite perceptions | Political elite perceptions |

of the desirability of specific goals that may require, unintentionally cause or preclude change at the global and/or regional levels [4]

These in turn are affected by:

Ideologies   **Interests**   **Imperatives**

The extent to which compettition can occur can be crucially affected by the **type(s) of political system** within and between which it is conducted

Fortune - this can be defined as the in many ways unpredictable interplay of natural events, complex group and individual interests, emotions and concerns within the global arena

Opportunity Factors - these can be defined as those things which instantly or incrementally greatly alter popular and elite perceptions of the world and make it easier to introduce significant changes. Such factors include **modernisation, global interfusion, economic growth, economic stagnation/decline, wars, environmental crises, government personnel changes, revolutions and coups, the evolution of ideas, and policy changes of state governments, multinational corporations etc. (which might result from one or more of the preceding opportunity factors) which are perceived by the populations/elites of other states as having major implications for them.** This list is not exhaustive.

ALL of these can act as **Blocking Factors.** These are factors which, through their impact on populations/elites within states, can obstruct or eliminate government or other elite policy alternatives that otherwise would be available.

1) It is theoretically possible for no differences to occur between any of these views, but the author's own experience in policy research suggests that there will nearly always at least be differences of degree.
2) This term here refers to relations between non-governmental actors, such as business corporations, across state boundaries.
3) This term here refers to relations between government bureaucracies across state boundaries.
4) Most of these can include various interest group perceptions.

PLAYING THE GAME – THE GLOBAL CHANGE MAP

Competition in global politics

The purpose of this chapter is to set down a portrait of how the game of international relations can be played via the device of the Change Map. The latter will be explained from top to bottom, given that this would seem to be the most logical way to approach matters.

Wars, trade deals, economic sanctions, the size of financial transfers between rich and poor states, are all the outcome of competition between and within elites,[1] and sometimes between elites and the wider populations around them. This process of competition can occur within states, between states and across states. Within the United States, for example, the North American Free Trade Association, which was set up in 1993, provoked fierce battles between sections of the Congress that supported NAFTA and sections that opposed it, between various government departments with different interests in the deal that was being struck, and between sections of the business elite that supported the deal and sections that opposed it. There was also strong pressure on Congress and the presidency from labour unions that felt that NAFTA would result in the loss of thousands of jobs in the USA, together with the mounting of a large-scale carrot-and-stick campaign by the President in order to persuade men and women in Congress to support the deal. In addition, the President did his utmost to persuade the wider electorate to support NAFTA for the simple reason that he needed to retain their support if he was to have a chance of winning the next election. The Congressional vote that finally authorised the deal was therefore the result of sustained and large-scale competition between a range of key business and political elites, with the additional involvement of American workers via their trade union representatives. All of this is an example obviously of competition between different elites and also sections of the wider population *within states*.

The 1993 GATT negotiation on the expansion of global free trade arrangements was a good example of competition between the elites and sections of the wider populations within several states, *and* of competition *between* them and the elites and sections of the wider populations in *other* states, a competition *which was conducted mainly through state governments as the primary external representatives of internal interests*. The European Union's common agricultural policy, for example, was a major source of disagreement between the Union and the United States, and to a lesser extent, between various states actually within the EU. Wider public opinion in the form of farmers' lobbies in both the USA and France strongly lobbied the political elites within their respective states to try and ensure that their particular aims were secured. Equally, those elites tried to compete with and modify the perceptions and demands of their farmers. The GATT farm deal ultimately was to a significant extent a result of competition between these groups *within* the two states, and between their views *as represented externally by the governments* of those two states (the USA independently, and France within the EU framework).

Wars are another example of competition centred around specific policy goals that is conducted via the governments of states with the external role of wider populations traditionally mainly restricted to that of cannon-fodder.

An example of competition between elite perceptions conducted *across* state boundaries, where groups *other than governments* are the main agents of that competition, might include the activities of multinational business corporations. These are firms that produce goods and services in several states (a fuller definition will be offered in Chapter 3). Where the elite in charge of a German corporation perceives that its interests require it to set the latter the goal of securing the largest share of the EU market for cars, and that in charge of an Italian rival decides that this is undesirable, given that it wants that share itself, obviously the stage is set for competition between the holders of those perceptions. One might decide to export key parts of its manufacturing activities to a low-wage Eastern European economy in order to undercut its competitor in price and thereby gain that share. The other then probably will be forced to follow suit. Such moves, if they were imitated by a sufficient number of additional corporations, could push unemployment in the states losing jobs to levels where political and social stability became threatened. The destabilisation of a major state such as Germany would obviously change the global security environment considerably.

The competing attitudes and perceptions of political elites, administrative elites, business, technical and cultural elites and the wider population with regard to the desirability of specific goals that may affect global change – the battle for dominance

The terms 'popular attitudes and perceptions',[2] 'business, technical and cultural elite attitudes and perceptions', 'administrative elite attitudes and perceptions' and 'political elite attitudes and perceptions' are intended to reflect the reality which underlies the above examples of competition. How members of each of these broad groups see particular issues and their interests within them, together with the competition which occurs between members of the groups in order to try and ensure that their particular interests are reflected in government policy, is crucial within democratic societies. Such competition can also be important in authoritarian societies, although the degree to which it is allowed to operate will depend obviously on the extent to which the particular authoritarian government in question will allow it to. Equally, as has been shown above, the competition that occurs between such groups across and between state boundaries can be highly important with regard to global change, affecting the shape of anything from the international economic system (e.g., the GATT and NAFTA negotiations) to key regional security systems (as was shown with regard to Germany).

The term 'popular perceptions' of the desirability or otherwise of specific goals which can affect the possibility of global or regional change refers here to the views of populations or non-elite sections of populations[3] (including non-elite members of interest groups) on such goals which political, business, technical, cultural or administrative elites become aware of and which they regard, or are forced to regard, as significant. For political elites, for example, such views may be seen as being significant because they are believed to be relevant electorally within democratic societies, or because they might be seen as potentially threatening to the stability of the state in either democratic or authoritarian societies, or because a particular political elite might believe that popular attitudes can be harnessed or manipulated for revolutionary purposes. In the democratic society of France, for example, the attitudes of French farmers to agricultural reform in general – and their perceptions of the implications of any new proposed specific reform measures – are regarded as of high significance by French governments because, among other things, of the effectiveness of farmers as an interest group and their preparedness to take highly disruptive direct action in support of their interests. Similarly, it has been argued frequently that one of the main reasons why the authoritarian Argentine military junta invaded the British-run Falkland/Malvinas Islands in 1982 was to try and defuse growing popular hostility to its failed economic policies by means of an inspiring nationalist adventure.

During the French referendum of 1992 on the Maastricht Treaty on European Union, the pro-European sections of the political elite found themselves in direct competition with the large section of the French electorate which opposed the treaty. To an even more marked extent, the Danish government found itself in the same position, and while the French government succeeded by a very narrow margin in obtaining a yes vote, the Danish government was unable to persuade the population to vote yes until it had secured some substantial concessions from the other EU member states.

'Business, technical and cultural elite perceptions of the desirability or otherwise of specific goals' refers mainly to the views on such goals of those who control the means of production of goods or services within and/or across societies, or those responsible for directing scientific and technical research, or those who lead and direct influential and/or societally respected bodies such as the major religious faiths, or key business, scientific, technical or cultural interest groups. (It is important to realise, of course, that religious faiths themselves are capable of acting as interest groups.) Governments may regard the views of such people as important for a variety of reasons. For example, leaders of non-violent religions with substantial national member-ships may be regarded by politicians as being capable of tarnishing their electoral image by means of widely reported public statements and sermons criticising the morality of their policies. Religions which sanction violence might be regarded as significant because they are capable of mobilising physical aggression against government interests, as in the case of fundamentalist Islam in present-day Egypt, or in Iran during the late 1970s. Where such aggressive competition with government ideas is directed solely towards the achievement of 'moral purification', one might argue that the leaders behind it remain part of the cultural elite. But where, like Ayatollah Khomeini, their aim is both competition with and the *overthrow* of an existing regime, then they also become part of a new *political* elite.

Equally, multinational firms which are large employers and investors in particular states may well be regarded as significant because of their ability to switch production to other states if they do not like particular government policies which affect their interests adversely. Such potential relocations might be costly to democratic governments in particular marginal con-stituencies, forcing them to consider adopting some of the multinationals' competing ideas of what their policies should look like.

In addition, some multinationals are so large that they can seek to completely undermine particular governments whose policies they perceive as being against their interests. The alleged activities of the American ITT corporation against the Marxist regime of President Allende in Chile during the early 1970s is an oft-quoted example in this regard. With ITT's help, it has been alleged, Allende was undermined[4] and the army eventually intervened to overthrow his government and replace it with a 'business-friendly' authoritarian regime. The ruling Marxist political elite found that its plans for reshaping Chile in a socialist manner were blocked, among other things, by the actions of business elites who believed that such plans would endanger their interests.

Large corporations also engage in high-powered lobbying in open societies such as the USA in order to ensure that their interests are safeguarded or promoted. For example, when influential sections of the US Congress tried to react against the brutality of Saddam Hussein's policies towards the Kurds in the late 1980s via a Prevention of Genocide Bill, several US corporations lobbied hard to help defeat their efforts.[5] In such circumstances, obviously, specific business elites are competing directly with particular political elites for the ability to determine the direction of particular national policies which they see as affecting their commercial interests.

It should also be realised that competition can occur not just between business, technical or cultural elites and governments, of course, but between those elites and populations, as pointed out in the previous section, or between themselves. The largest multinational corporations have the power independently to cause significant global change, and particular changes can be the outcome solely of competition between, for example, the elites directing two or more corporations.

The notion of 'administrative elite perceptions of the desirability or otherwise of specific goals' refers to the views held on such goals within the bureaucracies which governments rely on to advise them and to administer and implement their policies. The complexity of many of the issues which confront governments, together frequently with the sheer *volume* of issues competing for their attention, mean that presidents, prime ministers, chancellors, juntas and the ministers below them would be unable to digest all such issues, let alone try and make sensible decisions on them, without massive help from civil servants. While formally they are in control of the latter, the extent to which frequently they have to rely on them to do detailed policy research and supply appropriate advice means that potentially there is considerable scope for officials to shape the policy options of their political masters in the way that most suits them. Some analysts, such as Graham Allison, have seen a policy decision game frequently occurring within pluralist societies in which officials compete to try and push policy issues and advice into the 'channels' of government most likely to produce the result which they want.[6] This would seem to be a useful perspective to bear in mind when thinking about the way in which administrative elite attitudes and perceptions can be important.

Those attitudes and perceptions, it has been argued, can be crucially affected by such things as personal ambition, the role of an individual within a bureaucratic organisation, and the interests of that specific organisation as opposed to those of the government as a whole.[7]

It has been argued also that institutional factors such as the ethos of long-established bureaucratic organisations, which restricts the range of views which officials are permitted to advance, and the criteria for selection of civil servants, can be important in helping shape officials' perceptions of the desirability or otherwise of specific goals. With regard to the first point, it has often been said of the British Foreign Office that it has been characterised by a pragmatic approach in its reactions to policy problems and the advice which it has offered to ministers concerning them,[8] which has tended to produce an incremental approach to change rather than one characterised by sudden massive changes in policy. The gradual wind-down of the British Empire and the cautious step-by-step and limited reorientation towards Western Europe are two examples of this which are quoted frequently. Such an approach, it is argued, has had little time for long-term planning and in the past those who tried to think in such terms within the FO frequently found themselves marginalised. In addition, policy goals requiring substantial change frequently have tended to be dropped as a direct result of the FO's pragmatic institutional ethos. As far as the second point is concerned, one might note the fact that for much of the Foreign Office's existence, the basis for being selected as a new official seemed to be a background which at least included a degree from one of Britain's top two universities, and preferably also a childhood spent at one of its leading public schools. It has been argued that this tended to produce an institution characterised by a class-based and thereby inevitably limited view of Britain's place within the world.[9]

Overall, therefore, it would seem to be useful to keep institutional factors in mind when thinking about how administrative elite attitudes and perceptions are shaped. One might note also that such things as background might be useful when trying to understand how the attitudes and perceptions of business, technical and cultural elites (henceforth these will be referred to frequently as BTC elites) and political elites are shaped. The extent to which it is possible to probe matters to such depths, however, will be dependent upon whether or not there are the time and resources available to individual researchers to investigate matters in the required considerable detail. Where such things are available, the results of such an analysis may well be extremely useful.

Finally, it should be remembered that administrative elites within one state can compete more effectively with, for example, their own governing political elite, by forging an alliance of common interest with the administrative elite of another state. In the past, for instance, British and American defence officials have collaborated in this way to try and modify specific policy goals of their respective governments. Each group has lobbied its own government to intervene with the other on specific policy goals – in the manner desired by its administrative elite counterpart in the other state.

The notion of political elite perceptions of the desirability or otherwise of specific goals refers here mainly to the views of various groups composed of the politicians competing for power *within* states on such goals, and to the views on the same of politicians competing for power in relationships *between* states. (For the purposes of this analysis it can refer also to the views of the leaders of influential interest groups concerned solely with promoting ideas and policies which traditionally have been seen as of national political interest but which are not of a predominantly business, technical or cultural nature. The main concern, here, however, is with party politicians and the remainder of the discussion is focused on them entirely.) As implied by all of the above, those views will be affected by politicians' perceptions of popular views on the goals in question and of the views of administrative and business, technical and cultural elites and the damage they believe might be done to their electoral chances, or their ability to forestall coups/revolutions, if they do not take sufficient notice of them. (As will be shown shortly, political elites' views will be affected also by the degree of power and influence which they believe to be held by themselves and other groups and states.) This might be regarded as an overly cynical view of matters, and one ought therefore to allow for those politicians whose view of the perceptions of others might be determined by the extent to which these would seem to be of merit in themselves, rather than by their electoral significance.

It is important to realise that even within a political elite of the same broad ideological persuasion, as in the case of the British Conservative party, for example, there can be considerable differences of opinion on some issues such as the pros and cons of European integration. Equally, within business, technical and cultural elites, there can be marked differences between members of the same business association on matters such as environmental pollution, with the managing directors of some firms seeing economic and/or public relations advantages in becoming more environmentally friendly, while others hold exactly the opposite view, regarding environmental concerns as being simply one more form of economic cost. It has been implied already that administrative elites also may be host to a variety of views on specific issues.

In addition, it should be realised that some of the most powerful political and BTC elites operate across state boundaries and not just within them, and may choose to act in unison with their extensions or counterparts in other states in applying pressure on several states at once. When acting in a non-governmental context, such groups generally are referred to as transnational actors in the international relations literature.[10]

It should be remembered also that while, in an intra-state context, competition over particular policy goals within and between different political elites frequently is conducted according to the formal and informal rules and customs of particular democratic systems, that competition also can be conducted via such violent, non-democratic means as military coups and revolutions.

Finally, it was pointed out earlier that competition between elites can occur to different extents within different types of political system. Before going any further, it is perhaps useful to contemplate briefly something of the range of types of such systems that can exist. At an obvious and surface level they can take the form of the various *liberal democratic* systems of Western Europe, the USA, India and Japan, where free and open election contests occur regularly between a range of political parties with a variety of different beliefs, the *military dictatorships*, within which talk of democracy can be a reason for imprisonment, which have at different times characterised states as varied as Greece, Argentina and Chile, the *one-party systems* of states like the People's Republic of China or Cuba, in which elections are held, but in which candidates of only one political persuasion can be found, the *'family businesses'* of states like Saudi Arabia or Kuwait, which, while being on the whole less repressive than military dictatorships, nevertheless characteristically enforce strict limits on political activity, or the *partnerships between elected politicians and organised crime* that to varying extents have characterised Italy, Peru and Columbia in recent years. The less open and tolerant of diversity a particular political system is, then obviously the less will be the opportunity for competing elites to operate peacefully within it. A protest against government policies that will be regarded as a perfectly constitutional event in the United States, for example, may well result in the jailing (or worse) of the protestors in China.

The above is not an exhaustive list of the different types of political systems that can and do exist at national level, but it gives an idea of the wide range of possibilities. The scope for competing elite activity varies in accordance with that wide range.

The role of ideology, imperatives and interests

The views on the desirability or otherwise of specific goals with implications for global change that are held by members of each of the above groups – the wider population, BTC elites, administrative elites and political elites – will be affected crucially by three things – ideology, imperatives and interests – concepts which overlap and inter-react, but which nevertheless frequently can be clearly identified.

There are well-established debates about how ideologies and interests should best be defined and a variety of different ways in which authors use these concepts within the literature.[11] For the purposes of this book ideologies are defined simply as political, economic and religious belief systems which help shape the values and perceived interests of individuals. It should of course be remembered that ideologies themselves are shaped by the values and perceived interests of those who devise and develop them.

Imperatives are factors internal or external to individuals which lead them to conclude that they have no choice but to attempt change or preserve the status quo. They can include such things as impending environmental disaster, the danger of lethal attack from an enemy if defensive measures are not taken, and ideologies.

Interests are defined as those things which people believe likely to be to their advantage in a political, economic, moral, spiritual or simple hedonistic sense. When people act on the basis of perceived interest, an imperative might determine what their *most important* interest is. Where imperatives are absent, interests can be ranked on the basis of free choice.

All of these factors are capable of shaping the attitudes and actions of individuals across societies and must therefore be fundamental in any attempt to understand the motivations which lie at the heart of competition within and between political, administrative and BTC elites, and sections of the wider population.

Something which it is important to realise is that, as emphasised above, internationally, political processes and the way in which they operate are widely varied, even when apparent 'like' is compared with like – in terms of the American-inspired democratic system of Japan and that of the United States itself, for example – and this variety means that the role which ideologies, imperatives and interests play as facilitators or obstructors of change differs greatly from one society to another. In Japan, for instance, it takes much longer to bring about significant changes in many policies than in the USA because of the stress that is laid upon the notion of consensus in Japanese society.[12]

Change in international relations generally is the outcome of competition between interests within states and between the victors of that competition within one state and (unless there is complete agreement on a particular issue) the victors of the corresponding competitive processes in other relevant states.

The role of power and influence

This now leads us to a fundamental point. At the heart of any change map must be the question of how competing demands within and between different groups and states can be resolved. The tools which the discipline of international relations has produced in order to provide an answer to this question are the concepts of power and influence.

Politics for many politicians and writers has been most fundamentally about power. But what is power? There is a wide-ranging debate on this question.[13] For many ordinary citizens, a state's power is a quantitative matter, the sum of its military hardware and fighting forces and its economic strength. This understanding of the term is important, because it is the sum of states' economic and military strength, and others' perceptions of it, that will crucially affect the extent to which particular governments are or are not able to bring about change within the global arena.

But power also frequently is defined as a *relationship*. For Stoessinger, for example, 'power in international relations is the capacity of a nation to use its tangible and intangible resources in such a way as to affect the behaviour of other nations'.[14] It could be argued that one of the simplest and most useful ways of thinking of power is as the capacity to compel someone else to do something that they do not want to do – or not to do something they wish to do. But what is necessary to have this capacity?

Military strength has been a traditional requirement. With it you can persuade somebody to do something or not, either by the credible threat of military force or by the use of the same. You can try and use economic strength for the same purpose. Or you can use political strength. For example, the United States used the political strength that derived from its military success in the Gulf War to force Israel to the negotiating table at the Middle East peace conference. The Israelis could not afford to ignore the USA given (amongst other considerations) its sudden increased influence with its Arab opponents.

In a purely domestic context, a government may use its ability to manipulate available information – or its ability to persuade others to manipulate information on its behalf – to undermine the electoral chances of rival political groups.

How successful any attempted exercise of power will be depends upon three things: the skill of the user, whether he or she has adequate power resources for the task in hand, and whether the resources that are used and available are the right ones for the job.[15] One of the reasons the Soviet Union had to withdraw from Afghanistan, for example, was because it had the military resources to protect the government, but not the political leverage and credibility with the indigenous population to undermine the support which sustained the rebels.

Another factor which can be used to resolve competing demands within and between states and other global actors is influence. Influence is perhaps most simply defined as the ability to get someone to do something you want via simple persuasion rather than the implicit or explicit threat of or use of sanctions.

A frequently quoted example of alleged influence (although it must be noted that some regard the claims underlying it to be something of an exaggeration) has been that of then British Prime Minister Thatcher with regard to US President Bush prior to the Gulf War. It is claimed by some that she 'steeled' the wavering determination of the President to use military force against Saddam Hussein should it prove necessary. Clearly, if this allegation is true, she had no means of compelling the President of a far more powerful state to do as she wished. But on a personal level, she was renowned as someone capable of browbeating into submission those within her particular ideological camp who failed to show sufficient zeal in pursuit of a Thatcherite agenda. George Bush was most definitely within the same ideological camp, and because of that, vulnerable to pressures from a fellow ideologue. He was also, in her eyes, lacking a Thatcherite steel spine. It was in her perceived interests to prevent the Middle East being carved up by an Arab leader who might well use his growing power to try and hold the West to ransom in the future. So for her, it has been argued, President Bush had to be reminded, in terms that would have appealed to his immediate predecessor, that 'a man's got to do what a man's got to do'.

So, having defined these two factors, the question remains as to how they interact with ideologies, imperatives and interests in promoting or impeding global change. It has been answered partially with regard to influence in the above discussion of Mrs Thatcher's alleged US role prior to the Gulf War and the relevance of a commonly held ideology to that. One might go a stage further and look at the relationship between influence and imperatives.

The Roman Catholic Church is an interesting and ancient example of a non-governmental actor that operates on a global scale which can be used for this purpose. In the 1980s, it was imperative on religious grounds for the Roman Catholic hierarchy and many prominent lay Catholics in Ireland to try and prevent abortion from becoming a general right for Irish women. The hierarchy had a degree of power in so far as it could remind practising Catholics that global Vatican law decrees that to support abortion is a sin and that to ignore their instructions on the matter would be to invite divine retribution. This prevented many Irish Catholics from supporting any general abortion law. But there were many also who only half believed in Catholicism or did not believe at all both within the electorate and in the Irish parliament. The Catholic Church was able to use a certain amount of power against the latter by reminding them that it might well be able to turn a dangerously large part of the electorate against them on the issue. But it also used influence in trying to reawaken within the minds of ex-Catholics the specific moral conscience which their Catholic childhood education had been designed to implant within them. It could not compel them to reaccept the claimed virtues of this conscience, but it was able to try and persuade them of the same, and in so far as it did this, it was exercising influence in pursuit of the goals dictated by the imperative of its global religious laws.

As far as power is concerned, one might look at the interaction between it and ideologies. The policies of governments, and the alternative policies advocated by those outside government, obviously frequently derive from ideologies as they have been defined here. For example, the prescriptions for wealth creation advanced at state and global level are based upon economic ideologies which currently predominantly take the form of different varieties of liberal capitalism.[16] The military confrontation between the United States and the Soviet Union that dominated much of the post-Second World War period arguably resulted predominantly from the two governments having radically different ideas of how the world should be run, both politically and economically. Those ideas derived not just from differing interests but from incompatible value systems.

What it is crucial to realise is that while the process of political problem-solving can only progress if the ideas shaped within ideologies continue to develop, those ideas can play no role in global politics unless they are either taken up by those wielding political power or by those seeking to replace them. Politics (defined here simply as the process by which competing demands are resolved), power and the ideas which derive from ideologies, three of the key engines of global development or disaster, are inter-dependent.

One might look also at the relationship between power and the interests of states. An interesting way of doing this is to take the global problem of aggressive regimes and the question of to what extent they can be prevented from seizing the territory of others. The United States has the military capability both to keep Saddam Hussein in check, as it showed during the Gulf War when expelling his forces from Kuwait, and to expel Bosnian Serb forces from the territory which they have seized in Bosnia. In terms of a necessary ethical justification for doing the latter, there is overwhelming evidence that Serbian fighters have committed even more atrocities than Hussein's Iraqis would have been likely to have done had they stayed in Kuwait.

But ethics has proved to be peripheral in the American response to the problems of the former Yugoslavia. The simple fact is that the US government deemed it to be in its interest to use massive ground forces against Iraq, which it perceived as threatening the security of its oil supplies, but not to be in its interest to do the same in Bosnia, which has the misfortune of being without oil. Its huge potential power as a global righter of wrongs therefore only becomes relevant when American governments decide that it is in their interests to use it.

These are but some of the ways in which power and influence can interact with ideologies, imperatives and interests within the framework of the political processes of states. This brief hint of the enormous range of possible permutations gives some initial idea of just how difficult the solving of global problems via the device of substantial change in policies and policy directions can be, given that solutions depend significantly upon appropriate and often complex interactions between the above factors.

The role of fortune

However it should not be thought that the above factors alone determine whether or not change can occur within global politics. Also of crucial relevance are fortune and opportunity factors. Fortune can be defined as the *unpredictability* that frequently lies at the heart of the interplay (and the factors affecting it) of complex group and individual interests, emotions and concerns within the global arena. It can be observed at work frequently via unforeseen non-human natural events such as earthquakes, famines and floods and via the largely unforeseen global military consequences of such human-facilitated disasters as the international economic mire which helped create the conditions for Hitler's rise to power in Germany. Fortune can produce a temporary coincidence of interest between two or more states which allows each to achieve something that otherwise would not be possible, providing they act before that coincidence vanishes. Fortune is perhaps most visible during time of war. For example, during the 1982 war between Britain and Argentina over the Falkland/Malvinas Islands, the British were saved from military embarrassment by the fact that a great many of the Argentine airforce bombs which found their targets were incorrectly fused and failed to go off. In far earlier times most of a then militarily inferior Europe appears to have been saved from conquest by the

Mongol armies of Asia by the timely death of Kublai Khan, the leader who had been the main driving force behind the idea of carrying the invasion forwards. Fortune can affect the future of whole continents.

The role of opportunity factors

Opportunity factors can be defined as those things which instantly or incrementally greatly alter popular and elite perceptions of the world and make it easier to introduce significant changes. Foremost among these perhaps are the related phenomena of modernisation and global interfusion, together with the processes of economic growth and economic stagnation, the occurrence of major wars, revolutions, the evolution of ideas, significant changes in personnel among key world leaders, as in the case of the emergence of the reformist Gorbachev during the mid-1980s after a long period of conservative rule in the former Soviet Union, and, more for the future perhaps, environmental crises *which are fully recognised as such*.

While some extremely useful definitions of modernisation have been provided within the international relations literature,[17] the definition offered here will be kept simple to avoid unnecessary overlap with the concept of global interfusion.

Modernisation

For the purposes of this book, modernisation is defined simply as the continuing process of development of those aspects of science, technology and manufacturing and service provision processes which have an impact on national and global societies. It is a process which is capable of reducing and potentially even of eliminating the technological and economic gap between some societies and thereby reducing power differentials. This is what is happening at the moment in relation to the relative position of the Four Tigers of the Pacific (Hong Kong, South Korea, Singapore and Taiwan) and the rich Western states with regard to economic power for example.

It has been argued frequently that the labour-saving aspects of modernisation potentially are capable of causing social and political unrest, and of providing the necessary breeding-grounds for extreme ideologies, such as right-wing nationalism, if they result in too many people becoming unemployed and alienated from their societies. Some press and other commentators argued that the success of an alleged neo-fascist group in the

1993 Russian parliamentary elections was a direct consequence of the process of modernisation that followed the fall of the USSR. Modernisation, therefore, could be argued to be capable of causing changes in the power relations between states and of causing changes in people's perceptions of their own and global society which are large enough to provoke in turn domestic political changes which, in the case of a militarily powerful state like Russia, could prove to have momentous implications for international relations. These are not the only possible consequences of the process, as will be seen as the book progresses.

Economic growth and economic stagnation/decline

Economic growth and economic stagnation can both result from modernisation. The Japanese economic 'miracle' of the 1960s and 1970s is a good example of growth deriving considerably although not entirely from modernisation (which in turn originally was greatly facilitated by the USA for its own reasons). Equally, as already pointed out above, the economic doldrums that Russia found itself in during 1993/4, with key sections of its economy stagnating or in serious decline, increasingly is being seen as a result of a confused and over-rapid modernisation programme, even by sections of the reformist Russia's Choice party.

However, it should be remembered that theoretically it is possible to have economic growth independently of modernisation, and that economic stagnation and decline can most certainly occur without modernisation, as key sectors of many third world economies demonstrate powerfully.

The most positive side of the coin with regard to economic factors takes the form of the opportunities for significant beneficial global and regional change that can be facilitated by sustained periods of growth in the world economy. For example, the growth experienced by the six Western European states that originally formed the European Coal and Steel Community during the 1950s was partially attributed by the governments concerned to their membership of that Community.[18] It thereby helped persuade them of the wisdom of trying to use integration as a growth-booster in other sectors of their economies as well by setting up the much more wide-ranging European Economic Community, the forerunner of today's European Union. While there are many who do not see the European Union as 'beneficial', the majority within the ruling political elites of the Union continue to regard it as both politically and economically indispensable to the pursuit of crucial national interests. The substantial economic growth which the original member states enjoyed during the early years of their membership of the EEC in turn persuaded the British Conservative government of the day that it would have to reverse its previous policy and apply to join in order to share in the growth process that it and the various member states associated with economic integration.[19]

Potentially, therefore, it would seem that economic growth, economic stagnation and economic decline are all capable of having significant effects on the business of global change.

Global interfusion

The term 'global interfusion' should not intimidate the reader. It simply refers to the fusing of a wide variety of human activities, values, structures and concerns on a global scale. The idea behind it, in other words, is very simple. The complexity lies entirely in the processes by which global interfusion occurs within the 'real world'.

If an overall definition of the concept is sought, it can be said that global interfusion can involve the fusing of one or more of the following: (1) the economies or part or entire sectors of the economies of two or more states; or (2) of the values and practices of one society with those of another; or (3), directly or indirectly, formally or informally, of states' people and their interests with a variety of power structures beyond their individual boundaries; or (4) of problems in one part of the world relating to anything from pollution to religion with the fund of human concern in another; or (5) of attitudes or concerns in one state with those in others. The extent to which factors fuse will vary greatly according to specific circumstances of course. How global interfusion processes can operate will be explained shortly.

There is no perfect concept available for dealing with *processes* as complex as those encompassed by the idea of global interfusion. Language is simply too unsophisticated a tool for such a thing to be possible. However, while it is not immune from inadequacies of its own, the concept of global interfusion is preferred over the term 'globalisation' because the fashionable nature of the latter has led to over-use and abuse, whereby it is employed so generally and so imprecisely by many (with the exception of analysts such as Anthony McGrew, Michael Smith and Paul Hirst[20]) that its worth as a tool of analysis is devalued greatly. There are also fundamental problems with the application of the concept which Hirst identifies.[21]

The idea of global interfusion is preferred also over the traditional notion of interdependence because of the explanatory limitations of the latter. The very *word* 'interdependence' does not convey adequately the flavour of a world where, for example, the *problems* of one society can become *fused* with the *concerns* of another without the latter becoming *dependent* on the former. A simple example of this is the concern many felt in the USA over starvation in Somalia after TV news coverage, and their subsequent pressure on the Bush administration to act. A Somali problem fused with US public concern without the Americans being in any way dependent upon the Somalis. Across the globe there is a continuing fusing of problems and concerns, values, economies and so on, that is in its entirety too complex a process to be described adequately by many of the less manipulable definitions of interdependence.

Global interfusion can occur via four main types of process. First, it results from the growing subversion of many states' and nations' values and practices by values from other societies transferred by the media and/ or global economic mechanisms. The interfusion of values and practices *with societies* that occurs is often a one-way process, due to the superior media and economic capabilities of its sources compared to those of the recipients of the alien values and practices. (However, it need not always be – militant varieties of Islam, for example, have been extended into some parts of the developed world partially as a result of news coverage in the Western media of events in the Middle East and the Persian Gulf.) Such subversion can be accidental or intentional, and beneficial or harmful to the people within the affected areas.

Second, it is the consequence of a continuing process whereby more and more decisions affecting any one large or small state and its people, that were taken previously by that state or firms within it, are now being made by or in other states, or by other types of international actor partially or wholly outside that state's control. In other words, it involves the direct or indirect, formal or informal interfusion of people and their interests around the world with a variety of different power structures which originate from beyond their own state boundaries. As will be seen in detail later on in the book, the process also is causing considerable international economic interfusion via the global structures, outlook and operations of multinational business, service and finance corporations. The interfusion, in which the states' citizens who are involved effectively become *subject parts* of another state's or other international actor's power structure, may arise only with regard to one instance, or over a range of instances.

Third and relatedly, global interfusion is also the result of a process whereby issues, decisions and crises are becoming increasingly global in their impact as a result of the communications/technological revolution. This process affects crucial matters as diverse as economics, pollution, politics, religion, and health (as a result of increased travel). It can lead to the international interfusion of efforts to deal with issues which it places on the global agenda which are perceived as being serious and best resolved (at least partially) on a global level by those in a position to act. It can also lead to the interfusion of attitudes (the growth of a negative global perspective on nuclear power after a widely reported serious accident, for example), or to a variety of other effects, some of which will be explained later on in the book.

Finally, it is the result of interfusing ideologies such as economic liberalism being taken up by those governments with the power to spread and implement them around the globe. This can in part occur as a result of the first of the above kinds of global interfusion process. It can also be the entirely independent and 'non-subversive' result of, for example, states simply deciding for themselves that economic liberalism is the system which they and others have to adopt in order to maximise their wealth.

From the above analysis, therefore, it can be seen that, potentially, global interfusion (on occasion henceforth referred to as GI) can create opportunities for change in a wide variety of ways. For example, it can create the conditions within which changes in states' foreign aid and military policies can be brought about, as in the case of the dramatic shifts in US policy on Somalia which were mentioned earlier. In the latter instance, GI changed US popular perceptions of Somalia and its needs which in turn forced the government to change its perceptions of what American policy on that state should be. Equally, GI can result in new opportunities for the spread of ideologies (as in the case of the previously cited example of the increasing global reach of militant varieties of Islam). The changes in popular and elite perceptions of the world which such a spread can occasion can in turn cause significant changes at the global level, as in the case of the significant upgrading of American and Soviet concerns about and reaction to the popular anti-Westernism and anti-Marxism of Islamic fundamentalism in the wake of the successful Iranian Revolution of 1979. In addition global interfusion can change and/or diversify the power centres to which the world's people are subject. Ultimately, such a process may well lessen the extent to which citizens are committed to the idea of the nation state, given that it is demonstrating actively that other centres of power are important to their lives as well. That in turn may increase the opportunities for regional integration, as in the case of the European Union. Potentially, therefore, global interfusion is a highly important factor within any change map of global politics.

Wars

Throughout history wars have been significant factors in the business of global change. For example, the ravages of the First World War, and the contribution which the incompetence of the then Russian government made to them, helped discredit the Russian monarchy to such an extent that the opportunity which revolutionary forces had been looking for to organise the government's successful overthrow was provided. Thereafter, following the success of the Bolsheviks, one of the most potentially powerful states on earth was governed for over seventy years by an ideology and by leaders that were felt to be a serious threat by its major competitors, and from that fear ultimately the Cold War and all of its momentous consequences – including the burdening of the planet with a joint super-power arsenal of over fifty thousand nuclear warheads – was to follow. The result of the Russian Revolution was that Western governments and many of their people ultimately came to see Russia as the major threat to world peace. This in turn prevented the United States from returning to its traditional policy of isolationism after the Second World War and prompted its emergence not only as the world's policeman, but also as the most awesome military power the planet has ever known.

The Second World War also had a major effect on the global political map. It so devastated the Western European great powers – it cost Britain alone a quarter of its national wealth for example – that they were forced to change their perceptions of their role in the world and to accept US primacy in the business of 'world leadership' during the entire period of the Cold War.

Clearly, therefore, major wars, as the consequences of the war-facilitated Russian Revolution demonstrated, can set in motion perception shifts which provide the opportunity for significant social and ideological changes in global or regional great powers, which, by virtue of the size and influence of some of the latter, can in turn have substantial implications for the world as a whole. Furthermore, as the Second World War demonstrated, such wars also can so damage the economic position of states that the global balance of power is changed completely.

Environmental Crises

As will be seen later in the book, environmental crises potentially can take many forms. They can be man-made, as in the case of the 1986 explosion at the Chernobyl nuclear reactor, natural, as in the case of the aftermath of massive earthquakes, or a mixture of both, as in the case of the soil erosion resulting from a deadly combination of inappropriate farming practices and natural processes that is adding to problems of famine in some parts of Africa. The section on global interfusion has explained in preliminary detail already how environmental issues can be brought to global attention and can become serious items on the agenda of world politics because of this. Should some prominent scientists' fears over matters such as global warming or the depletion of the ozone layer prove to be well-founded,[22] then it will only be possible to tackle these problems effectively on a global level, given that their *causes* are of a *global* nature. In such circumstances, it is likely that the industrial and many of the industrialising economies will be left with little choice other than to change some of their industrial and economic practices in order to reduce the severe environmental dangers facing them,[23] and if fears of unequal burden-sharing in the matters of such changes are to be precluded, to do this by means of a cooperative global agreement. So, potentially, some possible environmental crises can be argued to be likely to have the capability to create perceptions of the need for both changes in global economic behaviour and greater international cooperation. Al Gore, among others, has suggested that changes in both of these areas could be quite substantial should fears over phenomena such as global warming indeed prove to be justified.[24]

Equally, the over-exploitation of some of the planet's limited natural resources could result in severe shortages in a number of key raw materials in the next century. Remembering how the West was prepared to fight a major war with Iraq when it felt its oil supplies potentially to be under threat, it might be reasonably speculated that such shortages will provoke an increased incidence of resort to the use of military power in international relations as states become desperate to secure access to the remaining supplies of those materials that are not easily or completely substitutable. In this instance, therefore, abuse of the environment's resources which creates a crisis of supply ultimately could make it easier for democratic governments to justify the use of force to their populations – as a means of protecting the living standards of the latter by securing continuing access to raw materials in the midst of such a supply crisis, for example.

Environmental crises potentially, therefore, can be the causes of both more cooperative or more violent behaviour internationally, depending upon the circumstances of the case.

Changes in government personnel

Any number of relevant examples can be cited under this heading. Perhaps two of the most important during the twentieth century are the cases of Adolf Hitler and Mikhail Gorbachev. Substantially, although not entirely as a result of the former's rise to power in Germany during the 1930s,[25] most of Western and non-Soviet Europe fell under German military domination for several years, and the United States and the Soviet Union were forced to change dramatically their perceptions of their roles in global politics and to start to turn their potential military superpower status into a reality. As a direct result of the latter event and the high economic cost of the war, the Western European Great Powers were reduced to secondary status in the years that followed. As pointed out already, this in turn resulted in a change in their perceptions of their global role to the extent that most of them were prepared to accept American leadership in East–West security matters. These are but a few of the major global changes that resulted from Hitler's plans for empire. Had an individual of Hitler's charisma, ruthlessness and greed – and ability to eliminate or play off against each other domestic forces that might have restrained him – not risen to power in Germany, then even had the attack on Pearl Harbour by the Japanese still taken place, the United States government would not have been provided with the opportunity that followed in the wake of the Second World War to change the isolationist perceptions of the American people to such an extent that the USA was able to supplant the old Western European states in the military leadership of their half of the continent. Because Hitler's aggression forced the emergence of the Soviet Union as a regional superpower, and because the USA came to regard the new-found military muscle of the latter as a serious threat to its security after the Second World War, it was possible for the American government to change the perceptions of both Congress and the electorate on the need for a long-term large-scale American military presence in Europe. Had Hitler and all his deeds not afflicted Europe, then the emergence of the USSR as a regional superpower would at the very least have been delayed greatly, the old Western European Great Powers probably for some time would have remained able to hold their own against it, the USA would not have had any grounds for involving itself in Western Europe as a major military presence and the global security system therefore would have been a far more multipolar one (that is, power probably would have been more evenly divided within it) than was the case during the 1950s, 1960s, 1970s and 1980s. The opportunity for radically altering domestic elite and popular perceptions concerning the need for an American peacetime world role that presented itself to the USA after the Second World War is but one of several major 'windows of change' whose opening may substantially be attributed to Hitler's ill-fated aggressive interventions in global politics.

In the case of Mikhail Gorbachev, then most obviously the opening up of Soviet and East European society and the greater economic and political freedoms which he introduced provided the opportunity for the emergence and growth of the anti-Communist forces that were to liberate Eastern Europe, destroy the Warsaw Pact, ultimately humble the Soviet Communist party, end the period of Soviet global influence and terminate the Cold War. While the chronic problems of the Soviet economy quite possibly would have caused many of these things to happen anyway at some stage in the future, the bold radicalism of Gorbachev undoubtedly greatly accelerated their occurrence. His policies so changed perceptions in the USA, the former Soviet Union and Europe that it was possible to completely restructure global security relationships.

Revolutions

For the purposes of this study, revolutions might be defined as spontaneous or planned popular uprisings which occur with the intention of deposing an existing government. In the section on major wars, some of the change consequences of the Russian Revolution of 1917 were outlined, revealing several ways in which revolutions can change the perceptions and policies of those in states other than that which is the host to a particular revolution.

But it is important also to think of the way in which revolutions can alter the perceptions of the populations of the states in which they occur. The 1917 Russian Revolution, for example, altered the perceptions which many of the Russian people had of the way in which an economy should be organised and of the friendly or hostile nature of the major states which surrounded their country. In relation to the latter point, their views were affected greatly by the fact that the Soviet Communist party had a monopoly control over the media and thereby was able to present a strongly biased view of national and international events. It could be argued that this was of assistance in securing the active and passive popular support which helped legitimate the anti-American/Western policies which were a mirror image of those directed at the Soviet Union by the USA, and thereby contributed directly to the Cold War after 1947.

In addition, the success of the revolution in Russia had a knock-on effect in that it helped inspire communist revolutionaries in other states to launch and sustain struggles against their own governments, some of which ultimately proved successful, as in the case of the People's Republic of China. In other words, it created the perception that Marxist–Leninist revolutions could be successfully carried out even in the most powerful states. The combined success of the Soviet and Chinese revolutions meant that a massive slice of the world's population for many years was governed by a collective rather than an individualistic approach to wealth creation and distribution and thereby offered a radically different model for economic development than that preferred by the capitalist states of the West. The success of the Chinese revolution in the late 1940s also greatly increased the fear of the United States of what its leaders frequently referred to as 'world communism' and thereby exacerbated the Cold War.

Potentially, therefore, revolutions which occur in major states, or whose ideas spread to and are adopted by the leaders of the same, can produce highly significant changes in global perceptions, politics and economics.

Governments also can be replaced as a result of *coups d'état*. For the purposes of this study these can be defined as the forced removal from office of the leaders of states by rivals from within the political or military elite around them. These also can produce opportunities for significant change. Had the attempted coup against the Soviet leader Gorbachev succeeded in the dying days of the USSR, then that state would have reverted to a hard-line communist direction and Western perceptions that the Soviet Union was now becoming so 'friendly' that the Cold War could keep on being wound down would probably have been replaced by a perceived need for a continuing vigilant containment of Soviet power and a high level of conventional and nuclear military preparedness.

The fact that coups frequently are carried out by highly conservative forces within states should not obscure the fact that they are often instruments of change in the policies of states and of the perceptions and policies of other states around them. Whether policy switches are in a conservative or radical direction obviously they still constitute *change*.

The evolution of ideas

Opportunities for change do not come only with dramatic events like wars and revolutions, but can result simply from the evolution of human ideas. The fact, for example, that liberal capitalism, in a variety of forms, is the dominant mode of economic thought at present does not mean that it will retain this position indefinitely. Capitalism, like its current less successful competitors and its predecessors, is a framework of economic thought that seems to leave important problems of wealth creation and distribution undealt with or poorly dealt with. For this reason, it is probable that some out of the world's many economists will keep trying to produce a superior economic ideology to replace it. Should they succeed, and should the virtues of the latter seem sufficiently attractive to governments, then it is likely that economic behaviour across the world will start to change in the same way that it did when mercantilism[26] was replaced by new ideas in earlier times. The result of such a change would be significant for the world's populations. For example, should capitalism be faced with a competitor ideology that offered a variety of *credible* incentives to entrepreneurial activity that did not involve simple personal wealth accumulation, then the groundwork would be laid for a sea change in popular attitudes, within states such as the USA, to those who justify personal fortunes on the grounds of their alleged role in overall economic growth. Such an ideology, by providing a means through which perceptions of the virtues of personal wealth accumulation could be changed on a societal and cross-societal basis, would in turn provide an opportunity for a massive change in global policies on wealth accumulation and distribution.

In other words, the fact that economics and the politics of economics is constantly a subject of debate and rethinking in itself could at some stage in the future − as it has done in the past − provide the means by which governmental and popular perceptions of desirable or permissible forms of economic behaviour are altered drastically and thereby create significant opportunities for change in the global political−economic system. Similarly, ideas on how people should be governed − within democracies, for example − are constantly being debated, and these debates also periodically have the potential to change perceptions on desirable and undesirable forms of government and, if they convert those with the power to effect change to new ideas, to bring that change about.

Policy changes of state governments, multinational corporations, etc.

The particular policy changes being referred to here are those which are perceived by the populations/elites of other states as having major implications for them. Such changes might result from one or more of the opportunity factors already outlined.

This type of opportunity factor is almost self-explanatory, but an example might nevertheless be useful. As was touched on earlier in the chapter, the momentous changes in the foreign and domestic policies of the Soviet Union introduced by Mikhail Gorbachev ultimately were seen by the government and electorate of the United States as offering an opportunity for greatly improving relations between the two states and for making substantial progress on arms control. Gorbachev's policies significantly reduced the threat which the United States government and population perceived as being presented by the Soviet Union.

The role of blocking factors

These are factors which, through their impact on populations/elites within states, can obstruct or eliminate government or other elite policy alternatives that otherwise would be available. All of the above opportunity factors can act as blocking factors. For example, economic stagnation within the European Union has greatly dampened popular and political elite enthusiasm for further European integration and could well severely hinder progress towards the goal of economic and monetary union. Even economic growth can act as a blocking factor. For example, if it is achieved under non-interventionist governments within the developed states, the resulting satisfaction of those parts of their electorates benefiting from it can, for as long as the growth lasts, make it difficult for interventionists to get into power and switch the economies of the developed world in the direction which they believe to be most desirable.

Using the map

Now that the core elements of the Change Map have been laid down it is time to apply them and see what they reveal about some of the most pressing issues currently at the heart of global politics. However, it is important to bear in mind that the investigation here is primarily an illustrative and a preliminary one geared very much to the need to keep the application of the Change Map at a level that is comprehensible to new students of international relations as well as those who are more experienced in the subject. Accordingly, while the map will be applied in such a way as to demonstrate key aspects of its value as a means of increasing one's understanding of international relations, it will not be deployed in as comprehensive a manner as would be required if, for example, one were attempting to show how all of the world's problems could be solved (always presuming that such a task might be possible!). In any case, it would not be practical to apply the map in full to each chapter in the present volume, given the broad nature of the topics covered. The aim is simply to demonstrate enough of the map's utility for readers who are new to the discipline of international relations to be stimulated to think creatively both about that discipline and about the problems of change that confront global society, and for experienced researchers to judge whether it might be of use to them in their own work.

Accordingly, different but appropriate sections of the map will be applied in the various chapters of the book in order to demonstrate their analytical power. The guiding principle behind the author's selection of sections of the map for application will often be one of looking at an issue which he wishes to analyse *in parallel* with the map in its comprehensive checklist function, and then making a judgement as to what the available evidence concerning that issue suggests might be useful sections to apply. The obvious immediate justification for such an approach is the above-stated primarily illustrative nature of the analysis to be conducted in the present volume. However, from a researcher's point of view there are other rather more weighty justifications that can be offered for this strategy and these are explained in the appendix on the wider uses of the Change Map at the end of the book.

Finally, primarily with the interests of undergraduate readers in mind, it is intended to broaden the range of questions asked about some specific global issues beyond those concerned simply with the book's central focus of change. This should provide important background understanding of those issues which otherwise would be missing.

Chapter 2

The American pivot

American military power has been a double-edged sword which has both cost and saved many thousands of civilian lives during the present century. For some the United States is remembered most for the My Lai massacre in Vietnam[1] or because of the thousands of ordinary people who died as a result of direct or indirect American and Soviet involvement in the other regional wars which became bloody arenas for their Cold War ideological competition. For many of those over 60 it is remembered more with gratitude for its mid-century part in liberating substantial areas of Europe and Asia from frequently brutal occupying forces and for the enormous contribution which it made to the rebuilding of those states that emerged shattered from the Second World War.

Whatever the rights and wrongs of America's various engagements with global politics during the past eighty years, there is no doubt about the key role which it has played in shaping the world that has emerged from that period. American power was crucial in helping determine the outcome of the two world wars in the first half of this century. It was one of the two dominant forces that most shaped global politics during the Cold War and it was the USA's defence and deterrence policies and the huge amount of resources devoted to them that helped destroy the Soviet economy and ultimately the Soviet Union itself by means of the superpower arms race.

In the post-Cold War world, despite the process of relative economic decline that started during the 1960s as new competitors emerged, in the form of Japan and the European Union for example, the United States remains the world's strongest economic power and, as such, a key player in the global economic system. It is now also the only state possessing super-power levels of weapons and forces in every dimension of conventional and nuclear military capability. Despite US troop and missile reductions in Europe, it remains a major player in that crucial region due to its continuing NATO security guarantee and its status as the most powerful member of that alliance. It retains also a substantial military presence in Asia. In the Middle East, the USA is a prime mover whose actions and backing have been and remain fundamental to the chances of achieving a lasting peace settlement. On a global level, American economic and military power allows it to retain a pivotal role in shaping the alternatives available for such bodies as the United Nations. Decreases, increases or simple non-payment of US contributions to the UN and its various agencies can have a significant impact on their effectiveness for example. Equally, the ability of the UN to mount or facilitate operations equivalent to the 1991 rollback of Saddam Hussein's forces from Kuwait is entirely dependent upon the willingness or otherwise of the USA to provide the core military power that is required.

In short, despite relative decline in some aspects of its power capabilities,[2] the United States remains and is likely to remain, for at least the immediately foreseeable future, the world's primary state.[3] This does not mean that it is capable of getting its own way on every issue, as it has found recently with the difficulties it has experienced in trying to persuade Russia and the European Union states to see the Bosnian question its way.[4] Equally, a constant ghost in the memory of all American policy-makers and generals alike is the defeat of massive US military forces by the relatively technologically backward state of North Vietnam in the mid-1970s. Nevertheless, the sheer size of the United States on every index of military and economic power means that the attitudes of its governments and people are of fundamental importance in determining the extent and the rapidity of global change with regard to many of the most vital issues facing the world.

However, given that the primary focus of this book is on global and regional problems rather than specific states, it is not possible to examine here the USA in all the aspects that its global significance otherwise might be seen as justifying. But this hardly means that it will be ignored. A glance through the index and specific chapters will reveal that the United States is referred to throughout the book with regard to each topic. Its importance in the change process is shown particularly in the chapters on the threats to the state from global economic, technological, scientific and cultural interfusion, the problems of the global environment, and the control of war, for example. The main concern here, having emphasised the extent of the United States' global significance, is to provide a necessarily concise insight into some of the core dynamics that determine the nature of America's often crucial contribution to global change processes. The intention is to provide the *background* necessary for an understanding of the types of political complexities that underlie the various American stances on global change that will be referred to at various points throughout the book. Given this primary background purpose, the Change Map will not be brought in in as much detail as in subsequent chapters. The chapter will conclude by considering briefly the importance of its content for those wishing to bring about global change.

What factors can influence US policy on global change?

The most obvious contributor to American decisions to support or oppose policies which occasion global change takes the form of the actions or perceived actions of individuals or bodies external to the USA, whether they be those of state governments, multinational business corporations, terrorist organisations or international organisations like the UN, to name but a few possibilities. The tactics and US market penetration of Japanese multinationals, for example, could be argued to have played a considerable part in influencing the shape of US–Japanese governmental relations during recent years. Equally, the invasion of Kuwait by Saddam Hussein's Iraqi forces in 1990 clearly was the major cause of the subsequent massive US military intervention in the Middle East, which in turn greatly reshaped the balance of power in the region. But what it is vital to realise is that the effect on American policy which the actions of any external body can have is crucially dependent upon how they are perceived by the various individuals, interest groups and other actors which can be involved in the shaping of US decisions in Washington. It is dependent also on the balance of power between these various forces as it operates at any one time. The main focus of this section of the discussion therefore will be on those factors operating within the USA itself which can determine how the actions of external actors should be perceived and reacted to, and which can themselves also help determine foreign policies which do not require any external stimulus in the form of the actions of states and other bodies to set them in motion, or which are devised primarily but not entirely in response to domestic concerns.

In this respect, the variety of factors which played a role in pushing through President Clinton's policy on the establishment of NAFTA has already been shown in Chapter 1. Reference is made elsewhere in the book also to some of the domestic influences that were at work on American policy towards Iraq prior to the 1991 Gulf War, a policy which arguably proved crucial in facilitating the war and the turmoil which it caused within the international system. Among others, Peter Pringle has set out to illustrate the range of these influences. He has argued that there were a number of signals that could have been sent by the Americans to Saddam

Hussein in the years immediately prior to the conflict which probably would have caused him to be much less sure of American tolerance of his move on Kuwait than he was. One such signal, Pringle contends, could have been the passing of the Prevention of Genocide Bill which the Senate Committee on Foreign Relations drew up in the late 1980s in response to the Iraqi military's use of chemical weapons against Kurdish civilians. Among other things it would have imposed economic sanctions on Iraq and demonstrated to Hussein that the USA was unprepared to accept aggressive action by Iraq against the region's peoples.

However, the bill never made it into American law. Pringle argues that this was due to a variety of domestic influences. First, those US industrial concerns which benefited considerably from trade with Iraq included powerful members of the oil and agricultural sectors who lobbied both government and Congress members strongly to persuade them to resist the bill. Second, its proposal for trade sanctions ran counter to the preferred policy of the House's powerful Ways and Means Committee who decided that they would oppose it also. Third, it ran counter to the economic and geostrategic aims of the President and other key members of the Republican government and so suffered also from them lobbying against it.[5]

One of the reasons why ultimately it proved impossible to change and contain Hussein's regional ambitions, Pringle argues therefore, was that in the rejection of the bill the United States government and Congress showed themselves unwilling to react effectively even against the most brutal and murderous use of force by the Iraqi military against women and children, and that was something that Saddam was to remember. Pringle's example illustrates neatly how domestic factors can interact within the American polity to block changes in policy that could be of enormous benefit to others within the global system, just as the NAFTA example in Chapter 1 showed how domestic factors can combine to push through changes that many argue will benefit both the United States and other states' peoples. In Change Map terms, the Iraq example shows how the degree to which global change is possible can depend crucially on interest-driven competition between BTC elites, political elites and administrative elites within the USA's political system.

Another example of the way in which domestic pressures within the US political system potentially can obstruct change at the global level is provided by the following newspaper extract:

'President Bill Clinton's refusal to come to London for the VE anniversary celebrations two weeks ago revealed less about the state of the trans-atlantic alliance than about American politicians and their special relationship with Israel.

Mr Clinton had a more pressing engagement at the Washington Sheraton: attending the annual conference of the American–Israel Public Affairs Committee (Aipac). He had to be there. Bob Dole, his likely rival in next year's presidential race, was going to address Aipac and there was no way Mr Clinton was going to let him steal a march on him. If there is one thing US politicians have learnt – literally half the members of Congress attended the conference – it is that you snub America's powerful Jewish lobby at your peril.

The last three weeks have witnessed three developments which Middle East experts believe will do little to promote peace between Arabs and Israelis: Mr Clinton imposed a total embargo on trade with Iran; Mr Dole announced at the Aipac conference that he would intro-duce a Bill in Congress to move the US Embassy from Tel Aviv to Jerusalem; and, on Wednesday, the US vetoed a UN Security Council resolution that criticised Israel's confiscation of Arab lands in East Jerusalem.

It is no coincidence that Aipac's current three main goals are the containment of Iran; ensuring Jerusalem becomes the capital of Israel, and preserving current levels of aid to Israel, which at $3bn (£1.9bn) a year – 20 per cent of America's total foreign aid budget – represents by far the highest amount received by any country.

Mr Clinton and Mr Dole made a point of reassuring the 2,500 delegates that they would not tamper with Israeli aid . . . Mitch McConnell, a Republican senator . . . recently proposed that aid to Africa, $1bn continent wide, should be slashed. Aid to Israel, however, was sacrosanct, he said. When McConnell last stood for election he received $213,900 from Jewish individuals and more than 50 pro-Israel groups. . . .

Charles Percy, a Republican who sat on the Senate Foreign Relations committee in the mid-1980s, won awards from Jewish groups for his devotion to the Israeli cause. When he started asking questions about the Israeli role in the West Bank, however, Jewish groups around the country, under Aipac's guidance, started distributing flyers denouncing him as Israel's biggest enemy. Funds poured into the coffers of Paul Simon, his rival in the 1984 elections, and Mr Percy was duly defeated. Tom Dine, the president of Aipac at the time, said in a speech: "All the Jews in America, from coast to coast, gathered to oust Percy. And American politicians got the message".'[6]

The above is an example not only of how powerful domestic interest groups can be in restricting the options of US politicians when foreign policies which might bring about change in the global system are being considered, but of the role also which foreign interests potentially can play within the US political system. Because Aipac promotes what it believes to be the interests of the people of Israel, it can be used as a conduit for pressure on the USA by the Israeli government and/or other Israeli political interests. When this happens it is an example of cooperation between members of one of the political elites of one state with the political elites of another, and of competition within the USA between their jointly promoted perceptions and interests and those of members of the American BTC, administrative and political elites who oppose their views.

Another similarly complicated example of how foreign-linked domestic pressures can affect American policies on change within the global system is that of the Irish lobby within the USA. Prior to and after the beginning of the IRA cease-fire in Northern Ireland during 1994, President Clinton on several occasions rejected overtures from the British Conservative government to drop gestures of friendship or encouragement which he was proposing to make towards Sinn Fein, a political party which the British believe to be an IRA front. He made a point of shaking hands with Gerry Adams, the party leader, on St Patrick's Day 1995, for example, a gesture which the British had argued was grossly premature. What was happening was that the President was prepared to help push the Irish peace process forwards more quickly than the British wanted, and despite their at times fierce opposition, in apparent deference to the powerful pro-Sinn Fein lobby within the United States. One view might be that he did so because he believed the views of the lobby to be correct and those of the British to be wrong in the matter of how fast the peace process should proceed. A more cynical view might be that, having noted the electoral power of the Irish lobby and his need to gain and hold on to support after his party's drubbing in the mid-term Congressional elections, he decided to point his policy in the direction of his own best interests. Whatever the truth of the matter, this could be argued to be another example not only of a powerful domestic lobby group at work in influencing US policy on change within the global system, but also of cooperation between it and part of the political elite of another land, in this case the leadership of Sinn Fein in the politically divided island of Ireland.

In short, what the above examples show is that the vulnerability to lobbying of the United States' political system makes the ability of American politicians to promote or obstruct global change potentially subject to the pressures exerted by a large range of domestic BTC and political elite interest groups, operating sometimes across state boundaries in harness with non-American interests. (A further example of the way in which external actors can play a role in the US political process was shown in Chapter 1 with regard to British Prime Minister Thatcher's alleged influence over President Bush prior to the 1991 Gulf War.) As will be illustrated shortly, administrative elite groups also can play a highly influential part in the decision-influencing process. Given that the extremely diverse ethnic composition of the USA makes it in many ways a United Nations in itself, there is a good chance that any significant proposed external policy will provoke lobbying from one group or another whose members in some way represent or are otherwise linked to nationals of another state and this has to be taken into account when attempting to understand American attitudes on change.

The Irish example cited above pointed also to the importance of the American electoral system, which can cause presidents to find their policy options severely complicated as a result of mid-term Congressional elections which go against them. The NAFTA example from Chapter 1 showed how external policies that are significant with regard to global change can involve competition and interaction between domestic factors at every level of American society, from the President down to the wider electorate, while the Somali example within the same chapter further reinforced the importance which the latter can have with regard to some foreign policy issues.

But these are just some of the domestic factors which can influence America's ability to shape global change. Additional to these, for example, are debates within any given administration as to which policies and involvements will best serve the United States' security interests, the ideological inclinations of the President and the balance between competing ideologies within Congress. The victory of Newt Gingrich and his fellow Republicans half-way through President Clinton's term of office, for example, resulted in considerable negative pressure being put on a number of American overseas commitments which carry significant budgetary implications.

In theory, as some of the above examples suggest, the foreign policy process in the USA has become highly democratised, with the presidency often being checked in its ambitions by Congressional power and with plentiful opportunities for interested individuals and groups to try and influence the key foreign policy players in both government and the Congress. In reality, however, the picture can be somewhat different. First, the balance of power between the Congress and the President varies according to the political circumstances of the moment and the issue involved. For example, as the primary player in the foreign policy process and the Commander-in-Chief of American military forces, presidents can actually use military force against another state before telling Congress of their intentions. It is true that on less dramatic external issues there are several powerful Congressional committees, such as the Senate's Foreign Relations and Armed Services Committees, which have the potential to heavily limit a president's policy options by means of budgetary and legal devices if they so choose.[7] However, their ability to do this is dependent upon their political will to stand up to the government at any one time and the skill and determination of particular presidents in trying to outwit their efforts. During the 'Imperial Presidency' of Richard Nixon, for example, the President was able to ignore Congress and its committees to a far greater extent than successors like Jimmy Carter, who tried to do the same but did not have the necessary know-how in the face of a Congress that was determined not to be trampled on.

Equally, those who are most listened to by the President and/or Congress often can come from a highly restricted selection of elite groups. Those favoured with top politicians' ears are frequently heard because they are regarded as 'experts' or because they are electorally significant, which, in the latter case, often simply means that they have economic muscle, while those who do not possess these qualities are marginalised.[8] Experts come frequently from within the many government agencies that can be involved in foreign affairs issues and which can have their own agendas based on career ambitions, differing perceptions of the national interest, and so on. Frequently (although not always – government experts can agree to an extent sufficient to produce a consensus view on the US national interest on some issues) there will be competitive jostling for influence between the various expert groups in the manner suggested by the Change Map. Experts can come also from industrial or financial concerns, for example, with specialist knowledge on, and interests related to, particular topics. Many foreign policy issues now are so complicated that their very complexity effectively rules out all but those few experts who understand them from the decision-making process.

As far as electorally significant groups with economic muscle are concerned, examples have been given already of the role played by Aipac on Middle Eastern matters and the influence of industrial and agricultural groups on the USA's pre-Gulf War policies towards Iraq. Government agencies also can lobby for Congressional support highly effectively because of their economic muscle. The Department of Defense, for example, can hint to Congressional opponents of their ambitions that they can place valuable defence contracts within their constituencies if they support them – or, alternatively, withdraw existing contracts if they do not. In this way they too can be 'electorally significant'.

Even where non-elite groups are able to make an impact on the government and influence a particular policy decision, the various agencies charged with implementing that policy can, if they wish, frequently subtly change and even subvert it by their chosen means of implementation.

Maidment and McGrew summarise much of the reality of American foreign policy making when they state that:

> the degree of effective participation and democratic control varies considerably according to the type of policy issue involved. It is least with regard to crisis decisions and the employment of military force, but greatest on those intermestic issues (i.e. those which are clearly of both a domestic and an external nature, such as trade or drug trafficking) which now tend to dominate the foreign policy agenda. But in relation to the latter participation and democratic control is often restricted both by inequalities in the distribution of political and economic power and the structural constraints inherent in the nation's role as the world's dominant capitalist power, with the consequence that some aspects of foreign and national security policy tend primarily to reflect the interests of the most powerful elites. Even in the post-Cold War era the realities of the foreign policy process are not entirely in accord with the principles of liberal democracy.[9]

How important is all of this for global change?

Overall, to return to the beginning of the chapter, all of the above factors which potentially can affect US policy on global change are significant internationally simply because of America's political and economic 'size'. To give but one illustration, despite the end of the Cold War, the United States retains a substantial military presence in Western and Central Europe. As the situation in the former Yugoslavia, together with the conflicts that have occurred in European areas of the former Soviet Union such as Georgia and the Chechen Republic, has demonstrated, Europe remains an area with deep divisions and inherent instabilities, some of which, if they ever run out of control, have the potential to escalate to major conflicts in the future, depending on the overall political circumstances within the continent at the time. In the light of this fact, unless the European Union hammers itself together into an effective security organisation, then the extent to which the USA remains committed to NATO, together with the decisions which it makes as to which conflicts it might be prepared to try and prevent or become involved with as part of the alliance, will be crucial in determining the future security of Europe as a region. Should Russia regenerate itself and become a benevolent regional peace-keeper, then the problem will obviously be less. But should it become once more a hostile power for any reason, then, in the absence of any integrated European Union force, only the United States would be capable of guaranteeing the security of Western, Central and possibly Eastern Europe.

The extent to which the USA is prepared to play a continuing European security role, on the basis of earlier sections of this chapter, is going to be dependent on the balance of forces within the US political system, whether they be internally or externally driven. Should there be at a time of approaching crisis in Europe a Congressional majority in favour of isolationism and withdrawal from NATO, together with a president who sees the USA's future economic interests as so concentrated in the Pacific Rim that Europe is expendable, together with a clearly articulated unwillingness of the American public to become involved in foreign wars and an absence of any strong enough counter-active pressure-group lobbying, then the Europeans would be in trouble.

In Change Map terms, therefore, because the United States has the potential to be a powerful blocking factor in the way of global change in a number of areas, then, unless they have at their disposal economic or military power and/or political influence that can be applied directly on the US government from abroad, and that is sufficient to make that government listen to them on its own, it is important that those around the globe who wish to facilitate that change, or to persuade the USA to become or remain a blocking factor in its way, are able to develop and exploit strong channels of influence within the partially open but highly competitive American political system. Many of the potential channels, such as lobbying through interest groups with cross-national linkages, have been covered briefly within this chapter. More detailed elaborations of these are readily available for those who wish to act on them.[10] In exploiting such channels, however, those who wish to preserve or change particular American foreign policies need to bear in mind one important factor which could influence crucially the success or otherwise of their efforts. Some of the US pressure groups which they might find themselves in competition with have formidable resources at their disposal with which to try and buy the support of American politicians. Aipac, for example, has 50 000 members and an annual budget of $15m.[11]

By way of a final comment, the implications of this chapter need to be borne in mind whenever US governments' attitudes on global change are referred to within the discussion which follows. If those attitudes sometimes seem strange or difficult to understand, the complexities of the

American foreign policy process explained here should help provide a key with which readers can unlock at least part of the puzzle, in so far as they show something of the extent to which US foreign policy is frequently the result of competing pressures rather than any logic-driven 'rational actor'[12] view of the world.

For those who wish to study the subject matter of this chapter further three useful texts which they might like to look at are G.T. Allison, *Essence of Decision* (Boston, Little, Brown, 1971), R. Maidment and A. McGrew, *The American Political Process* (London, Sage/Open University, 1991), and J. Spanier and J. Nogee (eds), *Congress, the Presidency and American Foreign Policy* (Oxford, Pergamon Press, 1981).

Chapter 3

Can the state survive?
The threat from economic global interfusion

Introduction

States can arouse great passions. Millions of people die in their name. During the Cold War, the military superpowers ultimately were prepared to threaten the world with the global catastrophe of a thermonuclear war in order to preserve their right to exist (even though the right itself might have been one of the only survivors of such a war). Yet developments are now underway which threaten the existence of states in their traditional form without a single shot being fired. It is these which form one of the central concerns of this and the next chapter. Before they can be considered, however, a definition of the state and a few initial thoughts are in order.

A state in its traditional form is, for the specific purposes of this study, perhaps most usefully described as a clearly defined territory which (i) is *recognised internationally* as a state, (ii) is presided over by a government able to make and enforce independent decisions concerning domestic policy and law and foreign policy and (iii) is permanently occupied by a specific population.[1]

The point about international recognition sounds obvious but is highly important. In practice, for the state to have any meaningful existence, its boundaries and its exclusive right (via its government) to make and enforce laws and policies (including, to the extent determined by its government, economic policies) within those boundaries, *together* with its right to be the international representative of its people, *must be respected by a sufficient number of the major players in international politics (such as influential states and international organisations) to make it viable as a political body.*

How many is 'enough' will vary from state to state, according to the particular nature of its political, economic and strategic environment. The Bosnian Republic, for example, scored some major successes during 1992 in terms of being recognised by major powers, but nevertheless ran into huge problems threatening its viability as a result of its failure to gain the recognition of the Serbs.

States as a group are not homogeneous in terms of population or territorial size, or the extent of power and influence which they possess. For example, the very smallest, such as Luxembourg, have populations equivalent only to a single relatively minor city in a continental state, such as the USA, while the largest, the People's Republic of China, has over a billion people within its borders. Equally, the United States is able to use substantial military power anywhere around the globe if it so wishes, while many poor states find it difficult enough simply to defend their own borders adequately.

But as implied at the beginning, as well as trying to answer the question of what is the state, there is a need for analysts to investigate the problem of whether or not it can defend itself against increasing competition from alternative power centres in world politics, such as the giant global corporations and the rise of a new part state, part intergovernmental organisation style of institution, in the prototype form of the European Union.

This and the next chapter, therefore, will ask and attempt to answer the question, 'can (and to what degree can) the state survive in the modern world?' The two chapters will focus specifically on the threat posed by the growth of global interfusion, first in the overlapping fields of politics and economics, and second, in the realms of technological, scientific and cultural affairs.

Global interfusion has been defined already at some length in the section on opportunity factors in Chapter 1. The types of global interfusion referred to above are not the only threats which states face, but the size of their importance justifies their place as focuses within this chapter and Chapter 4. We exist, after all, in a world in which many states are dwarfed in economic terms by giant global business corporations, in which the traditional values of ancient societies can be challenged by the simple action of their peoples buying television sets and switching them on, in which many policy problems are beyond the capacity of even the most powerful of states to solve on their own, and in which the economic welfare of all states is affected crucially by what happens in the world beyond their boundaries. We live, in short, in the age of global interfusion. Furthermore, the checklist function of the Change Map draws analysts' attention to the need to consider the concept's potential importance when undertaking any investigation of potential or actual global change, given that it is often a crucial opportunity factor.

The concern of this chapter and the next, therefore, is to examine the ways in which global interfusion can undermine the power and/or credibility of the state and to illustrate the ways in which this process can alter popular and elite perceptions concerning the most appropriate role for the state in global and domestic politics. The findings derived from the completion of these tasks should provide a useful answer to the question of whether or not the state can survive in the face of the challenges it now faces as a result of this process.

Conclusions on the significance of the threat posed by each type of global interfusion for the long-term health or demise of the state as a form of political organisation will be drawn at the end of each appropriate chapter. In addition, the effect of their combined threat will be emphasised at the end of Chapter 4.

The Change Map emphasises that opportunity factors, like everything else within it, can be important not only on their own, but also in the context of their interaction with other variables. While the predominant concern in the study of the state that follows will be with global interfusion, in order to demonstrate something of the analytical power even of this single aspect of the Change Map, such potential interaction is something that needs to be kept in mind and elucidated at relevant points of the analysis.

Preliminary questions

As far as the economic aspect of the global interfusion process is concerned, closely integrated international trading systems are nothing new. The Roman and British Empires in their respective heydays were two prominent authoritarian examples of such systems. Equally the global corporation, as a device that is increasing economic interfusion greatly, is not something that has sprung up overnight. A significant number of such bodies were operating by the beginning of the twentieth century. What is new is the growth of an international economic system that is both truly global in scope and which, through the interlinkages that it is creating, is reducing significantly the ability of even many of the largest states to control their own economies. With the post-1989 changes in Eastern Europe, most of the former Marxist state capitalist[2] countries are in the process of becoming full members of this 'liberal/capitalist' economic system.

The fact that the 'liberal capitalist' system with its interfusing tendencies (to be explained shortly) has become globally dominant does not mean that it is everyone's favourite way of doing things, but rather that because many have chosen to belong to it, others have been left with no real alternative if they want to participate fully in world trade. There are some who believe the system in its present form is a real threat to their state and its citizens.

The first question to ask therefore is what is the precise nature of the threat to states which this interfusing system might be seen to pose? Part of the answer must be that it is not only a threat, but also an opportunity for states, otherwise the former Soviet bloc members would not be joining it. Another part is that the threat, if it exists, must vary with whatever interpretations of the capitalist system are being applied at any one time at the global level. For example, the economic concerns of the version which predominated during the two Reagan presidencies, *declaredly* at least, were focused on the business of pushing for as complete a system of global free trade as could be obtained, to the point where ultimately, at some time in the possibly quite distant future, there would be virtually no incidence of one state restricting imports from other states. Taken to its logical extreme, this would have involved the complete global interfusion of states' economic practices with regard to trading rules, something which, as will be explained shortly, was regarded by many critics as being likely to be much more damaging to states than the consequences of other less ambitious views of how the system should be run. As will be seen towards the end of the chapter, this version of the liberal system did not just have economic goals, and this fact has had tremendous negative implications for the Soviet Union and its successor states. What will be seen also is that there is often a significant gap between declarations and intentions, and that by the mid-1980s the Reagan presidency's free trade commitment was noticeably constrained by strong protectionist domestic pressures.

Whether or to what extent the global economic system is seen as a threat or an opportunity for states depends also on one's ideological perspective. The intention here is to compare the views on this question from the standpoint of those who may be broadly termed traditional liberals with those of interventionist liberals (including the views of those who will be defined as semi-protectionists), and to outline also the particular concerns of many less developed states. Such a comparison will hardly encompass all the various economic ideologies existing to one extent or another currently across the globe, but it will illustrate effectively the importance of ideological perspectives in relation to the above question. A cautionary note for students takes the form of a warning that the terms 'traditional liberals' and 'interventionist liberals' *as employed here*, together with some of the characteristics attributed to them, would not be agreed with by some political economists – the broad meanings used within the analysis which follows are designed purely for the purposes of this chapter. It is necessary to realise that liberalism in its various forms can be defined in other ways by analysts who view it differently.

It is important to realise that, as implied in the Reagan example above, the global political economy tends to be the ever-changing outcome of an ongoing struggle between various shades of traditionalists, interventionists and out-and-out protectionists. Jones describes matters in the following simplified but usefully illustrative way. He observes that the potential benefits offered by unrestricted trade relations make liberal exchange an attractive proposition, while the negative consequences of free trade act as a counterbalancing factor. There is therefore a tug-of-war at both the domestic and international levels involving those individuals who stand to benefit and those who stand to lose out from free trade. The overall trade regime that is in evidence at any one moment in time is the result of the power balance between these forces.[3]

To reiterate the above point, if it is argued that there is a threat to the state from the global capitalist economic system therefore, the severity of that threat can be expected to vary according to the nature of the balance between traditionalists and interventionists or others at any one time. Why this is so will be explained fully below.

The threat to the state posed by the global liberal capitalist economic system: the view of traditional liberals

If the traditional liberal recipe for international economics was applied fully within the system, many interventionists would see it as a massive threat to the authority of the state in economic policy matters. But traditional liberals argue that there is *no* threat posed to the state by their strong emphasis on the need to move ever closer towards the fusion of the world's economies into a single global free trade economy and their concern to avoid any effective regulation of multinational business corporations, the great economic interfusers of the late twentieth century. This is so, they claim, because economics is an area in which the state should only minimally be involved. Shifts in the forces controlling national economies, resulting in increasing global economic interfusion, a characteristic of the global economic system in recent times – do not undermine state authority because liberalism dictates that the economy should be as independent of the state as possible anyway. The state's role, for traditional liberals, is to establish the conditions in which free market economics theoretically can flourish by removing as many impediments to competition as possible at both the national and international levels. Its role as an interventionist authority ideally should be restricted to that of establishing laws to prevent dishonesties, such as fraud, and anti-competitive practices. It should exhort and encourage entrepreneurs to establish successful businesses but should not get involved in the enterprises. The idea is that market forces, not governments, are the most efficient producers of wealth and that the taxation revenues from successful business will provide the means by which the state can finance its various policies in the fields of health, education, defence and so on.

If an economy falls under the control of foreign multinationals as a result of its membership of the liberal capitalist international economic system, this is nothing to worry about, because as the traditional liberal state always tries to leave control of its economy to market forces anyway, nothing has changed. What are still governing the economy, providing monopolistic abuses do not arise, are market forces and products of those forces in the form of the multinationals. The country of origin of the businesses within it is irrelevant – all that is important is that entrepreneurs are at work within the economy and that their activities are creating wealth and funding state policies. The market is all and it is believed to work best if allowed to operate globally rather than just nationally.

To get a more concrete idea of just precisely what traditional liberal ideas look like in practice it is useful to consider briefly the example of Peru. The listing by the prominent liberal journal *The Economist* of Peruvian economic reforms during the 1990s can be quoted for this purpose. Something of the extent to which interventionist liberals would question the journal's highly favourable interpretation of the appropriateness of some of the reforms will become apparent in the next section.

'In 1990 Peru was in a sorry state. Economic mismanagement, political infighting, corruption and a vicious guerrilla insurgency had left it on the brink of economic and political collapse. . . . Five years later, no country outside the former communist block has changed as much. Economic growth in 1994 ran at 12.9%, the world's highest; this year it is set for 7–8%, and many believe that it can continue at 5–6% a year for the rest of the decade. Tight monetary and fiscal policies have brought inflation down to an annual rate of 11.4%, its lowest level since 1973. In Lima, blocks of offices and flats that stood unfinished for a decade have been completed, and new ones started; in the shanty towns that ring the city, people are once again adding an extra room, or a concrete roof. . . . In the past three years foreign and local mining firms have staked out 20m hectares for exploration, four times the area prospected since Peru became a republic in 1824. Outside investors have become enthusiastic. . . .

Considering that it started with the most statist economy in South America, Peru's progress towards the free market has been particularly impressive; much more so, in some respects, than that of Chile and Argentina. Unlike Chile, it has lifted all capital controls, freed the exchange rate, and started privatising state-owned oil and mining companies. In all, the government has sold 51 state companies (and parts of another dozen) for a total of $3.6 billion; the purchasers have committed themselves to new investment totalling another $4.1 billion. The remaining government holdings – which include the oil company, some electricity generators and water companies – should be sold or leased to private firms by 2000.

Unlike Argentina, Peru was quick to cut its bloated central government payroll. . . . Under Carlos Bolona, who as finance minister in 1991–93 was responsible for most of the market reforms, the number of taxes was cut from 200 to half a dozen, and collection tightened up. . . .

Officials at the World Bank and International Monetary Fund (IMF) – which have supervised and advised on reforms – express awe, even trepidation, at the speed with which Peru's government has rushed their recommendations into practice. There are no subsidies now, nor are there import quotas and bans. Tariffs have been cut from an average of 75% to either 15% (applying to three quarters of imports) or 25%. Subsidised credit for agriculture and industry is no more, and restrictions on foreign investment have been scrapped, along with reams of internal regulations. A private pension system is starting to boost domestic savings. Last month the government moved to free the labour market, by scrapping rules protecting workers from dismissal.'[4]

The article later acknowledges that despite all of these reforms, Peru remains a very poor country with a huge external debt and with almost half of its population still living below the poverty line. Interventionist liberals argue that a different, less 'extreme' strategy is needed for effectively tackling such poverty, as will be seen during the course of the discussion below, and that this can only be implemented when states are allowed full freedom to intervene in their economies when they think fit.

The views of interventionist liberals

In the 'real world' economic liberalism houses many varying schools of thought within it. While traditional, relatively unrestrained liberalism was

close to the hearts of many American Republicans and the British
Thatcherites during the past decade, for example, much more interventionist
strains of the doctrine predominated elsewhere around the globe. In thriving
liberal capitalist northern Italy during the 1980s, for example, there was
extremely heavy and frequently misdirected government involvement in the
running of the economy by means of large state corporations and various
forms of protectionism. In Japan, the partnership between government and
industry has long been seen as a key ingredient of the Japanese economic
success story. Japan also has been notorious for limiting imports from other
states via a variety of formal and informal barriers to trade, while *declaredly*
supporting free trade. In the 1990s, one of the early concerns of the Clinton
Democrat administration in the USA was to try to push through Congress
an unashamedly interventionist package of economic measures in an attempt
to set the American economy back on track for growth. Many of these kinds
of mixed-economy approaches were stated to be heresy by the Reaganite
and Thatcherite liberals of the 1980s (although in practice US govern-
ment/industry relations were close in the field of defence). The simple key
point is that, by definition, interventionist liberals of all kinds wish to see the
state having a significant degree of control over its economy.

So, as will be seen below, from the points of view of many interventionist
liberals (including those who advocate a degree of protectionism), the main
threat presented to the state and its ability to influence its economy by
the global capitalist system arises whenever there is any attempt within
the latter to implement virtually unrestrained economic liberalism. As
pointed out already, this is seen to involve the interfusion of states' economic
practices concerning free trade to the point ultimately where none would
be able to restrict imports from other states. Neither ultimately would they
be able to provide 'unfair' subsidies to protect 'lame duck' industries. In
addition, multinational corporations would be likely to remain free of any
effective international system of regulation. (The consequences of this latter
point will be examined towards the end of this chapter.)

The biggest threat from attempts to apply traditional liberalism, therefore,
is seen by those social democratic liberals and others who believe the state
has a responsibility to intervene to strengthen or shore up its economy when
necessary in order to guarantee that it can meet its obligations to its citizens.
They believe that while market forces can greatly help in the creation of the
necessary resources to supply adequate health, education, welfare and
defence services, there is a definite limit to their usefulness. If left unfettered
completely, then such forces can begin to undermine the state's ability to
generate sufficient wealth to maintain such services. When this happens, the
state needs to step in.

They argue that one of the main reasons why an unfettered market can be so damaging is because the theoretical model of traditional liberal economics does not fit the real world. It assumes that competition under unrestrained market forces will be 'fair', and will be conducted between homogeneous parties. However, in the real world the parties are frequently not homogeneous. Some states' cultural attitudes, for example, give them a considerable 'unfair' advantage over their rivals. The extraordinarily competitive ethos of Japanese society is an oft-quoted example. Cultural attitudes can not be changed overnight, and this has put societies such as the British, whose cultures are much less competitive, at a severe disadvantage in a number of key industrial sectors over the past twenty years. The cultural differences between Britain and Japan, and even the United States and Japan, it is argued, make it both ridiculous and dangerous for any economic theory to presume them to be homogeneous competitors. Accordingly, some liberal interventionists contend that if such states are to survive Japanese competition, then either their governments may need to introduce or preserve various forms of protectionism, or the Japanese government should intervene and 'adjust' its own economic impact on other cultures in order to make this less damaging.

Equally some states may be at a considerable 'unfair' competitive disadvantage to others because of differing governmental obligations. Homogeneity, in other words, does not exist because there are some states where the population has come to expect and demand a substantial and expensive welfare state, adequate health and safety provisions in the workplace and a minimum wage, while there are others which suppress or ignore many such demands (or where they simply are not made) and which do not have to add the cost of such things on to the price of their manufactured goods and services. In the early years of the Clinton administration, for example, the problems created by this kind of difference in social welfare provision were raised by powerful voices in the US Congress (even though by European standards, *American* social welfare provision is relatively limited). There were serious concerns that Mexico's relatively poor social welfare and health and safety provisions were giving it an unfair advantage over US competitors who were legally bound by much higher standards.

Again, in the absence of international measures to offset the disadvantageous effect of such social obligations in a global market-place where many states are not hampered by such burdens, interventionist liberals may want to take protectionist measures at state level. Otherwise, with such irremovable[5] burdens on their backs, some states may find unfettered market forces do them nothing but damage in the face of increasing competition from new rivals with much smaller social obligations.

However, many interventionists in the United States and elsewhere have felt that traditional liberalism has had too much of a sway over the global economic system in recent times and that this has limited greatly the extent to which states have been able to protect their industries against such 'unfair' competitive advantages. This, they claim, has been because of the formalised pressures against the extension of existing levels of protectionism exerted through the long-established General Agreement on Tariffs and Trade, an agreement (and a process) with the avowed purpose of *fusing states' trading practices* in order to produce fully open world markets.

Traditionalists would dispute this however by pointing to the fact that in 1985, for example, the USA was applying protectionist measures to 15.1 per cent of its imports, while Japan was doing the same with 8.7 per cent and the EC was weighing in at the top of the league with one form or another of protectionism being applied to 41.9 per cent of its imports.[6]

On a more general level, one prominent interventionist economist explains his overall views on how the traditional liberalism of the New Right has damaged states and their citizens as follows:

'the right has created an international economic structure in which assertions of state or community interest seem at best self-defeating – at worst impossible. The global market place insists upon conservative . . . and free market . . . economic policies – with the Group of Seven [a group comprising the US, Japan, Germany, France, Italy, Britain, and Canada with the stated goal of coordinating domestic economic policies in pursuit of steady growth and minimal inflation], the Bank for International Settlements, the IMF and the OECD as willing cheerleaders.

Heard any of them mention full-employment as an objective? You won't have – and with respectable parties of the left apparently offered no choice but collusion, electorates are fearful of their powerlessness in the face of the inexorable rise in unemployment.

But markets have no better self-stabilising properties internationally than domestically. As the Japanese stock market reached dizzy heights in the late 1980s – itself partly a result of financial deregulation – the cost of raising investment funds fell absurdly low.

The resulting investment boom has equipped Japan with a manufacturing sector that is far too large for any probable market at home or abroad; and which presages a major price-cutting war.

The shrinkage of British and American manufacturing was the mirror image of the explosive growth in Japan. In the Anglo-Saxon world, the equities boom [equities are stocks and shares which pay dividends related to a company's performance] cheapened capital too; but the response was an orgy of deal making and asset stripping.

In any case, in both the US and UK, interest rates and the exchange rates were allowed to reach ridiculous levels as the cost of stabilising prices at the same time as deregulating the financial institutions. First in Britain and then in the US, important segments of the industrial base were eliminated. . . .

In sum we need an international order that allows communities to assert their needs over the caprice of unregulated markets. The paradox, as it has always been, is that markets work best where there are rules and where they are managed; even though their apologists always insist that they work best when free. But if "freedom" means what we have today – a fat lot of good it is.'[7]

Other ways in which recent versions of the liberal capitalist global system have been argued to have reduced the ability of states to influence their economic affairs perhaps have been less obvious. The periodically troubled European Monetary System is a useful example here. Basically, at the core of the EMS is an agreement amongst those European Union (EU) members who wish, or are able, to participate in it to keep their exchange rates within agreed narrow bands of fluctuation and not to move beyond those bands without common consent. As such this aspect of the EMS represents a clear example of the interfusion of the participating states' exchange rate policies. While originally introduced as a response to such things as German currency problems and what were seen as the vagaries of US economic policy and leadership in the late 1970s, the European Monetary System subsequently came to be regarded as an important strand of Europe's strategy to survive in the face of increasingly fierce competition from Japan and the newly industrialising members of the liberal capitalist world economy. (Its perceived stabilising effects on EU currencies were seen as beneficial to business confidence and because of this, to encourage economic growth.) In this sense, the continued survival of the EMS *and its interfusion of fully participating member states' exchange rate policies* can be seen as a direct result of the global spread of the liberal capitalist system and its spawning of new and challenging economic competitors. What has been important about it from the point of view of interventionist liberals is that it has driven an arrow right through the heart of past patterns of interventionism in that it has removed the ability of those member governments who adhere to its core provisions to affect their country's levels of exports and imports via independent exchange rate adjustments.

Together these examples illustrate how considerably some of the inter-fusing tendencies present within the existing version of the international liberal capitalist system, and that are even more particularly inherent within any attempt to move towards implementing 'full-blown' traditional versions, can be argued to limit states' abilities to control their own economic destinies. (The major interfusing impact of multinational corporations will be covered in a separate section shortly.) For some interventionist liberals, tendencies such as the above have meant not only that states' abilities to influence their own economies have been constrained, but that their ability to meet their health and welfare pledges to their citizens has been reduced. This is believed to be the case, for example, for the simple reason that if home-based industries or services are damaged severely by 'unfair' foreign competition because an appropriate level of protection or whatever is not possible, or by free-market exchange rate or interest rate prescriptions that ignore their needs, then the revenue which they can generate to meet such pledges via taxes declines in parallel.

For some interventionists, recent versions of the liberal capitalist economic system have been a very real threat to the survival of *their* concept of the economically and socially interventionist state.[8] While traditional liberals argue that the global economic system is not, nor has been, nearly liberal enough, some interventionists in the USA and Europe, worried by the growing economic challenge from Japan and the Pacific Rim states, believe that the influence of the traditionalists is too great and dangerously so.

A key question, obviously, is whether any threat which traditional liberalism might be argued to have posed to the state has been or yet might be capable of undermining popular and elite confidence in it as an institution. A case might be made for saying that to a degree this has happened in the case of the United Kingdom. Britain, as well as being a leading supporter of the traditional liberal concept of economics under the Conservative rule of Thatcher and her successor, has been keen to emphasise its commitment to national sovereignty. Yet its relative economic power and related political muscle has continued to decline within the context of traditional liberal policies, leaving the British with little option but to continue to surrender sovereignty to the European Union.[9] While this has not been popular with some sections of the major political parties and the electorate, the decline in the UK's capacity to 'go it alone' on many issues has so changed attitudes among key sections of the political and business, technical and cultural (BTC) elites that such continuing surrenders have been accepted as unavoidable, even if they are disguised frequently by nationalist posturing and a variety of other 'diversionary tactics'. In this sense, the interfusing tendencies of traditional liberalism might be argued to have created the basis for significant change in the role and institutional nature of one of the international system's major second-rank players.

The British example therefore might be used to try and demonstrate that traditional liberalism threatens the sovereignty of even some of the larger states. However, traditional liberals outside the UK might well argue that Britain's decline has not been the result of traditional liberalism as such, but rather its failure to implement the doctrine appropriately. Severe distortions of the British economy occur, for example, because of the continuing failure to reform its investment structures in such a way that would allow for the medium- and long-term investment that is necessary to allow many British firms to develop and put into production a range of innovative new products that could rival seriously those of their major competitors. Vested interests so far have been simply so strong that they have been able to prevent this from happening. Britain also has long-established weaknesses in the field of industrial training.

However, such counter-arguments do not deal with (a) the simple fact that the global market-place consists of non-homogeneous actors and (b) the interventionist criticism that the examples used to illustrate this fact above demonstrate that anything resembling full-blown traditional liberalism involves 'unfair' competition in which the disadvantages inherent to some actors mean they could lose out severely under such a system. If one were to accept that in some cases such disadvantages are both irremovable within the short/medium or even long terms and unfair, then traditional liberalism begins to look both extremely negative as far as the seriously disadvantaged are concerned and a serious potential threat to the sovereignty of such states. From this point of view it could be argued on the basis of, for example, the earlier cited point about cultural differences between Britain and Japan, that the British Conservatives' recent pursuit of traditional liberalism has been damaging for their own economy, even if it is now beginning to copy some Japanese work practices. Equally, the point about social welfare obligations has relevance here. Britain in the recent past suffered economically as a result of many of its jobs being exported to areas where such obligations are minimal or suppressed, but made little effort to do anything about this due to its commitment to the traditional liberal ethos. With each full-time job lost spending power and taxation revenue within the British economy has declined. From this point of view, aspects of traditional liberalism have helped to undermine the British economy which in turn has undermined domestic confidence in Britain's ability to 'go it alone' on many issues, which in turn has created an acceptance of the need to surrender some sovereignty to organisations such as the EU.

The British Conservatives' commitment to the key interfusing tendencies of traditional liberalism has therefore helped remove their state's ability to retain the substantial sovereignty that they desire. The fact that this has been able to happen in the case of a relatively powerful state can therefore be taken as an indication of the dangers of traditional liberal policies, and most particularly of a full-blown traditional liberal global economic system, for the many states that are less economically powerful than the UK. In this sense, the interfusing tendencies of the traditional liberal approach to economics are a real danger to the survival of many states in their existing form.

The views of the less developed states

The General Agreement on Tariffs and Trade, previously and appropriately described both as a treaty and a negotiating process, has been a keystone of the post-Second World War liberal capitalist system. Along with other global economic institutions, it has been used as a means of applying considerable 'interfusing' pressure against protectionism during recent decades. However, many less developed states have greatly resented such pressure as applied to themselves. They have felt that it has been a neo-colonialist recipe for keeping them underdeveloped, and that it has been designed to put them in a position where they are unable to protect adequately their infant industries, where these exist, until they are large enough and advanced enough to compete against foreign firms without being overwhelmed by their greater levels of resources and know-how.

Some of them have pointed to the example of the United States' treatment of Japan after the Second World War. The USA, they point out, had a strong interest in redeveloping Japan because it wanted it to become capable of supporting an indigenous military establishment for deployment alongside American forces in the Pacific anti-communist defensive shield. Accordingly, the USA did not tell the Japanese that if they wanted to prosper economically they should adopt immediately the key prescriptions of free-market economics – the advice which in the past frequently has been given to less developed societies by the US-dominated International Monetary Fund when laying down the conditions under which it will help bail them out – but instead allowed them to protect their infant industries heavily until they were ready to take on foreign competition. In addition, it allowed Japanese goods *extremely preferential access* into its own markets.

Japan was thereby able to lay the foundations for the spectacular economic growth of the 1970s and 1980s. The fact that the liberal capitalist system has not been prepared to allow the former African and Asian colonies such a helpful prescription except on a very small scale has been seen by some as a way of denying them full statehood, of keeping them at least partially in the role of economic dependencies of the wealthy states. Instead of granting them the widespread preferential access they need into the economies of the developed world, many rich states have even gone right against the spirit of GATT, which supposedly they believe should be applied to themselves as much as anyone else, and have busied themselves erecting protectionist barriers against key exports of the less developed states.

From the point of view of the less developed states, therefore, important strands within both the traditional and the interventionist liberalisms that have been infused into the global economic system by the rich states within recent decades could be argued to have been threats to their ability to exist as viable independent states. As will be seen in a later chapter, during the 1960s and 1970s there was a concerted attempt by a large number of less developed states (often referred to as LDCs) to alter the balance within the global economic system to enable them to strengthen the economic structures of their own societies. The power of the vested interests in favour of the existing economic system, together with its continuing growth as what is in many ways a multinational corporation-driven interfusing force and the LDCs' own inability to act in a sufficiently united manner ultimately led to the failure of the attempt. Some LDCs simply decided that they could not beat the system but could gain some benefits from it and set out successfully to do so. The vast majority of the LDCs, however, particularly many of the African and Asian states, have remained seriously economically disadvantaged within the system. It will be shown later on in the book that in the case of many this has been partly their own fault, but that it is partly also the result of the way the existing system works. In combination with their own disunity, the strength of the vested interests behind that system and its continuing growth as an interfusing force via the multinationals (their role will be explained shortly) therefore ultimately modified the views of many third world elites as to the degree to which change is possible in the global economic arena. In doing so, the system and its backing interests persuaded them that there was a limit to which they could strengthen their own states and thereby ensure their long-term viability. In helping take the steam out of the search for greater equality by such elites, therefore, the existing system and those behind it have ensured that a large question mark remains against the ability of some LDCs to survive into the future, given the internal pressures that may well build up in some of them as a result of their continuing inability to meet the needs of their peoples adequately.

The plight of the former Soviet Union

The global liberal capitalist economic system had a particularly dramatic effect on the Soviet Union during its final decline. One of the key institutions of the liberal capitalist global economy is the previously mentioned International Monetary Fund, dominated by the United States, Canada, Japan and the largest European economies. One of the IMF's key functions is to furnish loans to members in difficulty, providing such conditions as it may set are accepted. Under Gorbachev, the USSR tried to obtain membership of the Fund in order that it might secure much-needed loan assistance. However, in early August 1991 the dominant IMF states refused Gorbachev full membership until the Soviet Union had made greater progress towards a Western-style democracy and market economy. In order to join, in other words, the Soviet state was being forced to first achieve a rapid fusion with the world capitalist system and to try and accelerate a programme of reform that was already causing internal chaos as the means of doing this. Some have argued that these humiliating conditions strengthened the determination of the August 20 plotters to mount their coup. The combined result of the coup and its failure was the substantial strengthening of the nationalist movements within the republics, and the guarantee of the break-up of the Soviet state. In his previous attempts to make the USSR a viable applicant to join the liberal capitalist system, Gorbachev had already moved too quickly in the field of democratisation, and that had released at one almost uncontrollable swoop the demands for independence in the first place.

Thus, the attempt of the then political leaders of the global liberal economic system to force the Soviet Union to move rapidly towards their own economic ideology in order, among other things, to destroy the remnants of communism and thereby to further the prospects for the interfusion of the global economy, could be argued to have contributed significantly to the destruction of the USSR. It created the conditions in which ultimately many of the peoples and significant sections of the elites of the then USSR were to lose confidence in the notion of the Soviet state, thus leading ultimately to its break-up.

The threat from increasing global economic interfusion – multinationals under the microscope

Perhaps the most fundamental problem posed for supporters of the independent nation state by recent, and indeed, current developments in the liberal international economic system is the increasing extent to which economies are becoming woven together by the operations of the world's 4500 multinational enterprises. These are companies which individually create goods or services on a major scale in several state economies and which are recognised for statistical purposes (by such bodies as the Organisation for Economic Cooperation and Development, otherwise known as the OECD) as being significant actors in the global economy. Often, their headquarters and main centres for research and development are located in one (home) state; with subsidiaries distributed among other (host) states judged to offer economically favourable locations. The largest corporations are mostly American, with the Japanese, Germans, British, Italians and Dutch sharing a smattering of notable presences in the 'big league'. General Motors, the biggest multinational of all, has a turnover that is larger than many states' gross national products. In 1990, for example, General Motors' annual product was $125 126m while Bangladesh's gross national product in the previous year amounted to only $22 579m. A total of 43 other multinationals also had larger annual products than Bangladesh's GNP. Twenty-five multinationals also had annual products that were larger than Kuwait's GNP during 1989/90.[10]

In recent years the structure of multinationals has become increasingly diverse. One recent survey of their activities noted:

'The United Nations Conference on Trade and Development, which keeps a permanent watch on what it dubs "transnational corporations", distinguishes between simple and complex integration. Simple integration means that companies contract-out routine production to the developing world but keep their most sophisticated operations in the home country. Nike, an American sportswear maker, keeps all its product development and marketing in Beaverton, Oregon, its home town, but sub-contracts production to 40 different locations, mostly in South and South-East Asia. If wages in one host country rise, the firm simply shifts production. In complex integration, companies locate all their activities according to the logic of the market, and disperse decision-making throughout the organisation. Their hallmark is the endless flow of information in all directions instead of a command and control system.'[11]

The dominant, although not universal, tendency has been for multi-nationals to split the production of any one complex product between several economies. This means, for example, that no single state builds an entire vehicle for General Motors' European volume car subsidiaries – the engine may come from the United Kingdom, the body panels from Germany, and so on. The effect of this on the state is perhaps most visible in the case of the European Union. By 1985, the activities of the 2500 multi-national corporations at work in the EU had helped bind the member states' economies together to the point where further integration was seen not only as a logical response to external competition, but also as a simple acknowledgement of the way the EU economies were going. The further EU economic integration proceeds the more it pulls a follow-on process of political integration behind it, for reasons that will be explained in the two chapters on the future of European integration. The effect of this economic and political interfusing or binding process, a direct result of the international liberal capitalist system as it has been operated, has been to reduce significantly the prospects for the survival of the nation state in Europe as an entity comparable, say, to France in the early 1960s. A sign of this is that the political, administrative and BTC elites, together with significant sections of public opinion, have in a number of key states come to accept that this continuing interfusing process will reduce the sovereignty of those states. Because of the scale of the implications of multinational corporations, they will be discussed in some detail below.

However, before this is done it must be emphasised that the implications which will be investigated are based on an examination of the world as it is and recently has been (rather than how it might be in the future), with regard to the nature and presence of multinationals within it. This picture may change over the medium to longer term, in which case the nature of any threats which states may be under from multinationals' activities will be affected accordingly. Multinationals have been undergoing a con-siderable degree of change recently in terms of 'downsizing' and moving towards 'flatter hierarchies', which means basically that they have fired large numbers of staff, in particular middle managers, and have dispersed decision-making more widely. Some management experts now think that this process of radical change will go considerably further and that the days of huge multinationals operating as single integrated firms are numbered for the simple reason that such arrangements do not foster the flexibility that is required to preserve companies' competitive edge: 'A better structure ... may be a supportive family or federation of companies, loosely linked through cross-shareholdings, along the lines of the Japanese keiretsu ...'[12]

Such an eventuality, because of its less centralised nature, may well be perceived as representing less of a challenge to state authority than multinationals as they currently exist. The concern in this section of the chapter, however, is the situation as it stands at the moment and in the recent past, and it is this that will now be discussed.

If multinationals did not bring benefits with them, then presumably their continued existence would be violently opposed by states, given the growing realisation of the costs that accompany them. Inward investment by foreign multinationals was encouraged by states like Britain in the late 1980s because such corporations were seen as bringing jobs, exports, new thinking in the field of industrial relations and tax revenues which otherwise would have been absent from the state's economy. In the UK case, the increased revenues that they could provide were seen not only as essential compensation for tax income lost due to the decimation of sections of Britain's industrial base during the early 1980s, but as a useful means of strengthening the state's ability to deliver on its pledges to the electorate.

Equally, American, Japanese and European multinationals have repatriated vast amounts of valuable profits from their overseas operations during recent years and thereby have made crucial contributions to the economic wealth of their home societies.

Less developed states also have received investment, training, jobs and revenue from multinationals which otherwise simply would not have been present within their economies. Such benefits have strengthened their ability to survive as states. Some poor states, for example, which easily could have slid into chaos and possible disintegration, have been able to prevent this by buying off their urban elites with the benefits of foreign direct investment.

So, given all the benefits of multinationals' activities, is it really fair or relevant to think of them in terms of the ways in which they might be seen as threatening the state? It is time to expand the discussion with which this subsection began.

Their main potential threat is to the range of economic and political options open to the state and, as has been seen, to states' independence. If these things are sufficiently reduced, of course, then the viability of a particular state is called into question. Its elites and people may well be forced to consider a new role for it as part of a larger organisation such as the EU in order to survive. If such an option is not available, it may find itself reduced to being an ineffectual pawn on the political and economic chess-boards of world affairs.

So, how can such apparently negative effects occur? First, it is worth looking at the economies of the Irish Republic and the United Kingdom.

Both of these states have actively encouraged a situation in recent years in which a very large slice of economic activity within them has become dependent on foreign multinationals. As such, they have greatly increased the extent to which their economies are interfused with those of other states. They have done so in pursuit of the kinds of benefits outlined at the beginning of this subsection. The price they have paid is to put themselves in a position whereby many of the decisions affecting growth, jobs and the taxation revenues available for public spending are taken by headquarters far outside their borders and largely out of their control should they wish to try and exert pressure on them. While this has been of no worry to Irish and British traditional liberals, it is a cause of considerable nagging concern to more interventionist liberals within these states. For them, the independence of both states in making economic decisions and resource-dependent political decisions has been reduced.

States may find also that significant chunks of their economies are downgraded to 'screwdriver operations' by multinationals. These are 'manufacturing' activities which consist largely of the import and assembly of bits made elsewhere and arise as a result of multinationals' tendency to interfuse economies by producing components for single products in several states and assembling them into one unit wherever politics or economics deem it expedient to do so. Some states may be deemed most suitable for mainly assembly work on several possible grounds, including the desire to disguise and thereby make more acceptable imports by building the façade of a manufacturing presence in a particular state. Some of the electronics manufacturing operations conducted by foreign multinationals within the UK, for example, amount to little more than screwdriver assembly. As a convenient case in point, the UK-'manufactured', Japanese-brand, printer on which the first draft of this manuscript will be run off appears to have only the casing and the roller as British-made components. Such operations can be beneficial in that they at least give some states partial presences in high-tech manufacturing and exporting sectors from which they otherwise would be completely absent.

However, what they can do also is to give economically ailing states a false sense of security. Should the multinationals in a particular 'screwdriver' sector such as electronics find that another state has become more desirable as an economic location, they can 'up and off' extremely rapidly. Screwdriver operations mean that firms do not have to worry about shifting vast amounts of expensive plant to new locations, or about lengthy and complicated training programmes for new employees in the countries they are moving to. Mobility is relatively easy. This type of cost-led rapid relocation abroad can quickly deprive a state of a presence in a whole industry when the same reasons for moving that tempted one firm to move lure firms in related and rival fields to follow. Over-reliance on screwdriver operations runs the risk of part or all of an economy being destabilised by a withdrawal of investment that is too rapid for measures to be taken in time to try and fill the gap when it occurs. It is a risk that arises directly from the fact that multinationals are much more closely interfused with the global economy than they are with most national economies.

In addition, any part of a workforce that possesses only screwdriver skills will be a prime candidate for low wages. This means it will be capable of supplying only a small tax yield to the state. Many states can not afford to let too great a proportion of their labour forces become engaged in screwdriver assembly work therefore, and will be severely damaged by multinational policies that result in their moving towards a 'screwdriver economy'. Allowing multinationals to turn anything more than a very small part of a previously advanced economy into screwdriver production can also be very dangerous as far as the economic independence of a state is concerned. A concentration on screwdriver production means that vital research and development work is not being done locally, and the economy in question will not only find itself being deskilled but also losing its innovation base. It will become entirely dependent on research done in other economies for its well-being. Should multinationals choose to move elsewhere on any scale, the state will be without the skills and innovation base necessary for local firms to be able to spring up and fill some of the gap. The resources necessary for some of the state's key political objectives to be realised could simply vanish. The future of the screwdriver economy is potentially a bleak one.

There is another potential snag for states which become over-reliant on multinationals. Those less developed states in which a few large multi-nationals are the prime source of their wealth-generating capacity, and whose economies thereby have become substantially fused with the latter, can find that some of the corporations succumb to the temptation to throw their economic muscle around to influence the domestic policies of the government in their favour. In extreme cases, as in the famous alleged involvement of the American ITT corporation in the overthrow of President Allende of Chile in 1973, they can actually try and decide who will hold power in a particular country.[13] When this kind of thing happens, the state arguably has ceased to be viable as an independent political actor. In this sense, large corporations potentially are a very serious threat to less developed states.

For developed states, this type of problem is generally less overt because of the much greater diversity within their economies. But a developed state that becomes heavily reliant on multinationals, to the extent that significant sectors or part-sectors of its economy are fused with multinationals and thereby become dependent for their health on the continued presence of the corporations as producers within them, can still find itself significantly constrained. While not necessarily being told what to do by the big corporations, it may well have to do voluntarily what it knows will please them if it wishes to retain their presence. This means a government may not be able to meet some of its electoral obligations to its people. So in this case also, the independence of the state is reduced. Britain and the Republic of Ireland are rather more affected by this kind of problem than states like Germany or France because of their greater reliance on foreign multinationals.

In both developed and less developed states, multinational corporations can be, and have been, used by their state of origin to reduce the policy options of host states. For example, on a number of occasions over the post-Second World War period, the USA tried to stop Western European states from engaging in high-tech trade with the Soviet Union by instructing its corporations to refuse to let their European subsidiaries supply components vital to such trade which were available only from them, or to refuse European companies permission to export goods made under licence from US corporations. The Americans also attempted to hinder France's independent nuclear weapon programme by these means at one stage during the 1960s. In these cases, the USA was trying to use the interfusion which had occurred between sectors of its own and foreign economies, and which was controlled by companies with HQs within its jurisdiction, to determine what other states could and could not do.

A combined effect of the multinationals' ethos and the present liberal capitalist system of which they are a part is that states can find themselves prone to considerable social dislocation as a result of the corporations' mode of operation. Social dislocation can, arguably, help to undermine electorates' confidence in the idea of the state, or certainly of the particular states which are affected. How can such dislocation occur? Well, while multinationals characteristically fuse part-sectors or even sectors of the economies of several states together, they are under no obligation at present to retain all of those component economic sectors or part-sectors within their web of operations. As noted already, as one state becomes a less desirable location to the multinational the latter may well simply disengage from the state and fuse a replacement part-sector from another state into its global framework of operations. For example, for some time European, American and Japanese multinationals have all been shifting significant amounts of their production to lower-cost economies in the more developed world, and very low-cost economies in the less developed world. The US Hewlett Packard corporation, for example, now manufactures bubble jet printers in Singapore and the transformers required to operate them in Mexico. Another American company, Hoover, has transferred part of its European production from France to lower-cost Scotland. The German Bosch corporation manufactures power tools in Mexico and transformers in Taiwan. The giant Japanese Matsushita corporation has shifted significant chunks of its productive capacity abroad and now manufactures hi-fi speakers and vacuum cleaners in Spain (as a low-cost producer behind the EU tariff wall), and record/radio/tape decks in Singapore. Philips similarly now manufactures many of the audio products that used to be made in Europe in Asia. While to some extent this phenomenon has benefited the new recipients of the investment, it has left some of the evacuated economies in considerable disarray. Whole areas, such as the Ohio Valley in the USA or Kirkby near Liverpool in the United Kingdom, for example, have been left rapidly with almost no sources of employment after the departure of multinational firms. Bailey Morris recounts the experience of Elkhart, Indiana, USA:

'This Mid-Western city of 45,000 used to be the home of Whitehall Laboratories Inc, a subsidiary of American Home Products Corporation. The plant produced popular non-prescription drugs for its parent company. The average tenure of its workforce was 20 years and the average wage was $14 an hour. In short, the employees thought they had a secure future.

But last November that dream was shattered. Whitehall closed its plant and laid off all workers. The explanation by American Home Products was that the plant was inefficient. For Elkhart, the closure was a big economic blow. Unemployment rocketed, fewer than half of the workers have found new jobs and the shutdown has had a ripple effect, depressing retail sales and smaller businesses.

However, the final chapter has yet to be written. The outraged former employees, claiming that their plant was a highly efficient profit centre, have filed a $1bn federal suit against American Home Products which alleges that the plant was closed illegally and that their jobs were moved offshore to lower-wage Puerto Rico, so that the company could take advantage of big federal tax breaks. US and Puerto Rican laws prohibit companies from closing plants on the mainland to take advantage of these special breaks. One former Whitehall employee said: These companies have no allegiance to communities, or to countries.'[14]

The enormous human costs for those on the losing side of this kind of relocation are not the only negative effect. The tax revenue-generating industrial production which states such as Britain have lost in the recent past, together with the significant amounts of money which they have had to use to fund the resulting unemployment benefits, has meant that there have been fewer resources available for such things as the defence of the state. Britain is a particularly useful example here. In 1982, for instance, after a massive economic haemorrhage, the UK government was only just able to muster the specialist items necessary to remove Argentina from British-claimed islands seized by its forces in the South Atlantic. Had the proposed defence cuts of the same year – to a significant degree a desperate response to a gathering momentum of British domestic production losses – actually been implemented prior to Argentina's invasion of the Falklands/Malvinas, then the specialist British military operations required for the reversal of that conquest would not have been possible. The production lost from Britain has meant that, despite periods of economic growth, the economy has been unable to keep up with escalating costs in the defence, health and education sectors, and that, in the defence field, the British political and administrative elites have had to accept that their state has become increasingly dependent on the assistance of others.

Production losses in Britain have not by any means solely been due to British and other multinationals shifting manufacturing elsewhere during previous decades. Many UK firms simply vanished during the early 1980s and early 1990s due to the economic mismanagement either of themselves or of the then Conservative government and its Labour predecessor. But at the same time, the multinational 'toll' certainly has been great. For example, over the past fifteen to twenty years, the Dutch electronics giant, Philips, has shifted a significant slice of its domestic appliance operations out of Britain, on one occasion during the 1980s removing 500 jobs at a stroke by doing so, Kraft and Birds Eye have moved sizeable chunks of their UK food production to mainland Europe, the Litton corporation has closed down key UK office machinery factories in favour of imports from Asia, General Motors and Ford have switched the manufacture of entire model ranges from the UK to other EU states (the latest 'British' Vauxhall super-mini, the Corsa, for example, is built in Spain) and much of that British-based presence in the tools, toys and mass sales consumer electronics industries which has been taken over by foreign or British multinationals, or simply replaced by multinational transplants, also has changed substantially from manufacturing its own products to sticking its brand names on products supplied from abroad. The 'reversal of the exodus' of production – the substantial compensatory inward investment by some foreign multinationals which has occurred during more recent years, and which has been of real benefit to the British economy, has had its impact reduced by the earlier factory and job losses of the 1980s in particular. These have meant that its beneficial effects have not been as great as they would have been within an economy that had not previously suffered from such significant evacuations of industrial plant and production, and unemployment within Britain still remains at levels which many people find socially and economically undesirable.

To reiterate the above point, a large part of the massive haemorrhage in Britain's manufacturing capability within the recent past undoubtedly has been due to a potent combination of incompetent politicians, bizarre ideological prescriptions, and uncompetitive trends within the British economy. But a not insignificant part of the explanation for its occurrence rests with such things as the fact that many multinationals came to realise increasingly during the 1980s that they could cut costs substantially by a policy of keeping on moving from low-cost production areas to newly arising, even lower-cost areas. For a variety of reasons, such 'hops' occurred mainly in the developed world for some types of production. But many multinationals became increasingly aware also that the less developed economies, offering their workforces relatively poor wages and frequently less in the way of health and safety provisions, enabled them to produce goods much more cheaply than in the developed world. For the reasons explained above, these realisations effectively contributed indirectly to a decline in the power of states such as Britain (although, as implied previously, some argue that multinationals have now once more become a force that is helping stem the UK's slide into deindustrialisation). In Britain's case, the power decline has resulted, post-Thatcher, in a grudging realisation among the Conservative political elite that the UK's bargaining position in the European Union has also declined in parallel, although not necessarily proportionally. Multinationals, therefore, when they contribute to such decline (which they can do also as the result of additional modes of operation to those listed above), can potentially be a very real threat to the power of the state and can be a cause of the elites of the latter having to surrender more power to organisations like the EU in order to try and fill the gaps in their effectiveness internally and externally resulting from that decline.

There are of course many more aspects of this subject that could be mentioned. What the above points have emphasised is that multinationals, with their various types of interfusing behaviour, are capable of doing severe damage to the state – in some cases even being able effectively to end the viability of particular states – if left entirely to their own devices in the manner prescribed by the traditional version of the liberal international economic system. But equally, as pointed out earlier, they would not have been encouraged by states in the first place if there were not believed to be benefits from their presence in terms of investment, jobs, revenue and exports. Indeed, the then European Community actively encouraged its multinationals to grow bigger in the run-up to the completion of the 1992 Single Market programme[15] in the belief that by doing so it would help Europe to better resist Japanese and American competition. Furthermore, to return to the British example, as pointed out above, some are now claiming that after having in some cases helped accelerate the decline of the UK's manufacturing base during the 1980s, multinationals, most particularly foreign corporations, are now helping rebuild it. For example, in August 1995 one commentator noted:

'The decision by Siemens to locate a £1.1 billion microchip plant on north Tyneside is a dramatic example of Britain's second industrial revolution.
. . .

That the investment came here at all overturns the proposition, plausible just a decade ago, that the UK can't compete with the economies of the Pacific Basin. The reasons are many. Automation has eroded the advantages of sending parts to the Far East to be assembled by cheap labour, while exploding capital costs have cut the percentage wages represent of the final costs. Nowadays, companies like to be near their suppliers because of Japanese-style "just in time" production techniques. And, finally, being located inside the European Union removes the need to pay the common external tariff.

The prospect of a minimum wage if Labour gains power was less important than the existence of infrastructure and skilled labour (including the government's promise to train future employees). In this way, competing countries like Singapore and Czechoslovakia (where wages are a 10th of UK levels) were ruled out. . . .

Many of our consumer electronics industries, including televisions and video recorders, have been taken over by the Japanese and are now flourishing.

These foreign-owned companies, helped by the devaluation of the pound, have been in the vanguard of the export-led recovery. Although there are dangers in hiving off a country's manufacturing heart, not least because we don't know whether in a crisis they would close down their overseas subsidiaries first.'[16]

However, if the above passage is 'turned on its head', it will of course be realised that Britain's gain could equally be seen as the Pacific Basin's loss, and that if such trends continue, then multinationals could start to undermine the economies of Asian multinational-dependent states by this latest variation on their liberal economic views of how most efficiently to locate industrial plant.

So what all of this seems to imply is that there is a balancing act to be performed by states in trying to limit and offset the costs of multinationals' globally interfusing behaviour while securing as many of the benefits as possible. The key question is whether states can achieve such a balance individually, or whether they need help from effective regional or global regulatory bodies.

For economically enormous states, such as the USA and Japan, there is considerable bargaining power at the disposal of government should it choose to use it. The US government, for example, is highly important to many multinational corporations, and therefore potentially in a strong bargaining position with them, because it is a significant purchaser of their products, and can also subtly and negatively affect the image which consumers have of those companies in its extremely rich market if it so chooses. The further one goes down the list of states' relative power resources, however, the more difficult it becomes to believe that many states can strike a good bargain with multinationals if acting alone. The extreme case of ITT and Chile has been mentioned already. But even states like France or Britain can have serious difficulties if they wish to take on the multinationals on their own over any serious issue. This appears to have been demonstrated as early as 1968 when, in a famous case, a number of American pharmaceutical companies' subsidiaries in Britain allegedly threatened to transplant themselves to other parts of Europe unless the then British government changed a policy which displeased them. Given the importance of their contributions to UK exports, the government allegedly had to accommodate their demands.

In short, there seems to be an urgent need for effective international regulations to try and produce a situation of fairer play between multinationals and many both developed and less developed states. There have been several attempts to do this so far, the most serious occurring within the United Nations and the EU. However, while several sets of voluntary guidelines now exist, no binding and effective system of regulation has been agreed. The problem has been simply that it has not proved possible to get sufficient agreement between states on any given set of proposals.

So, until states can reach the high level of agreement amongst themselves that is necessary to produce an effective system of international regulation

– an eventuality that looks extremely distant at the moment – a situation will remain in which multinationals, with their various forms of globally interfusing behaviour, are free both to provide great benefits to states – and to do them considerable damage. As the previously cited British example has suggested, they have the potential to contribute greatly to a situation in which key sections of the elites and populations of even the most sovereignty-conscious states are forced to conclude that it is necessary to cede part of that sovereignty to other bodies.

The threat to states from international finance

One of the most potentially destabilising aspects of the global liberal economic system of recent years has been the dramatic growth in the scale and impact of international finance. While it used to be the case that most of the current exchanges that were made related to the flow of goods, under recent versions of the global liberal system the daily volume of foreign exchange trading has become greater than the value of traded goods by a factor of several hundred.[17] With the instant access to economic information, political events and visible trends that computerisation has provided, speculators can buy and sell currencies on a massive scale literally within minutes. The slightest whiff of panic-selling will be picked up instantly by dealers and can lead to rapid 'mass evacuations' from one currency to others. When such huge movements occur, as was the case with the irresistible pressures on the pound sterling in September 1992, governments can find key elements of their economic strategies destroyed overnight. During the above-mentioned event, mainly caused by a loss of confidence by investors in the pound sterling and the UK economy, the British were forced to leave the European Monetary System despite the fact that membership of the system was a loudly declared cornerstone of government policy.

Britain's fate has been a salient reminder to the international community of the extent to which states have become dependent on the whims of speculators around the globe. Governments and their central banks have to think very carefully before introducing new tax measures or changing interest rates in case of hostile and damaging reactions from international investors, which now can occur so quickly and on such a scale that it is impossible for many states to block them.

From the viewpoint of some interventionist liberals, this situation is unacceptable because it means that states can find themselves unable to introduce or maximise policies that would help those of their citizens or industries who are in need. They can be forced to keep interest rates at a level which actually damages the employment prospects of their own people because of the self-interested machinations of those working the global financial markets.

Even the USA, which through its provision of the world's primary currency seems in a much stronger position than states like Britain or Italy, could easily find itself in serious difficulties. Should the policies of a future US government cause the international financial community to lose confidence in the dollar, then the entire global economic system could collapse, threatening to bring the US economy down with it. Contingency plans for such a collapse are in place globally, but only the test of experience will show whether they will be up to the task of preventing a disaster or not.[18]

In a way the situation is one whereby a genie has been let out of a lamp which it has since monstrously outgrown. What has happened has been that the expansion of the global financial market, together with the above-mentioned possibility of massive, rapid movements of funds in and out of states due to modern technological developments, has increased significantly the rate of progress at which the interfusion of state economies with the global economy has been occurring. The consequence of this is that states increasingly find themselves vulnerable to the financial decisions of other states and speculators from all over the globe. The only way in which the threats to the interventionist state from the present global financial system could be reduced significantly is through the design and implementation of new systems of regulation at the global or regional levels. No one state, with the possible exception of the USA, is economically powerful enough to deal with the problem on its own. But effective action would require a level of common agreement that will be difficult to obtain – either regionally or globally – without a significant ideological shift among the world's leading economic powers. Even with agreement on the need for reform, some states ultimately may be too afraid of the financial movements that might occur on the announcement of impending change to give their assent to any effective control regime.

In short, for the moment at least, international finance can provide a powerful constraint on the ability of the interventionist state to carry out many of its major policies. The interfusion of economies across the globe which the existing international financial system has accelerated has, through its potential for contributing to the undermining of elite and popular confidence in the effectiveness of the state, become an opportunity factor capable of helping to cause significant global change. Arguably, it is helping to create the logic of a situation in which, for example, the states of the EU might well be forced to accept that, whether they are greatly in favour of existing schemes for economic and monetary union or not, further economic integration is the most practicable response to the pressures that face them as a result of continuing economic interfusion fuelled by such factors as the global financial system.

The final balance – for and against the liberal system

What all of the above clearly suggests is that, for traditional liberals, if the present capitalist international economic system (that is, that in operation in July 1995) were to put what they see as its recent tendency towards protectionist 'heresies' behind it, then it would be able to do no wrong, providing it progressed towards the goal of almost complete non-intervention which they prescribe. For them, by doing so it would be promoting wealth creation without any threat to the authority of the state. However, as has been shown during this chapter, ironically, the attempt to move further towards a global non-interventionist economic system on the part of some states such as Britain has in fact helped to undermine those areas of state authority which traditional liberals within them see as crucial, most particularly as a result of the non-homogeneity of economic actors (in this case states) which the traditional liberal theoretical model presumes to be homogeneous.

As far as interventionist liberals are concerned, the present mixture of traditional and interventionist influences within the system means that it can do some right but also a worrying amount of wrong (Marxists have not been mentioned because for them threats to the state are in the long term irrelevant, given that it is supposed to wither away under true communism).

Whether one *believes* the present global economic system to be a threat to the state, therefore, depends upon where one sees it as going in traditionalist/ interventionist terms and whether or not one is some form of a traditional liberal or an interventionist. But what it is important to realise is that the fact that many interventionists believe there are problems with the present system does not mean they would not have faith in a modified liberal system. In fact many of them believe that rules and procedures can be introduced into the system which will counter-balance its ill effects. In these circumstances, they argue, the threat to the state and to the economic welfare of its citizens will be minimised or at least greatly reduced, and the liberal system will become the most effective means of wealth generation.

Opinions as to precisely what types of rules and procedures should be introduced depend upon which schools of thought amongst interventionist liberals are questioned. Some, for example, would say that much more substantial measures need to be taken to protect the less developed states from the full heat of foreign competition, and to allow them preferential access to developed economies, until they are in a position to take a full unprotected role in the global economy.[19] Others would argue that the primary need is for multinationals to be regulated at the international level in order to eliminate some of their more cavalier and damaging attitudes towards states and their workforces. What is significant, however, is that many of the key demands of interventionist liberals remain unachieved. From their point of view, therefore, the present liberal global economic system constitutes a significant threat to the kind of state they would wish to see dominating the international arena.

In short, overall, the interfusing tendencies of the present liberal economic system are not only a threat to interventionist notions of the state, but, as the example of Britain has shown, can be a threat also to traditional liberal aspirations concerning state authority. In both cases, as the European Union could be argued to demonstrate, the result can be to alter popular and elite perceptions in the affected states to the extent that there is a preparedness to consider surrendering degrees of state sovereignty to organisations such as the EU – where such bodies exist.

Chapter 4

The second challenge:
the threats to the state from scientific, technological and cultural aspects of global interfusion

Introduction

The industrial, scientific and technological revolutions of the twentieth century have produced a wide range of impacts on a global scale. Collectively, these are seen by some as threatening the state. Why this is so will be explained after a brief exploration of some of the key forms which global interfusion in these fields has taken.

The effects of pollution internationally

One obvious thing that has been international in its impact, and has become a significant factor in promoting global interfusion, is the *pollution* resulting from the huge industrial growth process that has occurred during the past ninety or so years. The most spectacular example of this perhaps was the international distribution of the radioactive fall-out from the Chernobyl reactor disaster in 1986. The health implications of the accident in the then Soviet Union could well prove to be extremely serious during the next fifteen to thirty-five years, and attempts to both deal with and monitor the threat have required an international effort.

The psychological consequences of the accident were global in that they appear to have increased both governmental and popular caution about nuclear power in several countries across the world's continents. The contamination problem also was no respecter of boundaries, causing restrictions on the sale of affected animals for food in areas as diverse as Scandinavia and the United Kingdom. The task of monitoring and studying the contamination in the former Soviet Union adequately has proved beyond the resources of any one state and accordingly is being undertaken by researchers from several. The accident indirectly also served to remind both politicians and populations around the world of the international implications which a limited nuclear war would have. Radiation showed itself very publicly to be a keen traveller. All of these consequences of the accident make its impact truly global and several of them have caused a significant fusing both of concerns and, in some cases, of responses at an interstate level.

But radiation is only one type of international pollution. The River Danube in Europe efficiently makes the toxic effluent from states upstream a problem also for all of those downstream. Scandinavia has long suffered from the destructive effects on its forests and lakes of the acid rain fall-out produced by the United Kingdom's coal-fired power stations. These are problems that require international cooperation if they are to be solved. But perhaps the most spectacular pollution issues after Chernobyl have been those raised by the debates over the depletion of the ozone layer by CFCs, and global warming, resulting allegedly from current patterns of personal transport and industrial activity. It has been argued that these are potentially extremely worrying problems that affect the entire world and that they can only be dealt with effectively through the cooperation of all the major industrial states.[1] The very seriousness of the issues raised is causing a fusing both of concerns and responses at an interstate level although, as the chapter on the environment will show, there is still some way to go before effective global solutions are produced.

The effects of scientific and technological developments

Technological innovation has become another aspect of the global interfusion process. For example, the advanced production methods employed in one state can rapidly cause a fusing of the options facing its competitors elsewhere into one common alternative, that is, they must adopt the new methods or lose out economically. New production methods introduced in Japan, for instance, can force all its competitors in the developed world to follow suit if they wish to continue competing with Japanese firms. Robotisation in Japanese car factories forced European and American factories to start robotising parts of their own production processes. That in turn caused the shedding of labour, which has increased the social problems of those states without new sources of employment to take up sufficient of the slack. This shows one way in which technological developments in the most advanced states can fuse with the economic well-being or otherwise of their competitors in the developed world.

Furthermore, robotics, as Kennedy points out,[2] is but one new technology in which advanced states are investing which could particularly severely damage poor states by providing substitutes for large numbers of industrial and agricultural jobs. Vigorous robotisation, for example, could so lower the costs of production that less developed states lose both their low-wage cost advantage and their factories as multinationals find it advantageous once more to locate nearer to their markets in the advanced states. Such losses would be a serious threat to the viability of some less developed states, and might so fragment the confidence of their elites and general populaces in their governments and political systems that they could become in danger of descending into a Somália-like anarchy during the subsequent period of social dislocation. The fusion of parts of the economies of developed states with parts of those of less developed states, via the activities of multinationals, has made the latter states extremely vulnerable to potentially damaging new technological developments in the former.

In addition, as technology has become increasingly sophisticated, research and development and often the production costs of high-tech goods have become extremely expensive in many cases. This has taken the ability to independently develop and manufacture several types of technology largely out of the hands of even some of the world's largest industrial states. France, Italy, Germany and the United Kingdom, for example, now prefer to cooperate in developing and manufacturing new fighter aircraft and large civilian aircraft, finding the cost dangerously high for any one state to try and bear on its own. The Europeans also are struggling to keep in the race with the giant computer corporations of Japan and their huge R&D budgets, and are having to become more cooperative in their efforts in order to do so.

So, to recap, from the above it can be seen that technological developments occurring in one state can have repercussions right across the industrialised world, causing a fusing of industrial thinking and forcing firms in a variety of states to adopt new production methods. In some instances this process can create severe social problems, which in the case of some states may even threaten their continued existence. In addition, the escalating costs of technological development increasingly are causing states and the firms within them to think about fusing their efforts and developing cooperative manufacturing projects with firms and governments in other states. This process could be argued to be adding to the effect of those specifically economic processes, already referred to in the preceding chapter, which have been altering the perceptions of the effectiveness and role of the 'independent' state of some elites and populations to the extent that they have been prepared to sanction limited surrenders of national sovereignty.

Technology has had a direct political impact as well. For example, *issues* have been given a heightened global dimension through the communications revolution that has occurred right across the developed and the less developed world. Famine in Africa can now become an issue for the populations of developed states as soon as the first warning signs appear through television and newspaper reports transmitted and published on the day of compilation. Pressures on governments globally to help other states which have suffered catastrophes, such as flooding or earthquakes, can also grow extremely rapidly through same-day television transmissions of the victims' plight from disaster areas. In the Soviet coup of August 1991, Russian President Boris Yeltsin was able to bring immediate pressure to bear on the conspirators who had surrounded him through skilful use of satellite telephone links to other world leaders and through his use of the world's television media. Issues that in earlier times might have taken so long to travel round the world that nothing could have been done about them by the time many got to hear can now be transmitted live directly into the average citizen's front room. The communications revolution has become the means by which problems in one state can fuse rapidly with public humanitarian (or political) concern in others, thereby creating new demands and items on the political agenda of the governments of the latter. In this sense at least, the world has genuinely become the proverbial 'global village'.

One of the most spectacular of the new technological developments in the field of communications has been the rapid recent growth of the Internet, which has provided high-speed access across the globe to vast amounts of information on a scale that is unprecedented historically. American citizens can even use the network to interact with the White House in a much more direct fashion than previously has been possible. But the Internet is not just one more adjunct to the great American computer society, despite the fact that it is US-originated, or to the information age in general. It represents also a major communications revolution in itself, allowing people to interact with each other instantly and relatively cheaply right around the world. Overall, the net now (in August 1995) has over 30 million users. The latest available figures suggest that 50 per cent of its usage is accounted for by social communication, 10 per cent by news retrieval and 10 per cent by those wishing to access or communicate pornographic material.[3]

When it is considered that the net is completely outside the control of states, all of this at first sounds extremely significant as far as traditional notions of sovereignty are concerned. Some have talked enthusiastically of the creation of new communities of both a social and political nature that cross not only regional boundaries within states, but national borders around the world. As such, it is argued, the state is being undermined by a new global consciousness that will spread dramatically further as net usage continues to expand. Equally, theoretically nations are being enabled to create closer unities across conventional state boundaries through the use of the net. Members of the Irish diaspora, for example, use it as a means to keep in touch in their various locations around the world and to try and create a cross-state community within cyberspace. During 1995 Mexican rebels used the Internet to bypass their national boundaries and spread their version of what was happening within their state around the world.

However, there are many who are highly dubious about the net's supposedly revolutionary implications. One critic, for example, has derided it as 'the CB radio of the nineties'.[4] This kind of view sees most of the communications usage of the net as being of a low-level 'chit-chat' type and claims that it is little used for the growth and exchange of ideas (although some are worried by its increasing use by extremist political groups across state boundaries). Others, far from seeing the Internet as the creator of new communities within and across state boundaries, believe it is yet another means by which traditional communities are being broken down. They argue that it is encouraging the growth of a new breed of cyber-hermit, people who lose the ability to communicate adequately on a face-to-face basis by becoming over-reliant on the 'bedroom/study-confined' medium of the net. Another view argues that it is irrelevant that the net itself is beyond state control and that people can communicate globally with complete freedom because, whether they like it or not, each of those individuals remains restricted by the laws of the state that they live in as soon as they step outside their artificial cyber-world.

It is as yet a little too early to make any definitive judgement on the extent to which all of these views are right or wrong. The net is still expanding in usage and what will be significant will be how far that expansion goes, what the precise nature of that expanded usage is, and whether or not states find a way of trying to get control over this new technological anarchy. What can be said with confidence is that the very fact that journalists, academics and various other groups of opinion-formers are included amongst the Internet's users means that it already has become part of the previously mentioned 'global village' phenomenon, and as such another avenue through which problems in one state can fuse rapidly with public humanitarian (or political) concern in others, thereby creating new demands and items on the political agenda of the governments of the latter.

Cultural factors and the age of global travel

The communications revolution also has facilitated greatly the global interfusion of certain cultural values and trends. This has been alleged to be particularly true with regard to the interaction of some aspects of American culture with other cultures, due simply to the worldwide distribution of American films and television programmes disseminating, intentionally or otherwise, the US vision of the good life. Those who resent the spread of the 'consumer society' have laid no small part of the blame at the door of American popular media influence around the world, arguing that some key US values have fused with and then supplanted key local ones. A number of governments certainly believe the media play an important role in spreading values. The BBC World Service continues to be regarded as a significant standard-bearer for Western values by British governments for example, although this seems to be less the case for recent Conservative governments than for some of their predecessors.

The problem with such manifestations of cultural interfusion is that they can create demands and expectations among the population which are beyond the immediate economic means of the affected states and thereby encourage domestic unrest. This is one of the ghosts that haunts those who fear for the future stability of Russia if it proves unable to generate a successful market economy along the lines of those which Russian television viewers are able to see on their screens when viewing programmes imported from the West, and America in particular. While it is unlikely that either the US government or commercial interests would wish to generate such unrest deliberately, given the obvious dangers of an unstable nuclear-armed Russia, it has been alleged frequently that both have an interest in globalising aspirations for the 'dream' aspects of the American lifestyle in order to create new markets for American goods. To the extent that they succeed in doing this, they change the cultural norms within which affected societies operate, a process which can in itself open states to strong counter-pressures which may threaten to blow them apart. At the time of writing, in 1995, an example of such an endangered state is often argued to be Egypt, given the growing Islamic fundamentalist reaction against what they see as the Westernisation of the governing classes and their supporters. But as Michael Smith points out, while cultural global interfusion (he does not directly use this specific term in his analysis but he talks about the same things that it refers to) can help to undermine the state by subverting its values or by causing a destructive backlash, it is useful to remember that equally it can strengthen it through provoking a revitalisation of nationalist or ethnic groups whose interests in 'purifying' the state coincide with the desire to make of it an effective political organisation.[5]

The revolution in the ease of travel has in certain respects (although, as yet, clearly not in all respects) fused states together into a global arena for diseases like AIDS and for terrorist groups. Both of these things have become significant international problems as a result of mass jet travel and, if they become widespread enough within a society, can seriously challenge the institutions of the state and their ability to govern effectively. A society devastated by AIDS, for example, may become faced by severe economic problems as a result of a decimated workforce and escalating health-care costs. Such problems obviously can drain away the vital resources governments need to implement other policies, as is being demonstrated in parts of Africa at the moment.

The collective implications of these factors for the state

The above are some, but certainly not all, of the ways in which scientific, technological and cultural factors are contributing to global interfusion processes. The question here is to what extent does their collective promotion of global interfusion represent a threat to the state. One part of the answer is that the fact that pollution issues such as Chernobyl or global warming can only be resolved effectively by international cooperation is emphasising the limitations of states individually as a means for trying to deal with such problems and suggesting strongly to political elites across the globe the need for their resolution within international forums. The more issues are placed in the hands of such forums then the more does the individual state's role as a decision-maker become circumscribed by the pressures and politics of others. Another part of the answer is that trends in technological innovation costs, whereby research and development and manufacturing processes increasingly are having to be shared between states, could be argued to be forcing the affected elites and populations to recognise that states on their own are not necessarily the most effective channels for the pursuit of some key economic goals and thereby speeding up the integration process in contexts such as the EU. The media revolution is in turn circumscribing the freedom of manoeuvre of some states by making it difficult to ignore famines or other disasters in distant continents which previously governments might have tried to turn a blind eye to. Arguably, it is also threatening the cultural values of many states through tempting populations with American consumerism and so on. The continuing growth of the Internet could add greatly to the existing impacts of the wider media revolution, although it is a little early yet to judge whether its full potential will be realised.

It has been shown also how the fusing together of aspects of developed and less developed states' economies via the operation of multinationals has created a situation in which new technological developments in the former may undermine the economic and even political viability of the latter, and how cultural interfusion may create backlashes which potentially could lead to serious political upheaval within affected states.

Taken together, while hardly abolishing the state as an international institution, even though they might in future contribute to the destruction of some individual states, these various factors could be argued to be altering the perceptions of key sections of political, BTC and administrative elites and populations to varying degrees in a way that is bringing about a change in the role and authority of many states. They could be argued to be forcing key sections of these broad groups to accept a reduced role for the independent state and to have circumscribed the scope for political manoeuvre of state governments. As a side-effect, such factors could also be argued to be strengthening global and regional institutions at the expense of the state by persuading crucial sections of some elites and populations that greater reliance needs to be placed on such institutions as a result of the growing ineffectiveness of some states in key policy areas, as is evidenced by the increasing role of international bodies in international relations.[6] The extent to which this is alleged to be the case will vary, of course, according to the size and power resources of any given state. The United States, arguably, is much less affected by many of these factors than a small state such as Portugal.

It is when the above factors are combined with the subject matter of the previous chapter, that of economic global interfusion, that the greatest threat to the state is seen. For some interventionist liberals, the danger of the challenge to the decision-making scope and powers of states presented by what they see as undesirable traditional liberal interfusing trends in the global economy can be reduced by modifying the capitalist international economic system as it is operating at present (1995). But even such modifications as most commonly are proposed would not remove the key elements of the logic pushing towards greater international cooperation and integration created by the above-mentioned technological factors. Nor would they counter the inherent logic of both traditional and many interventionist liberal prescriptions that ultimately the best route towards wealth maximisation is the creation of (for example) regional as opposed to national single markets for goods and services, and then of a truly global single market. While interventionist liberals would want to try and retain some powers of government interference within such contexts, even if only as last resorts during times of difficulty, the end result nevertheless would be a significant reduction in the role of many states as independent economic decision-makers. Already, as will be seen in the chapters on European integration, even some of the world's most powerful states are bowing to the pressures from the growing forces of global interfusion and, paradoxically, are trying to ensure their survival as effective actors, albeit with less power than many of them ideally would like, by voluntarily surrendering or compromising part of their independence through member-ship of organisations such as the European Union. The consequence of this is that *at the moment*, given that the states involved are some of the strongest in the world whose economic and military position is far superior to the great majority of states, the answer to the question 'can the state survive?' appears to be yes, but in most cases only with reduced powers if they are to remain or become effective actors.

Conclusions

Ultimately, however, the strength of individual nationalisms and the struggle between different economic ideological prescriptions and those supporting them for reasons of imperative or interest will be crucial in determining the fate of the world's states. This is because, obviously, the extent to which such single markets as those outlined above are achieved, or whether they fall victim to a possible future resurgence of the forces of long-term nationalist protectionism, or other present or not immediately foreseeable future ideological rivals of traditional economic liberalism, will determine substantially the degree to which the state is able to retain its powers into the next century. In this regard, it is important to realise that just because liberalism in its various forms is the dominant economic orthodoxy at the end of the twentieth century does not mean necessarily that it will remain so in the next century. Just as Marxism was largely undreamed of before the advent of its originator, it is quite possible that an ideology of which we have little conception at the moment may dominate global society in future, as a result either of the gradual evolution of political–economic ideas, or of a shock to the system equivalent to the Russian Revolution of 1917, or of something of the order of a global ecological catastrophe occasioned by the present system.

Overall, what can be said with certainty is that despite the increasing pressures on them from the forces of global interfusion, and such sovereignty decreases as have been voluntarily endured within the EU by Western Europe's 'Big Four', states remain the primary mode of political organisation within the international system. While many of them are under serious pressure with regard to their independence in the making of economic policy, they nevertheless still control most issues of war and peace, even if many of them have to join military alliances (which are at the moment all *interstate* and not supra-state organisations) in order to be able to achieve their military and security objectives successfully, are the predominant law-makers (in terms of the sheer quantity of laws made) and can in most cases open or restrict access across their borders according to their own preferences. While the future of the state may be uncertain, and the effectiveness of many states open to question in economic and other matters, those who are most crucial in the business of making war or keeping the peace are always those who must be regarded as being the most important actors on the international stage. A single decision to start a war can after all wreck or destroy thousands of human lives and leave whole economies debilitated. In this respect, for the present at least, to employ a much over-used American phrase, 'the state is still King' with only terrorist or other revolutionary groups as relatively small-scale rivals.

Nevertheless, the very weak position in which the world's poorest states remain is a persistently worrying problem for those who are concerned about the poverty of their peoples which flows from this. The extent to which it is possible for them to escape from their plight is something that will be discussed in the chapters on global poverty.

Chapter 5

Global environmental problems

Introduction

The human race is faced with grave environmental problems. Significant parts of the former Soviet Union are seriously contaminated by chemical and radioactive substances, as are parts of the former Eastern bloc. The environmental clean-up bill at United States' nuclear weapons facilities is estimated to be at least one hundred and thirty billion dollars. Motor vehicles are killing between forty and fifty thousand people every decade in the United Kingdom alone, and that is a state with a relatively modest accident rate. This makes them one of the most lethal technological intrusions into the natural environment. The depletion of the world's ozone layer is continuing and many medical researchers believe that the incidence of potentially lethal skin cancer is likely to keep on increasing as a consequence. Potentially catastrophic changes in climate and sea level are alleged to lie in wait if the world's industrialised and industrialising states do not cut back drastically on their use of fossil fuels. Species of plants that may contain substances with valuable medical uses are disappearing forever at an alarming rate. Huge tracts of the earth's surface are threatened with creeping desertification and millions of the world's people are without sufficient food for a healthy existence.

Despite all of this, there is a lack of universal agreement on the precise nature of the global environmental crisis. Some scientists doubt the accuracy of predictions concerning global warming and claim that fears in this regard have been greatly exaggerated. Some who do accept the more alarming forecasts argue that nuclear power is the safest energy resource because of the alleged negative climatic impact of fossil fuels, while others are horrified at the idea of bequeathing to an uncertain political and geological future large amounts of lethal nuclear waste, some of which will remain dangerous for 24 000 years. Many environmentalists point to motorised road transport as one of the great mass killers of our time, while some politicians still respond by portraying it as one of the most significant new enhancers of individual freedom to emerge in the twentieth century. Some criticise those who predict doom on one ground or another by claiming simply that they have left one or more vital considerations out of their gloomy equations which could change everything for the better.

What is clear and is often forgotten is that from the beginning of time the earth has been a hostile environment for humans. Natural radiation gradually ages us. Many plants, fungi, reptiles, insects and even inorganic substances such as lead or cadmium can poison us and in some cases prove lethal. Our health can be horrifically destroyed or our lives ended in decidedly unpleasant fashion by a variety of diseases. In various parts of the world people throughout history regularly have been drowned by floods, killed, injured or made homeless by hurricanes, earthquakes and volcanic eruptions.

Many of the means by which humanity has attempted to conquer or at least hold at bay nature's malevolent forces have themselves proved to be threats to health and life. Radiation provided medical science with a variety of life-saving options. It also killed at Hiroshima, Nagasaki and Chernobyl. Asbestos protected millions against fire and road fatalities across the industrialised world. It also ruined the lungs of thousands who worked with the material. Industry and the wealth it has created has improved the quality of life for millions of people and has given them more control over the environment around them than ever before. It has resulted also in the premature deaths of thousands, as in the case of the 3500 killed by a gas leak at Bhopal in India in 1984. In short, there is no available route to a safe planet. It simply is not a safe place. Even everyday natural forces like gravity are potentially lethal, whether in the context of aircraft, mountains, buildings or ladders. There are only two viable aims for environmentalists. One is to try and prevent any growth in environmental threats to humanity. The other is to try and reduce them, but with the realistic acknowledgement that it is not possible to make what is in many ways a 'user-unfriendly' planet completely safe for human habitation.

What is clear, in the midst of all the political and scientific debates that have occurred over the environment, is that there is widespread public concern over a variety of ecological issues across the globe and agreement that something should be done about them. However, despite all of this, particular types of nuclear reactor which many experts fear are unsafe still operate in places such as Ukraine and Bulgaria, the holes in the ozone layer seem set on an expansionist policy and the motor car and the business of fossil fuel-burning in general continues to thrive. The problem for ecology, some have argued, is that: 'governments calculate that while their electorates may say they are concerned, the feelings do not translate into a willingness to make actual sacrifices: and rather like supposed support for public spending over tax cuts, when it comes to the push the public will evaporates'.[1]

Bearing all of the above in mind, the intention here is to ask and investigate four questions. First, what are the major current threats to the global environment? Second, what, if any, are the solutions to global environmental problems? Third, what are the obstacles in the way of solutions? Fourth, how and to what extent might such obstacles be overcome? It is not possible in a relatively short book such as this to examine the issues raised in comprehensive detail, but the intention is to provide readers with access to the core of the environmental debate and the wherewithal for constructing an informed opinion on it. (A broader introduction can be obtained by reading the Porritt, Kennedy and Allaby texts listed in the references for this chapter.)

Before these questions are dealt with two things need to be borne in mind. First, many environmental issues are closely intertwined with economic developmental issues. Inevitably, therefore, there will be a degree of overlap between this chapter and the next. This interlinkage does of course complicate enormously the environmental debate, which is in many respects already politically and technically complex and extremely wide-ranging in the number of issues which it covers. As pointed out above, it is not possible to cover all of that debate here, given the economic limits on the length of this book. Accordingly, what will be done is to take a selection of the most prominent current environmental concerns as the main focus of the chapter. This does not necessarily imply that the author regards those issues which are left out as being of a lesser importance.

As in previous chapters, the Change Map will be used to aid the analysis wherever appropriate.

What are the major current threats to the global environment?

It is perhaps most accurate to refer to the major *alleged* current threats to the global environment if the full nature of the scientific debate concerning ecological issues is to be reflected. It has been pointed out already, for example, that there are those who do and those who do not see nuclear power and global warming as definite threats to human existence.

The issues to be covered here include motor vehicles and their ability to kill and injure via road accidents and air pollution, global warming, nuclear energy in both its civil and military applications and the consequences of unrestrained economic growth.

The motor vehicle has been chosen as a focus here on several grounds. First, because of its global reach, second, because it perhaps symbolises more than anything else the double-edged nature of the modern industrial world and its products, third, because it has had a massive impact on the way people live and the principles on which their environment is designed, and fourth, because motor vehicles kill and cripple large numbers of people.

The positive side of the car at the moment has the upper hand in the mind of the global public. People are attracted by its 'go wherever you like whenever you please' appeal, even though traffic jams and restrictions seriously limit this freedom now in many cities in both the developed and the less developed world. It has been the means by which many urban dwellers, who previously would rarely have seen much of the natural beauty of their home states, have been able to broaden greatly their horizons and the range of their experience. Many also are grateful for the escape from crowded public transport which the privacy of their own mobile 'room with a view' provides on commuter journeys. Even if they do frequently end up stuck in traffic jams, they at least have a seat and room to stretch out. For many firms, cars are the means by which they can most flexibly provide for the transportation of their sales force from one customer to the next, while trucks get round what they believe to be the shortcomings in state rail networks and vans provide for unrivalled access for products and services within both urban and rural environments. For some, cars are perceived also (or even simply) as a source of prestige. For others, they are perceived as the safest means of transportation for themselves and/or their children in areas where there is a real or largely media-hyped danger of attack by hoodlums. For others, cars are a potential source of excitement and pleasure.

Basic and obvious though many of these things may seem, it is important to realise that, in combination, they create the basis for an enormously powerful political force – a deeply entrenched belief among the many millions of vehicle owners across the world that their right to buy and use motor vehicles must not be severely restricted, despite evidence that that right provides a significant threat to themselves and their families. Research by the Environment and Forecasting Institute in Germany, for example, shows that every fifty minutes a new car is produced which will kill some-one on German roads, and that every fifty seconds a new car is produced that will injure someone.[2] Despite these somewhat terrifying figures, there is no mass popular pressure in that state for dealing effectively with the problem. Had the same death and injury rate been produced by a nuclear power station, one would have expected a loud public outcry from across all sectors of the German populace. Even in the UK, with its relatively low accident rate, on average almost 100 people die in motor accidents every week and 859 are injured.[3] In the United States the most recently available figures show an annual death rate of 46 385 and an annual toll of injured of three and a half million people.[4] Were the same fatality figures calculated as being likely in the event of a military operation, one would expect that most presidents would reject the use of force unless to do so would be a complete disaster for national interests and their reelection potential. In most other circumstances, the likely public outcry would be such that few politicians would feel able to go ahead. Yet for Americans, the right to a car is even more sacred than the right to own a gun. Across the world as a whole, *over ten million people are injured by motor vehicles every year.*[5]

But road accidents of course are not the only way in which road transport can damage people's health. It is now the principle source of pollution in many of the world's cities. There are already an estimated 500 million petrol-driven vehicles across the world and on the basis of current trends the figure is likely to rise to 1000 million by the year 2030.[6] The Heidelberg Institute calculates that even with a three-way catalytic converter, over ten years a single car averaging 13 000km per annum will produce 44.3 tonnes of carbon dioxide, 4.8kg of sulphur dioxide, 46.8kg of nitrogen dioxide, 325kg of carbon monoxide and 36kg of hydrocarbons. If the environmental impact of every stage of a single 'catalysed' car's life, from the extraction of the raw materials used to manufacture it through to its final disposal, is taken into account, then, according to the Institute, the total burden on the air which we breathe amounts to 59.7 tonnes of carbon dioxide and 2040 million cubic metres of polluted air.[7] The pollution produced by vehicles without a catalytic converter will of course be much higher. The chemical cocktail which the world's vehicles emit can damage lungs, exacerbate breathing and heart problems and can even cause cancer when sufficiently concentrated. Athens and Mexico City have been particularly severely affected during the summer months of recent years and traffic pollution frequently exceeds safe limits across much of Europe and parts of Asia.

The problem of the motor car to some extent overlaps with the issue of global warming, given that the exhaust emissions of the former are alleged to be a significant contributor to the latter. Global warming is claimed to be the result of the massive use of fossil fuels to service the world's industrial development, certain industrial processes, deforestation, an over-reliance on a meat-eating diet and the spectacular growth in the use of motor vehicles during the twentieth century. The methane released by flatulent farm animals, and the carbon dioxide, nitrous oxide and chlorofluorocarbons which result from various of the other above-mentioned causes, add to the earth's pre-existing atmospheric 'shield' which serves to trap infra-red radiation (i.e. heat) near the surface of the planet. While previously that shield has served to keep the earth warm enough to be habitable, and in that sense has been highly benevolent, the fear among many scientists is that the various additions to it produced by modern and modernising industrial and agricultural societies are gradually trapping more heat. If they are right, then highly respectable predictions exist which state that at best the earth will experience more rapid climatic change than at any time since the end of the last ice age, and at the worst, sea levels might rise (as a result of melting ice at the polar ice caps etc.) to such an extent that large areas of the world's low-lying land would become submerged.[8] While no one is really sure what the precise consequences for agriculture of any significant global warming might be, there nevertheless are strong fears among a not insignificant body of expert opinion that it might be severely disrupted in various parts of the globe and that one result may well be increased starvation in the less developed world.

While there are many areas of debate concerning global warming, there is a scientific consensus that between 1890 and 1990 average global temperatures rose by somewhere between 0.3 and 0.7 degrees Celsius.[9] In addition, the five hottest years in the twentieth century were all recorded in the 1980s. The complicating factor is that it is not yet clear to what extent these phenomena have been a result of the increase in the man-made greenhouse gases referred to above or of such things as solar phenomena, dust resulting from volcanic eruptions or natural changes in the climate. According to Stephen Schneider of the US National Center for Atmospheric Research, it will take another ten to twenty years to tell whether greenhouse gases have been the cause of the global temperature rise with 99 per cent statistical certainty. Until then, it will not be possible to prove conclusively that global warming is a man-made environmental problem. Cautious experts such as Schneider argue that it would be foolish not to allow for this possibility in thinking about how the world's agricultural, transport and industrial policies should be shaped however.[10] Given some of the potentially catastrophic changes that many experts fear might result should the planet's temperature continue to increase during the twenty-first century, it would be an unethical gamble not to try and reduce man-made greenhouse emissions just in case.

The third alleged major threat to the global environment to be examined here is that of civil and military nuclear energy. For some, even after

Chernobyl and various previous near disasters in the USA, Britain and elsewhere, there is virtually no danger in civil nuclear power. Michael Allaby, for example, argues that nuclear power generation generally has a much smaller adverse effect on the natural environment than is caused by the burning of fossil fuels. He points out that the smoke produced by the burning of coal, in its heyday as a domestic fuel, is known to have killed thousands in London alone. In addition, some coal-fired power stations emit up to twelve times more radiation than an equivalent nuclear station providing the latter remains accident-free.[11]

There are a variety of ways in which the civil nuclear power production process allegedly can produce a major hazard for humanity. First, the spread of nuclear power around the world has brought about substantial movements of nuclear materials between the various types of plants that are needed to make power generation possible. This has in turn increased the danger of such materials being seized by terrorists and used for bomb-making purposes (or, within the former Soviet Union, of being 'acquired' by the Mafia and sold to the highest bidder). Second, as Chernobyl demonstrated vividly, there is always the chance of human error occurring in nuclear plants. Third, an attempt to compensate for this by greater reliance on computer technology runs the risk of overconfidence in a tool that can turn out to have unanticipated software flaws in the same way that anything else can be less than perfect. These two things are important, because there is much less room for error in nuclear power generation than in other forms of energy generation. While the health risks of a safely operating nuclear power station appear to be relatively low on the basis of current evidence, a serious nuclear accident is capable of adversely affecting the health of thousands and even millions depending upon its precise severity, the location of the plant, prevailing weather conditions and the effectiveness or otherwise of the damage limitation measures that are taken by the responsible civil authorities. There are also the problems of particular types of reactor which are alleged to be defective in their safety provisions, as is the case with regard to the reactor type employed at Chernobyl and elsewhere in the former USSR. In addition, some reactor facilities are potentially unsafe simply because the states within which they are located cannot afford to bring them up to current minimum standards or because their staff are poorly trained and demoralised by low pay and so on. There is also the problem of guaranteeing the long-term safe and secure storage of the waste products of the nuclear industry and the nuclear military. The adequacy of storage provisions needs to be guaranteed for at least one thousand years if future generations are to be protected. It is, among other things, frequently argued to be folly to presume that political circumstances in the states containing the waste sites can be guaranteed to remain stable enough to deal with any unforeseen problems should they arise, or that the relevant states, if they remain as such, will necessarily be able to afford to deal with such problems. Finally, as was demonstrated by various threats issued during the Bosnian conflict during 1993, nuclear power stations potentially can become a severe liability during periods of war.

Some parts of the world are already a contamination nightmare. The territory of the former USSR in particular is littered with radiation hazards as a result of its post-1945 civil and military nuclear programmes. For example, the eighty square miles around the Chelyabinsk bomb-making facility on the edge of Siberia contain contamination equivalent to the output of anywhere between twenty and one hundred Chernobyl accidents depending upon whom one believes.[12] The accident at Chernobyl in 1986 contaminated significant areas of the Ukraine and Belarus in particular. Post-accident decontamination and contamination containment measures, while extensive, simply could not match the scale of the leakage. Apart from anything else, dangerously contaminated art treasures and other valuables were pilfered from the permanently evacuated nearby town of Pripyat and presumably are taking their toll of those through whose hands they have passed. Many clean-up workers who served in Pripyat and elsewhere simply were not adequately protected against the contamination with which they were dealing. The contamination of valuable agricultural land remains a continuing problematical legacy of the accident. Further away, in northern Russia, up to 200 000 people live uncomfortably close to an area where, somewhat incredibly, plutonium bombs were used to mine raw materials for export to Europe and America in the 1970s and early 1980s. Contamination in the vicinity of the mine itself is alleged to be at least as bad as that at Chernobyl's worst hot spots. Places as far apart as land in the vicinity of Archangel and parts of Kazakhstan are known to contain worrying radioactive hot spots resulting from past atmospheric nuclear bomb tests. There are serious contamination problems in parts of the Vladivostok area as a result of an explosion on a nuclear submarine in 1985. There is also an as yet unquantifiable danger from the nuclear reactors that have been dumped in the sea around the Arctic nuclear test base of Novaya Zemlya. Media reporters have observed that the average age at death around some parts of the Russian coast facing on to the dumping-grounds does not appear to exceed forty. Serious contamination has been found even in Moscow itself. The most curious discovery, perhaps, was a deadly quantity of radioactive cobalt found buried in Gorky Park.

The final major threat to be examined here can be explained briefly. Basically, those who argue that there is a limit to economic and industrial growth beyond which the planet's entire ecosystem, including humanity, is likely to come under severe threat, contend that unless industry and governments across both the developed and the developing world rapidly moderate their rate of exploitation of the earth's resources and their output of pollution, then humankind is likely to end up with a future made up of a lethal cocktail of severe resource shortages, inadequate food supplies and an environment that is poisoned beyond redemption in the worst affected areas.

What are the solutions to global environmental problems?

The most complicated environmental problems include technical, economic, cultural/social and political dimensions and thereby require effective action in each of these if solutions are to be found. Fortunately not every environmental issue is quite so complex, but nevertheless many of the most intractable are. If one were to take the UK policy debate in 1993 over the thermal oxide reprocessing plant (THORP), a spent reactor fuel-reprocessing facility situated somewhat incredibly in the English Lake District popularised globally by the poet Wordsworth, then one finds an immensely complex situation. The plant was under threat because, among other things, one of the key original civil nuclear justifications for its building, namely a projected future need to reprocess spent nuclear reactor fuel for use in fast breeder reactors, had been completely undermined by the course of events after the original go-ahead for its construction had been given in the mid-1970s. By 1993 the idea of plutonium-fuelled fast breeder reactors was effectively dead in the UK and there was no shortage of other fuel types. Nevertheless, local pressure in favour of the plant existed within immediately adjacent communities due to it being the only major employer in the area other than local government. Should the plant not have been licensed, then the fear among such communities was that the result would have been the creation of a significant additional social problem for their region in the form of more job losses and their wider impact on the community. The consequent local pressure became an important political consideration for the area's members of parliament who wished to keep hold of their seats, and many felt that this was reflected by the consequent campaigning for the plant in Westminster by people such as the Labour shadow minister, John Cunningham.

There were also believed to be three major economic problems that would have arisen should the plant not have been allowed to open in the form of severe negative impacts on the local community (which would be reflected in lower income for shops and other businesses dependent upon local people having secure incomes to spend, for example), on the plant's owner, British Nuclear Fuels, which saw it as bringing substantial profits from reprocessing the nuclear waste of Germany and other states and, relatedly, on the government's ability to find a private purchaser for BNFL. With regard to the latter point, the privatisation of British Nuclear Fuels was one of the Conservative government's priorities and it did not believe this would be possible without the alleged profits that were projected for the plant.

There were also two political–military dimensions. First, environmental groups and independent experts warned that the increased movement and storage of plutonium would create an opportunity for terrorists to try and seize some of it. Second, one of the original purposes for the building of the Sellafield complex, of which THORP is the latest part, was a military one, in so far as the plutonium extracted from used reactor fuel rods was to be used in the making of Britain's nuclear weapons. When THORP was commissioned it was seen by the Ministry of Defence as a useful up-dating of existing weapons production facilities. One presumes that such a perspective was advanced in the 1993 debate over the plant's licence.

There were also two international dimensions to the THORP issue. First, BNFL had already entered into a contractual obligation to process German and Japanese waste using its new plant. Second, governments such as those of the USA and Ireland had worries about the plant and made their fears known to the UK government. Finally there was a technical problem in the form of the radioactive pollution which the plant would create and its possible health implications. All of these factors fed into the then Conservative government's decision-making process and its debate whether or not to grant BNFL a licence to operate the plant.

Bearing in mind such complications, there are four possible levels of approach which might be utilised in an attempt to solve environmental problems. Very simply, change might be attempted at the individual level, or via the several influential environmental pressure groups that now exist within various states, at governmental level or through international channels. The advice offered by Michael Allaby, for example, includes the possibility of action at all these levels. But, at the individual level, in order for action to have a chance of success, he advises environmentally concerned people to join conservation or environmental groups with their ability to call on specialist advice, and the resources that are available to many of them, such as Friends of the Earth or Greenpeace. The larger and/or most respected of such groups will be able to influence governments at home, and in some cases abroad (together with international organisations) to a degree which is completely beyond the ability of the average individual. That campaigns conducted by such organisations can be highly effective is well-evidenced by past successes over international whaling and the reversal of Shell's determination to dump a contaminated oil platform at sea during the summer of 1995. Despite considerable controversy centring around the question of whether it might actually be more environmentally hazardous not to follow Shell's preferred sea-dumping strategy, Greenpeace and its supporters succeeded in forcing the company to take its advice and radically change its disposal plans. Part of the explanation for their success is provided in the following newspaper extract published at the height of the Greenpeace campaign:

'Greenpeace's international protest against the planned deep-sea dumping by Shell of the Brent Spar oil rig came to mainland Britain yesterday. Activists picketed Shell petrol stations across the country.

As the rig continued its slow progress across the Atlantic to the dumping site, with two Greenpeace members on board and a Shell flotilla trying to use water-cannon to prevent them being supplied by helicopter, activists launched a petrol boycott campaign like the one that has swept through Germany and the Netherlands in recent days.

Protestors carried banners outside garages, highlighting the effects they claim the dumping will have on the ocean environment. The 14,500-ton rig is estimated to contain at least 130 tons of toxic substances, including 100 tons of partially-radioactive oil sludge.

A Greenpeace spokesman said: "We are asking people to use their purchasing power to persuade Shell that their dumping of the Brent Spar is totally unacceptable."

In Germany, the garage boycott campaign has gained enormous support. Chancellor Helmut Kohl tackled John Major [the British Prime Minister] about the issue at the G7 summit which ended in Nova Scotia yesterday. Shell filling stations across Germany are deserted. . . .

One in seven petrol stations in Germany belongs to Shell, and the managers of Shell Germany talk of "drastic losses" as the result of the boycott. In Germany, Shell's action is almost universally regarded as an environmental crime.'[13]

Shortly after the article was published Shell judged that the loss of business that the campaign was causing was too great and reversed their decision to dump the platform.

Allaby argues that several conditions are necessary for campaigns such as the above to be successful. First, the campaign obviously must be well-organised and sustained; second, the issue must be clear, even if many of the arguments surrounding it are confused or contradictory; third, there must be a realistic alternative way for firms or states to behave to the one being protested about; and fourth, it is probably true that campaigning can only be an effective tool for accelerating desirable change if such change is inevitable eventually anyway. While the first three requirements seem merely sensible rather than contentious, environmental groups may well dispute his last point and argue that it is still too early in the history of large-scale environmentalist organisations to judge whether such a limitation applies. They might at the very least use the success of the Shell campaign to cast serious doubts on his belief. Finally, implicit in what he says is that it is much more practical to concentrate on a limited number of issues at any one time rather than trying to 'save the world' at one go.[14]

The effectiveness of individuals can of course be increased should they achieve governmental office. Perhaps the most spectacular example in this regard during recent years was the election of environmentalist Al Gore to the Vice-Presidency of the United States within the Clinton administration, and his ideas will be set out in some detail here as an example of a coherent 'global planning' approach to environmental problem-solving.

Gore is a strong advocate of the idea of a global 'Marshall Plan' for environmental protection. The original Marshall Plan was the means by which the United States provided extremely effective assistance to Western Europe in its economic rebuilding after the Second World War. One of the key features of the new plan, he argues, must be that it views the world's needs on a regional basis and addresses the needs of all of those regions. At root, he contends,

> The world's effort to save the environment must be organized around strategic goals that simultaneously represent the most important changes and allow us to recognize, measure and assess our progress towards making those changes. Each goal must be supported by a set of policies that will enable world civilization to reach it as quickly, efficiently and justly as possible.[15]

Gore goes on to outline five strategic goals which he believes must be pursued if the global environment is to be saved. The first of these is the stabilisation of the world population by means of the globalisation of literacy and education to give all sexually active adults (most particularly amongst the world's poor who have the highest birth rate currently) the means to think about family planning. He believes it is necessary also to develop effective programmes to reduce infant mortality and to ensure the good health of children. He argues that these should create a situation in which parents in less developed societies will no longer feel it necessary to have large numbers of children as an insurance policy to guarantee that at least some will survive to help them on the land and in their old age. Finally, he believes that the universal provision of birth control devices and techniques along with culturally appropriate instruction is a vital requirement.

The second goal is the rapid development of environmentally appropriate technologies. These must be capable of allowing for sustainable economic progress without simultaneously degrading the environment. Priority areas for such development would be energy, transportation, agriculture, building construction and manufacturing and any innovations would need to be transferred to all the world's states in order to make them effective. In order to facilitate all of this Gore argues that a Strategic Environment Initiative is needed, a crash global innovation programme equivalent in scale and funding to the massive US Strategic Defense Initiative.

His third strategic goal is a comprehensive change in the economic 'rules of the road' by which the world's people measure the impact of their decisions on the environment. He argues that there is a need for a globally agreed system of economic accounting which assigns appropriate values to the ecological consequences of both routine choices in the market-place by individuals and companies and the larger, macroeconomic choices of states. He believes that at the earliest opportunity world leaders should convene a global summit to discuss ways of implementing this goal. The agenda should provide for the immediate adoption of a variety of measures, which should include the changing of the definition of gross national product to include environmental costs and benefits, the changing of the definition of productivity to reflect calculations of environmental improvement or decline, the establishment by governments of programmes to assist companies in the study of the costs and benefits of environmental efficiency, and the accelerated use by governments of 'debt-for-nature' swaps to encourage environmental stewardship in return for debt relief.

His fourth strategic goal is the negotiation of a new generation of international agreements that will embody the regulatory frameworks, enforcement mechanisms, incentives and penalties necessary to make the overall plan a success. He stresses that these must not place any unfair burden on the poorer states and that they must be strongly sensitive to the vast differences of capability and need between developed and undeveloped states.

His fifth strategic goal is the establishment of a cooperative plan for educating the world's citizens about the global environment. The main purpose behind this would be to encourage new patterns of thinking about the relationship of civilisation to the global environment.

Gore emphasises that each of these goals is closely related to all of the others, and that all need to be pursued simultaneously. As the sixth, integrating goal he states that his global plan should establish, especially in the less developed world, the political and social conditions most conducive to the emergence of sustainable societies. These include adequate nutrition, health care and shelter, a commitment to human rights, social justice (including equitable patterns of land ownership), high rates of literacy and greater political freedom, participation and accountability. For Gore, all specific policies designed to achieve the above should be chosen to serve the central organising principle of saving the global environment.[16]

What emerges from these two sample approaches, those of Allaby and Gore, is a dichotomy between all-embracing strategies to try and solve comprehensively what might be termed the global environmental crisis and much more narrowly focused attempts to try and campaign on a limited number of issues at a time. Some argue that the latter approach is the best way forward if pursued by a sufficient number of well-organised and well-funded groups (and especially if it is taken up by governments also), in so far as picking issues off one by one is likely to be more effective than attempting cumbersome, all-embracing strategies that run the risk of becoming bogged down in the sheer complexity, attendant bureaucracy and frequently self-contradictory nature of what they are attempting. They point to the 1992 United Nations Conference on Environment and Development as an excellent example of how an all-embracing approach apparently can come to little, merely providing international diplomats, well-experienced in watering down measures their governments do not want, with an easier opportunity to bury proposals they find disagreeable in the mire of concessions, compromises and simple fudges that inevitably is involved in any attempt to gain comprehensive agreement between such a widely disparate group as the global community of states.

On the other side of the coin, those who support a Gore-style strategy argue that anything less is dangerously inadequate given their belief that the global environmental crisis, which they see as being well underway already, is in danger of running out of control within the near future. More narrowly focused approaches are criticised on the grounds that not only do they risk creating a situation in which some vital problems are not attended to while people concentrate their attention in limited directions, but they do not even greatly solve the problem of complexity in the way that their supporters allege that they do. The range of interests involved in the issue of global warming, for example, is large and the interactions that occur between those interests often extremely complicated. Furthermore, because the global warming question overlaps with other environmental problems, the only realistic way to tackle it is as part of a wider whole of environmental issues.

The discussion above is centred on the most difficult half of equations which attempt to solve environmental problems, that concerned with the political/social/economic dimensions of the latter. The technical solutions, while themselves frequently complex and possessed of their own particular difficulties, are nevertheless often much easier to produce. The problem, of course, is that they can not be implemented in many cases without the first half of the equation being solved. (The extent to which the latter task can be accomplished is something that will be investigated in the sections which follow.) As far as cars are concerned, for example, the number of road deaths could be reduced by such simple measures as introducing traffic-slowing devices such as humps in the road into urban environments on a large scale, the more widespread use of photographic speed-monitoring devices on motorways and other intercity routes, and much more severe penalties for motoring offences which endanger health or life. Global warming could be countered, it is argued frequently, by restricting the use of motor vehicles (which should further cut road accidents) and by compelling industrial concerns to adopt more environmentally friendly production processes.[17] Equally, the actual and possible dangers from radioactive pollution could be reduced significantly by a globally funded programme to clear up the serious contamination problems in such badly affected areas as the former Soviet Union, by closing down or comprehensively modifying all of the potentially unsafe reactors in the world, such as those built to the design that failed at Chernobyl, and by reducing reliance on nuclear energy wherever possible by means which should minimise possible contributions to global warming. The threat to many species of plants that may yet prove to have valuable medicinal uses could be reduced greatly through the introduction of measures to halt the destruction of the world's rain forests. The threat to the world's ozone layer could be reduced dramatically if those factories which are still producing the chemicals which are believed to be causing the current holes were to switch extremely rapidly to available alternatives which are believed to be much less damaging to the atmosphere. All of these technical solutions to some of the world's most serious current environmental problems are perfectly feasible, as indeed are many more. As will be seen below, the difficulties in the way of their implementation frequently exist in the non-technical dimension.

What are the obstacles in the way of solutions?

The previous section demonstrated the complexity which can be involved in major environmental questions as evidenced by the THORP example. In terms of the Change Map this example showed that such questions can provoke a complicated interplay between *elite and popular perceptions*, which in turn can be influenced heavily by a variety of *interests* and *ideologies*. The latter factor was shown to be relevant, for instance, by the fact that the Conservative government's liberal orthodox ideology meant that it was interested in privatising the plant's owners BNFL and that it therefore looked at THORP's future with that consideration in mind among others. It was shown how such questions can also involve an *intermingling of national and international factors* by virtue of the involvement of the United States, Irish and other governments in the THORP case. Ultimately, despite significant popular opposition to the plant in the UK on the part of people worried by its negative environmental implications, strong arguments against it being commissioned were simply overridden by the British government through the use of its formal *power* as ultimate decision-maker within the UK.

The factors identified in the above example are, of course, only some of those that can be involved in environmental questions. If another nuclear issue is considered, for example, that of the debate over the future status of the Chernobyl power station in Ukraine, one can note that during 1994 the need to provide the Ukraine government with assistance to deal, in particular, with the problem of the leaking concrete sarcophagus covering the lethal wreckage of the reactor that exploded in 1986 was rapidly turning into an *imperative* as the leaks worsened. What is interesting in the case of this latter example is how the problems posed by the potentially unsafe reactors in the former USSR and, in particular, the questions raised by the dangerous state of the Chernobyl plant, were allowed to remain unresolved for so long. It seems that little of a substantial nature could start to be achieved until an imperative intervened. When one looks at a variety of other allegedly potentially serious environmental issues – global warming, the threat to the ozone layer and so on – one notices the slow pace of reactions to these also. This suggests that most such issues can only be dealt with adequately when imperatives intervene. But if this is the case, then what are the reasons for this?

One obvious explanation of why imperatives seem to be needed lies in the complexity of many environmental issues already referred to above. Problems like global warming, or the ozone holes, or deforestation, and the questions arising from the dangers presented by the nuclear industries of the former USSR, involve a variety of perceptions, interests and ideologies across a large number of states. The Ukrainian nuclear question, for example, involves all the governments of the European Union and the USA before one even starts to consider the issue at a local level. This often vast array of competing interests and perceptions frequently is a recipe for interminable debate or simple inaction because of an inability to find a realistic compromise position between so many interested parties. The intervention of an imperative becomes a vital necessity if the log-jam is to be broken. Furthermore, because the resolution of many environmental problems can be highly costly, squabbles over who should foot most of the bill can become extremely intractable given the large number of states that frequently are competing over the matter. The governments theoretically most able to pay are often reluctant to ask their populations for the large amounts that can be necessary. The question of why this is so leads into the second main reason why imperatives can become necessary to finally resolve environmental squabbles.

This was mentioned right at the beginning of this chapter. It takes the form of the apparent perception by many governments that electorates are not prepared to put their money where their mouths are on environmental issues. When it comes down to actually making the significant sacrifices that would be necessary to solve the most serious of the alleged emerging problems, popular enthusiasm for environmental reform, such as it is, begins to become heavily qualified. Paul Kennedy sees this problem as having an additional dimension. He points out that many of the forecasts for dire ecological consequences if our current use and abuse of the planet's resources are not reformed predict that matters will come to a head at the time when the present generation's children or even grandchildren become adults. So not only are politicians faced with asking people to make large sacrifices in their 'lifestyles' and the standards of living to which those in the developed world have become accustomed, but they would be requesting that they suffer such 'pain' on behalf of people thirty or fifty years into the future. Given the fact that there is scepticism among some scientists and economists as to whether many of the gloomy predictions that have been made are accurate, then it is easy for politicians to argue that to follow environmentalists' advice to the full would be merely to put their own careers at great risk for something that might never happen. If people are so reluctant to countenance increased taxation to pay for the various problems of the present then it would be singularly unwise to try their patience on behalf of an uncertain future. He quotes the example of UN environment authorities recently estimating that the less developed world would need one hundred and twenty-five billion US dollars a year to pay for necessary environmental programmes. Once they had considered fully the political realities in the form of the likelihood of developed states' governments being prepared to support such a large-scale programme, they cut back their request to a relatively miniscule five to ten billion dollars a year.[18]

Gore is aware of the above problems and of other severe obstacles that lie in the path of his proposed global Marshall Plan, a scheme that would require enormously complicated negotiations and vast amounts of money to get it off the ground in any substantial way. What is interesting is that he seems to agree with the idea that imperatives will be needed to free the log-jam. This does not worry him for the simple reason that he believes the arrival of such imperatives is almost inevitable. This part of his analysis – that concerned with the question of how imperatives can arise or can be made to arise – will be tackled in the next section. What will be done here is to show some of the key difficulties that he believes lie in the way of his plan being implemented in order to further expand this chapter's discussion of the obstacles that can impede environmental reform.

Given that the complications involved in trying to resolve single-issue problems have been shown to be frequently enormous, it should not be surprising that the difficulties of reform are many times multiplied when such issues are linked together within one overarching framework, as is the case with Gore's plan. In the first place, he sees the need for a politically and economically powerful prime mover to get the plan off the ground and to provide the leadership and momentum that will be necessary to keep it going. While he sees the UN as possibly having a limited role in this regard, he firmly believes that anything that involved the idea of trying to transfer policy-making powers on global matters to a world authority would be doomed from the start by the nationalism of such powerful actors as the USA. Despite its economic superpower status, Japan, he argues, could not fit the bill because of its reluctance to share responsibility for world political leadership. The European Union will be too bogged down in the business of trying to unify itself. Inevitably, therefore, the leadership role must fall disproportionately on the USA.

However, he argues, there are serious problems which stand in the way of the USA taking up such a burden. First, the United States is much less dominant in the world economy than it was at the time of the original Marshall Plan, and thus is less willing to shoulder large economic burdens. Second, the instinct and enthusiasm for world leadership that the USA was able to exercise in the early post-Second World War era has been dampened somewhat by highly negative experiences such as the Vietnam War, resulting in a high degree of caution before any such ventures are attempted. Third, there is the fear of interventionism that permeates a large part of the US political culture. Fourth, at present, public acceptance of the magnitude of the global environmental threat is still too small for truly effective measures to be taken. Fifth, even were the USA to try and get things going, it would be faced with the fact that public acceptance of that threat in the less developed world, where other immediate threats to existence might well make saving the environment seem a luxury for the rich, is quite probably far smaller even than that which exists in the developed world.[19] These difficulties are on top of the enormous problems that would be raised simply by trying to conduct successfully the vast multilateral negotiating process that would be necessary for agreeing on and implementing the plan.

Here, it is necessary also to consider in some detail an additional fundamental and potentially serious obstacle to the adoption of his plan globally. The extent to which it might be possible to overcome it via imperatives will be discussed in the next section. That obstacle is related to the fifth of Gore's points above and takes the form of the plan quite possibly being rejected by many less developed states on the grounds that it does not consider their interests adequately. Gore would argue against this on the grounds that, for example, the plan proposes to transfer resources from the developed to the less developed world to facilitate population control and the transfer of environmentally friendly new technology, and advocates that the former should provide debt relief to the latter in exchange for environmental reform. He would say that it stresses throughout the need to ensure that the problems of less developed states are taken fully into account in devising any global environmental programme. Surely, it could be argued, this demonstrates an adequate consideration of the needs of poorer states as well as those of the richer?

It is quite possible and even probable that many developmentalist critics would disagree. They could characterise Gore's plan as a means of trying to buy off the third world in order to save the developed world from environmental disaster. They might at the very least contrast the relatively modest resource transfers proposed by Gore with the much larger programme of assistance contained within the Brandt Reports of the early 1980s. The latter, to be examined in the chapters on world poverty, started from the assumption that the main threats to human well-being and existence, other than nuclear weapons and war, are the causes of global poverty (of which war in its turn is of course one), and that these should be at the top of the world's political–economic agenda. From a developmentalist perspective, the economic reforms contained in Gore's global plan could be argued to be relatively minimalist and to be shaped not by the aim of eliminating the suffering of global poverty but predominantly by the desire to end the environmental threat to the developed world by simply tackling those problems of world poverty that need to be dealt with in order to facilitate this goal. The rest, for all intents and purposes, 'can go hang'.

From this point of view, therefore, the concerns of the Gore plan could be seen as deriving from a first world bias. Many developmentalists would argue that the problem of global poverty should be given equal weighting to that of the global environment, because both seriously threaten human life. Therefore, Gore's plan should coexist with and to some extent overlap with a global poverty relief programme on the scale proposed by the Brandt Reports. Whether that relief programme would be based on the same economic perspective as that underlying Brandt would of course depend upon the particular ideology of the developmentalists in question. Gore's failure to suggest such a coexistence could be argued to be further proof of his developed world bias. The fact that past experience has shown that the implementation of a Brandtian-scale plan for poverty relief would seem to be unattainable within the short to medium term, given the present balance of global interests (see the chapters on world poverty), would not in itself prevent this argument from being raised as a powerful objection in principle to Gore's plan.

Leaving Gore's plan on one side now until the issues it raises are returned to in the next section, it can be noted that on top of everything else, another serious obstacle in the way of environmental reform is the fact that damaging the environment is seen as a necessary means to wealth by some powerful individuals and groups. In short, some entrenched economic interests see continued environmental degradation as offering them a source of rich pickings which they are not prepared to forgo without a fight. Motor vehicle manufacturers who see the potential for a growing global market, provided environmental controls do not become too strict, can be powerful lobbyists in their governments' ears, pointing out their importance as providers of employment, taxation and export revenues. It is often argued that cigarette companies, whose products have been a major global environmental disaster to date in terms of their effects on human health, are able always to point to the huge tax revenues that the industry provides in states such as Britain whenever governments threaten to become too strict about smoking.

In some areas of the world, economic interests can be horrifically brutal in the methods which they use to resist environmentalist pressures. In parts of South America, clashes between those pursuing deforestation and those opposing it have resulted in deaths among the latter. On one occasion during the mid-1990s over seventy Indians were massacred in Brazil by gold-miners anxious to get at their protected lands. The Brazilian government pointed out that it simply did not have the resources to be able to offer truly effective protection to the Indians. It is not unusual across the globe for economic interests opposing environmental reform to be able to bribe key politicians or to ensure that supporters of their interests find their way into government. During the post-Second World War period corruption has been a way of life in Italy, Japan, and most recently in Russia, to name but a few prominent examples of states where such opportunities have flourished (although a major attempt to change matters was being made in Italy during the mid-1990s). Among other things, this has facilitated the illegal dumping of lethal toxic waste in totally inappropriate locations. In terms of the overlap of economic and political interests, the Swiss parliament is often cited as an example of how far things can go in terms of powerful economic interests securing representation of their concerns at the highest levels, many MPs effectively being representatives of such interests.

A further problem is that once complex areas of the environmental debate have been mangled by a global media with news values that often do not facilitate adequate levels of explanation, and by politicians anxious to throw people off an inconvenient scent, many ordinary people are left simply too confused to become an effective ecological force even if they wanted to.

Finally, there is the problem that on some issues significant parts of electorates do their own cost/benefit calculations as best they can and come to conclusions which actively or passively support activities which can cause death or seriously injure the health of themselves or others. Protests over the mayhem that can be caused by motor vehicles, for example, tend to be isolated and provoked by particularly poignant incidences of carnage, such as the killing of children playing in the street by vehicles that are being driven too fast in urban areas. Largely people across the globe seem to be prepared to live with alarmingly high death and injury statistics because they value the convenience of the car over its possible ill effects.

How and to what extent might such obstacles be overcome?

As far as the chances of a comprehensive approach to the world's actual and potential environmental problems being implemented is concerned, Kennedy is something of a pessimist while Gore is relatively optimistic. The former does believe that if further substantial evidence of the reality of global warming arises, then it will be possible to overcome some of the reluctance which currently obstructs the taking of truly effective environ-mental protection measures. However, rather than any comprehensive plan on the scale envisaged by Gore, he sees the most likely outcome as being merely a number of piecemeal agreements on environmental matters which will tackle some of the problems globally, but leave most virtually untouched.[20] In this respect, he would seem to be backed up by the outcome of the grandiosely hyped 1992 UN Conference on Environment and Development, which produced binding conventions on biodiversity and climate change and a non-legally binding statement of principles on tropical rain forests, but no wider binding framework for these measures to fit within. A year after the UNCED Rio Summit, the then EC was still arguing within itself over the measures needed for protecting the climate and still had not ratified the modest set of proposals put forward in the UN convention, which had already been weakened as a result of American pressure at the summit itself. While the summit did adopt a wide-ranging environmental action programme known as Agenda 21, this did not bindingly commit individual member states to reform and one of the notable features of the summit was the range of issues on which there was serious disagree-ment between parts of the rich and poor world. In short, Rio seemed to suggest that, given the differences between the various interests represented by the world's states, it will always be a big enough battle trying to get agreement on single measures, never mind any comprehensive 'global plan'.

Gore on the other hand sees public attitudes as being subject to a process of continuing change, in which public recognition of the frightening magnitude of the global environmental threat is curving upwards and will eventually rise almost vertically as the dangers of environmental abuse become so apparent that the search for remedies becomes an all-consuming passion. He goes on to argue that the fact that the 'curve' of public aware-ness currently is only just starting to bend should not deter us from taking the strongest measures that are politically feasible in the present, even though these are woefully inadequate given the scale of the need. What it is important to realise, he argues, is that such measures can be upgraded as the public awareness curve rises. Equally, when that curve rises to a high enough point, which he strongly expects it will, something as comprehensive as his global Marshall Plan will become feasible and may indeed be grabbed at enthusiastically by a world anxious for an effective response to a lethal threat. To return to the earlier Change Map analysis used in the previous section, in other words he is arguing that elite and popular attitudes will be changed in favour of massive environmental action by the intervention of an opportunity factor in the form of a severe environmental crisis, which in turn will create an imperative for action.

So for Gore, a simple process should remove the complex obstacles that currently stand in the way of effective environmental protection. First, the scale of the threat ultimately will become so terrifyingly clear that the global public will clamour for drastic measures to avert ecological disaster. Second, the preexistence of a global plan in which such measures are incorporated will provide the means by which a worldwide response can be swung into action almost immediately in order to ensure that the planet can be saved.[21] What should be borne in mind, however, is that Gore's optimism is not unqualified throughout his book. Towards the end, for example, he expresses serious worries about the capacity of anti-environment economic interests to confuse the public through misleading propaganda and prevent them from seeing the full nature of the threats facing humankind. The only answer to this threat, he believes, is to ensure that a high enough proportion of electorates are sufficiently well-educated to be able to separate propaganda from the truth and to speak out for reform in numbers that governments will have to listen to.[22]

The kind of programme Gore envisages may well deal with some of the lesser obstacles to environmental reform as well as the bigger ones if it is successful. The momentum of a global initiative would quite possibly be large enough to brush aside the disinformation and bribery that some opponents of environmentalism engage in. Equally, the negative influence of people's apparent willingness to tolerate the high costs in human life and health wreaked by such devices as the motor car would be reduced significantly by the need to lessen reliance on cars as a result of a global warming initiative.

The big question, of course, is whether or not Gore is right in his belief that a massive increase in global public support for environmental reform is almost inevitable because the dangers of inaction will become so apparent that no one will be able to ignore them. He does admit that the battle with those who will try to use disinformation to undermine the environmentalist case will be a hard-fought one, and he admits implicitly that it just might be lost. The real key to the successful implementation of his programme, however, is the opportunity factor of a gross and clearly frightening deterioration in the environment of the *developed* world. Only then will the funds necessary for a global programme be released. Given that the developed world has been content to live with a situation in which it has most of the planet's wealth while the majority of the world's population live on or below the breadline for as long as can be remembered, it would seem unlikely that any global initiative on the environment will succeed if the worst environmental problems, such as the desperate plight of Calcutta or Mexico City, remain in the less developed world.

There is also the possibility that it might be too late to do anything effective by the time the environmental situation deteriorates so seriously for the danger to be unambiguous enough to become an imperative, in which case Gore's plan would be simply outdated when finally it became possible to implement it.

Overall, what is undeniable is that the globe is afflicted with appalling environmental problems – the territory of the former Soviet Union is sufficient enough illustration of that fact – and that there are strong, if not as yet irrefutable grounds, for suspecting that other even more serious problems, such as global warming, may be on the way. In the light of these considerations it is difficult to disagree with the logic of what Gore suggests – that the most effective environmental protection measures which are politically feasible across the globe should be implemented now, and that these should be uprated if the curve of public concern rises in the way he anticipates. It is also sensible that there should be coherent and comprehensive policy programmes sitting available on the shelf ready to take off to tackle environmental problems should concern rise to a sufficiently high level. The only questions are whether public concern will rise in the manner Gore hopes and whether his programme is the right one.

The first question can only be answered by the future, and is dependent, among other things, upon the extent to which those concerned about the state of the environment succeed in persuading those currently unappreciative of the dangers which they perceive that the planet is under serious threat. The second has been answered partially already at the Rio Summit where the Vatican led an alliance to ensure that birth control – a key ingredient of Gore's plan – never made it on to the agenda. This would seem to suggest at the very least that, when cultural/religious/ethnic differences are taken into account, some parts of his plan are not 'right' for everyone. Furthermore, as pointed out in the previous section, there is also the problem as to whether the less developed states might reject a plan such as Gore's on the grounds that it is too much in the developed world's favour. If a global plan was accepted under the pressure of imperatives, one suspects that it would have to be one which contained more concessions to the interests of the less developed world than Al Gore's offering.

In short, there are a number of areas within that programme which are likely to run into serious opposition from powerful global religious/ ideological or economic interests. This does not in itself undermine the value of a programme such as Gore's. It still represents a coherent basis for negotiation from which a truly workable global plan might emerge. Being prepared to try and achieve the most that is feasible is infinitely more useful than simply being so pessimistic that nothing of value gets done.

Having said this, one should perhaps not underestimate the potential usefulness of the UN in facilitating such negotiations, even if many environmentalists have tended to do so since what for them was the disappointingly modest outcome of the 1992 Rio Summit. For some, Gore included, the 'Earth Summit' was a turning point in the international community's awareness of the linkage between sustainable economic progress and development and as such an invaluable foundation upon which truly effective future developments might be built. What it did also was to bring the alleged global environmental crisis to the attention of virtually the entire world with access to television or newspapers or both. For people like Gore, in other words, the UN's Rio jamboree was not quite the failure that it has been made out to have been.

In thinking about the potential role of the UN it is important to realise that there are things it can not do and things it can, and to forget about the former in order to concentrate on the latter. Imber, for example, argues that the UN system is well-equipped to undertake such things as the consensus negotiation of norms and of rules in the form of treaty law (as an example of its usefulness in the latter regard he cites the UN's International Atomic Energy Agency's conventions on nuclear plant accidents), and the negotiation and implementation of safeguards and inspection regimes to monitor compliance with environmental treaties (one of the examples he quotes is the IAEA's safeguards regime which it operates under the Nuclear Weapons Non-Proliferation Treaty). He believes that the UN system is poorly equipped to undertake, among other things, taxation and other financial stick or carrot measures designed to encourage responsible environmental behaviour on the part of member states, the naming and publicising of states which have violated treaties and norms, and the imposing by vote or administrative procedures of credible sanctions on violators.[23]

Finally, it might be noted that for some time a number of academics and policy-makers have been warning that resource shortages and environmental quality issues could become major security issues in the near future. Imber points out that one consequence of this is that, using the concept of environmental security, it might be possible to elevate the environmental agenda to the Security Council itself, giving it a much higher international authority than it has so far been able to achieve.[24]

So, overall, it can be seen that attempts to solve environmental problems are dependent upon the extent to which they are compatible with the perceived interests of affected populations, governments and other relevant elites. While electoral pressure can change environmental reform in which a government previously had no interest into a policy option which it sees as being politically advisable to pursue, it is also the case that governments perceive electoral commitment to environmental reform to be too low at the moment for it to be worth their while to try and implement truly comprehensive national and international measures. While it is always possible that such commitment might eventually become so deep that it becomes an imperative forcing governments to act, it is equally the case that the influence which some of the large business concerns opposing environmental reforms are able to exert over the information flow in their societies might undermine that commitment through successful disinformation and so on. It also might be the case that ideological shifts among the major players in world politics, or the simple fact that developed states are not prepared to make big enough concessions to the poorer states in order to persuade them to join or remain in global environmental regimes of real effectiveness, might complicate severely the business of trying to achieve agreement on the nature of the most appropriate solutions to the alleged emerging environmental crisis.

In other words, as in most other major issues of global politics, the outcome of the environmental debate will be dependent upon the interaction between such factors as ideologies, imperatives, interests, power and influence. Environmentalists are faced with a battle in which those lined up against them have enormous resources at their disposal. The success or failure of their enterprise as a significant influence upon human affairs will depend upon the extent to which they can find the appropriate means to turn comprehensive environmental reform into either an interest or an imperative, or preferably both, for governments and polluters – and/or upon the extent to which nature and past and continuing environmental abuses by humankind create appropriate interests and imperatives.

Chapter 6

The political economy of death: what causes global poverty?

Introduction

Poverty cripples and kills both hope and lives on a massive scale internationally. The number of people who die from malnutrition is equal to the number that would be killed by dropping the Hiroshima bomb on an equivalent-sized city every three days.[1] One Indian magazine aptly described this situation as being equivalent to a Third World War: 'A war waged in peacetime, without precedent, and involving the largest number of deaths and the largest number of soldiers without uniform.'[2]

Despite the existence of charities such as Oxfam, or occasional global extravaganzas such as the Band Aid concert of the mid-1980s, when it comes to the crunch the lethal poverty of others seems remarkably low down the agenda of many of the world's electorates and politicians.

To a degree, poverty is a relative concept. The poor of developed states like Germany, which has a long tradition of substantial welfare provision, must seem fabulously wealthy people to the poor sleeping on the streets of Calcutta with little if any access to medical assistance, no roofs over their heads and no sanitation. Writing of the situation in the less developed world in 1984, for example, Kai Nielsen remarked that:

> The Brandt Report of 1980 states that 800 million people cannot afford an adequate diet [this figure is now accepted to be over one billion]. This means that millions are constantly hungry, that millions suffer from deficiency diseases and from infections that they could resist with a more adequate diet. . . . In some areas of the world half the children born will die before their fifth birthday. Life for not a few of us in the industrially developed world is indeed, in various ways, grim. But our level of deprivation hardly begins to approximate to the level of poverty and utter misery that nearly 40 per cent of the people in the Third World face.[3]

The conditions which Nielsen outlines are often described by using the term 'absolute poverty'. No matter what they are compared to they can only be viewed as characteristic of a situation of extreme deprivation. It is absolute poverty that will be the main concern of this chapter, given its horrendous cost in human health and life.

Nevertheless, it should be remembered that the worst forms of relative poverty (relative poverty is a term which for the purposes of this chapter is used to describe the situation of those who are considerably disadvantaged compared to those on the highest and average levels of income within their own and other societies, but who are not in the immediately desperate circumstances of those experiencing absolute poverty) can cause severe problems for the people and the states concerned also, and that these in turn can have global impacts. Within their own societies, those such as Britain for example, the 'wealth' of the relative poor compared to the absolute poverty of many of the people in the third world is often little consolation for a low-quality diet, the despair that can easily result from long-term unemployment, and the ill health that can arise from a combination of the latter, the stresses of coping with inadequate housing and the need to feed and clothe children on a low budget.

In Europe, many have long believed that if relative poverty is allowed to grow to too great an extent it will provide a fertile breeding-ground for political extremism, and the disastrous growth of Nazism in Germany between the two world wars often is cited as an example of the possibilities in this respect. The Nazi party was able to exploit the dire economic straits into which Germany sank during the period of the Weimar Republic to boost dramatically both its membership and its wider support. The consequence of Hitler's rise to power was the loss of millions of lives across the world (many historians now place the figure for Soviet deaths resulting from the Second World War at forty million for example).

Similarly it has been argued frequently that had Roosevelt not introduced his poverty-alleviating New Deal in the United States, then there would have been a popular uprising against the American government and the severe relative poverty for which it would have been blamed during the 1930s. A nightmare at the back of European minds in recent years has been that the extremism that has fed off the relative poverty resulting from German unification might lead to a resurrection of Nazism at the heart of one of the world's potentially most powerful states, with all its likely consequences in the form of oppression, war and loss of human life. In terms of its potential impact on human well-being therefore, and despite the fact that publishing economics means that absolute poverty must be the main focus here, relative poverty ought not simply to be dismissed as the much less important small brother of absolute poverty.

Absolute poverty and development

Some have tried actually to quantify absolute poverty, drawing a line above which, by implication, all other forms of poverty must be of the purely relative variety. The World Bank, for example, draws its dividing line at individual incomes of less than 370 dollars a year, a figure which places one billion or 20 per cent of the world's population in a state of absolute poverty.[4]

The idea of drawing a line at such an arbitrary level of income could be criticised as being unrealistic and unrepresentative of the true enormity of the scale of absolute poverty across the globe. But if a major purpose of such a definition is simply to illustrate the huge scale of such poverty to a world that needs to be reminded, then one which includes the mind-boggling figure of one billion people should be perfectly serviceable in this respect. It is a figure, after all, which is nearly equal to the entire population of the People's Republic of China.

Given that absolute poverty is always referred to as a problem of the *less developed* world, it would be useful also at the beginning of this discussion to consider what is meant by the idea of *development*. The UN Declaration on the Right to Development of December 1986 states that:

> Development is a comprehensive economic, social, cultural and political process, which aims at the constant improvement of the well-being of the entire population and of all its individuals on the basis of their active, free and meaningful participation in development and in the fair distribution of benefits resulting therefrom.[5]

The extent to which this definition is acceptable to different states and groups of individuals within them depends obviously upon the ideological positions which they hold, given that the UN definition itself is reflective of a particular stance. One problem with it is that many states which claim to be developing and even some of those which are regarded as developed, do not allow their entire populations free and meaningful participation in such a wide-ranging development process. Another difficulty arises from the fact that there is a wide variety of understandings as to what is and what is not 'fair'.

Some less ambitious but perhaps more practical definitions of development have started from the assumption that it is a mainly economic and social process, one concerned with modernisation in the manner of the industrialised West. Some have stated that any notion of development must include the targeted improvement of the living standards of those in conditions of absolute poverty. Others still have rejected such a specific concern and have seen the economic developmental process as simply being one which should help the less developed states to increase their overall wealth without any specific focus on the interests of the poorest people within them. In addition, increasingly there is concern with the idea of sustainable development.[6] This notion implies that economic growth has to be limited by environmental concerns, in order to ensure that gains made in economic performance are not simply neutralised by the severe environmental damage that can result from uncontrolled industrial and agricultural development.

So, overall, it will be important to keep in mind these different understandings of the term as the discussion progresses and to be clear which of them is being used in a specific context. The predominant usage of the concept here will be one in which a less developed state is judged to be one within which the per capita gross national product is considerably below the prevailing average in the developed world. Unless specified otherwise, this is what will be meant in this chapter whenever the term underdevelopment is used.

One should bear in mind also that when the less developed states are referred to as if they were a single community with strictly comparable members, this is a shorthand which, while in some ways convenient, disguises a wide range of differences. In economic terms alone, for example, there are some states where huge numbers of the population live in absolute poverty, where there is little in the way of industry or modern technology and little foreseeable prospect of any improvement in this situation, while there are others, such as South Korea, which while previously having clearly been members of the less developed world, now seem to be almost about to join the ranks of the developed states. There are also less developed states which contain some of the richest people in the world as well as some of the poorest, South America containing a number of examples in this regard. As will be seen, such disparities make it difficult for the less developed states to establish a sufficiently common interest to be able to present an effective united front to their developed counterparts. It needs to be remembered constantly that the poverty and specific needs of the less developed world vary greatly from state to state.

Now that definitions have been offered of the core concepts that will be used within this and the next chapter, it is possible to focus on the main questions that will be addressed within them. These are: first, what are the main causes of the global poverty problem? Second, what are the solutions to the problem? Third, what are the obstacles in the way of solutions and, finally, how likely is it that the obstacles can be overcome? The last three of these questions will be tackled in the next chapter.

What are the main causes of the global poverty problem?

While it might seem obvious to look at the role of the perceived economic interests of key societal elites nationally and globally when trying to understand the causes of global poverty, reference to the Change Map reminds the analyst that these frequently can interact with ideologies and imperatives, and that the role of all three therefore should be investigated. A limited but useful indicative analysis proportional to the necessarily finite scale of this study will be carried out here with regard to these three factors.

Opinions as to the causes of and possible solutions to the global poverty problem differ in accordance with whichever of various competing ideological perspectives individuals hold. Interests come into the debate on a number of levels. Frequently, for example, those who accuse the developed world of acting imperialistically towards the less developed states identify specific economic interests which they believe to be the driving force behind such behaviour. Imperatives come into the picture in the sense that some argue that there is a moral imperative for the developed states to assist the third world, while others have argued – in the Brandt Reports of the early 1980s for example – that there is an economic imperative that is at least equally strong.

It is ideologies that act as the starting point in attempting to provide an answer to the above question. Interests, which can both promote and result from ideologies, will be examined where relevant. Imperatives will come more into play when examining possible solutions to the global poverty problem.

In recent years the international political economy has tended to be characterised as a battle between elites adhering to competing ideologies. Confusingly, not everyone believes that precisely the same ideologies are at the heart of the debate and some ideologies are classified under different names by different authors. The intention here is to examine four major ideological perspectives and the contrasting explanations which an examination of them offers for the problem of world poverty. These are liberalism, neo-mercantilism, structuralism and what might be loosely termed the radical perspective, which includes different varieties of Marxism–Leninism. It is important to realise that not all writers will agree with the particular ways in which these various schools of thought are (necessarily broadly) characterised below, and that the system of classification and explanation used is one subjectively deemed to be most appropriate to the needs of this particular analysis.

Liberalism

There are a number of different variations on the theme of economic liberalism which are operative in the many states which now form part of the liberal capitalist international economic system. It has been seen in earlier discussions within the book that classic liberalism, which might be regarded as the root from which all these branches grow, has a number of core assumptions. In particular, it contends that the key to wealth creation is efficiency and that the most efficient economic situation is one in which the market is allowed to operate in an unfettered manner. This means that the laws of supply and demand must be the dominant decision-makers and competition, not monopoly, must be the condition under which producers operate.

At the international level, efficiency requires that trade between economies should occur without protectionist barriers, thus enabling the global market to grow to the limits set only by demand. Each economy should specialise in producing those goods and services with which it can compete effectively with others, those in which it has a comparative advantage. Politics and economics should be kept separate, because government interference generally will only reduce economic efficiency. The only role for governmental decision-makers should be to frame the rules and laws which will deter fraud and other crimes which are hostile to market forces, and such anti-market practices as attempts to establish monopolies. Sticking to these stipulations, it is argued, will maximise wealth across the globe.

While some varieties of mixed-market liberalism are happy to encourage substantial government interference where social considerations are deemed to make this desirable, together with the provision of wide-ranging welfare benefits for the poor, classic liberalism sees this as potentially damaging in so far as the high taxes necessary for the provision of a welfare state will reduce both the incentives for entrepreneurs and the purchasing power of consumers and will therefore restrict economic growth. This means that people across the economy as a whole will not maximise their wealth and if welfare expenditure and consequent taxation become too high, then poorer people will actually end up being worse off than if no such welfare safety net had been in existence. Classic economics argues that the best way to help the poor is to forget about grandiose welfare state ideas and simply to let the market work in an unhindered way. Wealth created by the virtuous circle that will follow will then trickle down to them because the increasing level of demand will force producers to take on the unemployed in order to meet it, thereby providing them with regular incomes.

So, the logical consequence of the above line of thinking is that the present enormous scale of absolute poverty and underdevelopment across the third world is the consequence of the above liberal economic policy prescriptions not having been followed in the states concerned.

Neo-mercantilism

Originally, mercantilism was a theory which had considerable influence in seventeenth- and eighteenth-century Europe. It equated the wealth of a nation with its possession of precious metals. In order to acquire these it was stipulated that governments must pursue interventionist policies designed, among other things, to maximise their surpluses on foreign trade, to promote their national commercial interests and to acquire colonies. All economic transactions at the international level should be regulated for the purpose of state power. Controls were imposed on the movement of precious metals across borders and on exchange markets. Tariffs, quotas and prohibitions of some transactions were employed to regulate individual and general commercial transactions. Governments provided subsidies for industries engaged in export and import substitution and on occasion engaged in trade or production themselves. The economies of their colonies were closely controlled by the governments that acquired them, production, exports and imports all being strictly regulated.[7] Mercantilism was the complete opposite of the liberalism which was ultimately to replace it as the favoured European economic doctrine.

Some policies characteristic of those espoused under mercantilism still operate in the global economy today, most particularly via protectionism and various forms of subsidies, even though the motives behind them might have changed to one extent or another since the demise of mercantilism in its original theoretical form. The United States, for example, has long criticised the Common Agricultural Policy of the European Union for damaging its export prospects by its use of protection and subsidies. American agricultural produce attempting to get into the EU market has encountered a tariffs system which has made it more expensive than European produce by the time it reaches the consumer, while many European farmers have been heavily subsidised over the years. Equally, both the

Europeans and the Americans have complained about Japanese protectionism during the past twenty or so years. There are also those who argue that while formal colonialism largely has disappeared, informal methods have grown up to replace it, effectively continuing to regulate the economies of the former colonies for the benefit of dominant states in the manner prescribed originally by mercantilism. Multinational corporations, which were examined in some detail in Chapter 3, have been argued to be key movers in this new imperialism. Other ways in which neocolonialism is alleged to operate will be explained in the next section on structuralism.

Neo-mercantilism is argued by its critics to be one of the key reasons why global poverty remains on such a scale. For liberals, its protectionist elements subvert the expansion of global trade which they believe to be one of the keys to economic growth. It therefore retards the relief of poverty in all sectors of the global economy. Neo-mercantilism competes with liberalism within the economically powerful states in particular, resulting in the dilution of liberal economics at both the national and the international level.

Such protectionism as the above does not necessarily derive from any one motive. It might be employed in order to obtain an economic advantage over one's competitors, as Japan's critics have alleged has been the case with its trade policies. Equally it might be used purely defensively in order to try and protect domestic industries against what is believed to be unfair competition (in this regard there is an overlap with structuralism, which, as will be seen below, argues that protectionism pursued for this kind of motive can actually boost the growth rate of poorer states). Or it might simply be the result of pressure from electors in a crucial marginal constituency who are worried about possible job losses if a particular inefficient employer is not protected against more efficient firms from abroad.

Another key criticism focuses on neo-mercantilism's neocolonial elements, whereby, it is argued, less developed states deliberately are exploited for the benefit of dominant states. This is seen as an obvious factor in the preservation rather than the relief of poverty in the less developed world.

Overall, the commonest criticism of neo-mercantilism is that, whereas liberalism at least sets out to harness selfish personal interests for the common good in creating the conditions within which individual greed allegedly can lead to the maximisation of the wealth of all, neo-mercantilism generally is driven by national and sectional interests which operate only at the expense of others, most particularly the world's poor. As was noted above, however, some aspects of apparent neo-mercantilism can be justified on structuralist grounds as means of trying to help poorer states and their people, as will be seen in the discussion which follows.

Structuralism

Structuralist theory could be argued to be a version, or indeed a variety of versions, of mixed-market liberalism. It looks at how liberal market economics works with regard to the less developed states. It notes that instead of trade being a boost to growth in the latter as the liberals promise, it tends rather to widen the gap between rich and poor. Inelasticity (i.e. inflexibility) of demand on the world market for the primary (i.e. such non-manufactured items as coffee beans and copper) products of the poorer states, together with the increasingly competitive nature of that market, has in recent years been driving prices for such products down. Simultaneously, it argues, economic interests in the rich world have cheated on classic liberalism and created a monopolistic market structure for many industrial products, which leads to higher prices due to the neglect of adequate competitive pressures. Rising demand for such products (outside periods of recession) also has helped drive prices up. So, while the income of poorer states has been declining under the current structure of the international trading system, the cost of the manufactured goods which they need to import from the richer states has been rising, a trend which has led to transfers of wealth from the less developed to the developed world.

Such transfers are added to by the fact that the debts which the poorer states have run up with the developed world over the past few years are now so large that they carry unmanageably large interest repayments. The root of the huge scale of their current debt problems lies in the quadrupling of the price for oil in 1973. This hit the less developed states particularly badly and they were forced to look abroad for loans to enable them to keep buying the oil that was essential to their needs. Simultaneously, the surpluses which the price hike generated for the oil-exporting states led them to invest heavily in Western banks in order to protect and enhance their gains. The banks in turn looked for new customers to loan the money out to and thereby make a profit on it.

The result of this sudden presence of equally enthusiastic buyers and sellers of loans on the world financial markets was a massive bout of lending in which the less developed states ran up huge debts with the banks of the rich world. One of the problems was that many of the loans were at variable, not fixed rates, with the highest interest rates being charged to the poorest states. This has meant that when the budget deficit and currency and interest rate policies of such large economic entities as the USA and Germany have caused global interest rates to rise sharply, as they have done from time to time, then the interest rates charged to the poorest states have shot up simultaneously.

On top of all this, there have been further increases in the price of oil over the years since and, during periods of recession, reductions in demand in the developed world have caused the price of third world exports to fall even more, making it even harder for the poorer states to keep up their debt repayments. This has meant that banks have granted further loans in order to enable the less developed states to keep on paying back their previous loans, if only to prevent the collapse of the world financial system which a mass default on the part of the latter would bring. But while easing the worries of the banks, the effect of this has been simply to push the poor states even further into debt. In order to try and cope with this situation, the latter have been forced to turn increasing amounts of land that previously was used for domestic food production over to the production of export crops in order to buy in the foreign exchange necessary to service their debts. This has exacerbated a pre-existing shift towards export crop production resulting from the fall in the revenue which could be earned for other third world exports (that has been occurring for reasons explained above). So the poor of the third world came to find themselves in a situation of deadly irony – at the same time as more than enough food was being grown globally to feed them, they were being forced to give up large chunks of their vital domestic food production, despite the fact that their earnings from exports would not enable them to buy in replacement food from abroad.

In addition, the developed world's solution to the growing debt crisis in the 1980s was to make any further rescheduling of loans to the poor states conditional on them undertaking economic adjustment programmes approved by the International Monetary Fund, a body dominated by the developed states. Such programmes, designed ultimately to make the economies of the poor states more capable of handling their debt obligations, characteristically involved restrictions on public expenditure, which hit the poor because of consequent reductions in things like food subsidies and even the limited social services that were available in some states. Furthermore, they tended to exacerbate the switch to export crops at the expense of domestic food production.

In short, structuralists argue, since the oil price hike of the early 1970s the less developed states have found themselves at the mercy of global financial and trading structures that have caused increasingly severe difficulties for the poorest members of their societies.[8] In November 1991, for example, the Catholic Bishops' Conference of England and Wales took up a firmly structuralist position when it expressed its 'grave concern at the escalating violence in Peru' that was then occurring, and went on to state that,

We believe that the social crisis of Peru is exacerbated and prolonged by the dire economic circumstances of the country where the external debt and structural adjustment policies have placed an intolerable strain on the country, and especially upon the poorest sectors of society . . . We ask western governments, the commercial banks, and the international financial institutions to release the people of Peru from the crushing burden of debt and to make available appropriate development aid to enable the country to return to peace and the people to live in dignity.[9]

Furthermore, structuralists argue, foreign investment generally prefers the greater security of the northern developed world to the less developed south, and that investment which does go to the latter often concentrates in economic sectors which do little to fuel the development of the rest of the domestic economy. Structuralism argues that much of the profit produced by such investment is repatriated to the developed north.

Structuralists therefore believe that the current structures of international trade and finance are a major cause of global poverty and are serving to increase it. They argue that those structures can and must be reformed from within. The structure of the world's banking system in particular needs to be made more responsive to the needs of the poor.

Even if their diagnosis of the causes of global poverty should prove to be the correct one, the problem which structuralists face is that their ideas clash with the interests of many of the world's most powerful elites as defined by the liberal or other economic ideological perspectives of the latter. (Equally, as pointed out previously, interests based on simple greed can in turn hide behind convenient ideologies such as liberalism and use them to generate support for their own self-concerned status quo positions.) The extent to which it is possible for structuralists to overcome these obstacles to the implementation of their ideas is one of the things that will be evaluated in the next chapter.

The radical perspective

Just as the above analysis necessarily oversimplifies the various bodies of structuralist thought that exist in order to make them comprehensible to readers encountering them for the first time, some selectivity here is necessary with the wide body of Marxist and Marxist-inspired thought.

For Marxists, the sole purpose of the international banking and trading system as it exists currently is to make the dominant classes within the developed world continually richer and to exploit the world's poor to as great an extent as is necessary to facilitate this goal. They identify all of the faults of capitalism pointed to in the above outline of structuralist theory and more.

For example, they see foreign investment as aggravating unemployment through its frequent concentration on capital intensive production. They also see the capitalist states as having set out to create comprador elites within the less developed states – dominant classes which would benefit from the capitalist structures oppressing their fellow citizens and which would therefore have an interest in maintaining those structures.

At root, Marxist theories argue that capitalism is a corrupting force because it legitimates and promotes greed as the key element in international economics. For Marxists, greed-driven capitalism leads ultimately to over-production and underconsumption, because the wages of the proletariat (workforce) do not rise as fast as capitalist profits do. Therefore capitalism has an absolute need to invest excess capital in the less developed states and to export excess production to the same. But it is driven to do this by the greed which lies at its heart also. Less developed parts of the world have by definition not yet been able to raise production to its full potential, so capitalists are able to obtain higher rates of profit for their surplus capital in the less developed economies. Furthermore, the latter also provide both raw materials and relatively cheap labour.

Under Marxist–Leninist theory as originally expounded, capitalism would lead to the developed market economies competing with each other to seize control of the less developed areas of the world in order to make sure that the desired benefits to be derived from the latter could be made secure. However, with the huge process of decolonisation that followed the Second World War, Marxist–Leninist theorists were forced to revise their thinking. What had happened, they argued, was that during the years of colonisation the dominant capitalist states had been able to lock the colonial areas into structures of dependence from which it would be virtually impossible to escape, and once those structures were established formal control became unnecessary and indeed an undesirable cost. They could therefore hand over nominal control of the less developed areas to their peoples while retaining effective informal control of their economic destinies. By such means capitalism continues to keep the less developed world in a state of poverty and subservience in order to promote the wealth of the ruling classes in the capitalist states. The proverbial leopard has merely changed its spots in order to pursue the same old goal of greed.

Liberal, radical and structural explanations for continuing global poverty all have their critics. Marxists, for example, criticise structuralism on the grounds that, while it identifies many ills of the capitalist economic system that are similar to those identified by themselves, it fails to identify correctly the ruthless and inexhaustible nature of the search for higher rates of profit that lies at the heart of capitalism and is the chief underlying cause of those ills – and therefore believes futilely in a solution that can be produced by peaceful reform.

In turn, among other things, Marxism–Leninism's critics argue that its concentration on a capitalist economic explanation for imperialism is in many respects out of tune with reality. In particular, looking at Lenin's original analysis of imperialism, critics have pointed out that most of the outward investment of the European imperialist states at the time he was writing was going not to their colonies in the overwhelmingly poor parts of the world, which for the most part were of relatively little economic significance to them, but to states such as the USA and Canada. Such an inconvenient fact greatly weakens the Marxist–Leninist analysis, they argue, in so far as it undermines the whole argument that capitalist economics is the taproot of imperialism.[10] It is further weakened by the question which writers such as Waltz have asked, namely, if imperialism in the form of the control and exploitation of other areas of the world occurred long before the advent of capitalism, as it did with the Romans among others, then why should the pre-capitalist motives for imperialism cease to operate just because capitalism comes on the scene?[11] Marxists do not deal adequately with the possibility that such motives might still be operating and that they might be even more important than capitalism as factors causing imperialism.

Liberals in turn are criticised for assuming that those motivated by a philosophy based on greed will be enlightened enough to see the arguments for allowing any significant 'trickling down' of its benefits to the poor. Surely, it is argued, greed will corrupt their reason and they will fail to appreciate adequately the subtle argument that increasing the spending-power of the masses will boost the opportunities for economic growth. Wages therefore will be kept as low as possible. Indeed, given that liberal theory assumes that people will make rational economic choices, is it not being presumptuous to argue in the first place that there might be any one common notion of rationality in a world of greatly different individuals and cultures? Furthermore, increasing automation means that significant boosts in demand now frequently do not lead to significant increases in employment within those states following the prescriptions of liberal capitalist economics. This is another factor obviously working against trickle-down.

However, it should also be remembered that many Marxists would agree that structuralism has at least got part of the picture right, and that many structuralists would argue that Marxism, despite its faults, does offer some useful insights on the global economy. Equally, prominent liberals such as Gilpin agree with the latter point,[12] while some Marxists, in China for example, argue that there are some good points in liberal economics from which Marxist economics must learn if it is to be more efficient in meeting the economic needs of the people. Readers must make up their own minds on the relative merits of these doctrines, having noted that, to an extent, each is a critique of the other, but the assumption here is that there is enough of validity in each of the above perspectives to merit a study of the usefulness or otherwise of their proposed solutions to the problem of global poverty in the next chapter.

Specific factors

What it is proposed to do now is to discuss briefly several specific factors, some of which can sit both inside and outside the above perspectives, and which would seem to have a particularly useful light to throw on the possible causes of global poverty.

The first of these is perhaps the most obvious, namely war. Frequently, during the period of the Cold War, wars in the less developed world were fuelled and prolonged by the superpowers as a means of extending their ideological competition into areas of the world where the use of military force would be much less likely to escalate to nuclear war than would be the case with Western Europe. The bloody Korean War of the early to mid-1950s, and the massively destructive Vietnam War of the 1960s and early to mid-1970s are perhaps the most spectacular examples of such conflicts. While the Soviets remained largely as arms suppliers and advisers in both cases, the United States inserted huge ground and air forces into each conflict. While South Korea seems to have recovered and thrived since, despite the destruction that occurred, and North Korea's precise economic position remains contentious due to the closed nature of its society, North Vietnam gained its military victory over the USA at the cost of a heavy economic defeat. The havoc which the war inflicted on the Vietnamese economy was greatly exacerbated by the subsequent use of American economic and political muscle to impede attempts at economic rebuilding.

In Africa, the involvement of the then two superpowers as arms suppliers and military advisers greatly increased the destructiveness and probably the length of bloody conflicts in Angola, Mozambique, Somalia and Ethiopia. In 1991, for example, the relief organisation CAFOD noted that,

Every five minutes a child under five dies in Mozambique as a result of war or its consequences. Since 1975 a million people have either died of starvation or been killed in the fighting. Three million have had to

leave their homes and four million are now at serious risk of starvation
... Many civilians in Mozambique have lost limbs by stepping on
mines.[13]

Such horrendous direct and indirect casualties of the war would not have
been suffered without the involvement of big-power arms suppliers. In
Asia, Afghanistan became the Soviets' Vietnam from the end of the 1970s
into the Gorbachev era, with the Americans exacerbating the destruction
caused by Soviet involvement by organising arms supplies to their Afghan
opponents. In Latin America, the Reagan administration deliberately set
out to bring the Sandinista regime in Nicaragua to its knees through the
provision of substantial aid to its internal military opponents. Out of all of
these conflicts, only South Korea seems to have managed to recover fully
from the huge economic setbacks which they caused.

But it would be wrong to see war in the less developed world as purely
a function of past superpower involvement. In Sri Lanka, for example, the
Tamil separatists and the Sri Lankan government forces have managed to
fight a vicious little conflict, in which 1.3 million people have been forced
to leave their homes, without any substantial outside involvement other
than that of the Indians. Similarly, long after Somalia ceased to be part of
the superpower chess game, local warlords found pressing reasons of their
own for pursuing a violent conflict that eventually so ripped the country
apart administratively and economically that the United Nations was forced
to intervene.

The simple fact is that no third world state can afford to engage in a war,
whatever its cause. The consequences of a substantial conflict for any
economy that lives on a knife edge are bound to be disastrous. Victory in
any conflict involving two or more impoverished states will by definition be
meaningless in economic terms. War has been and remains a significant
cause of impoverishment in the less developed world in the post-colonialist
period.

Corruption amongst government elites is another important contributor
to the poverty of ordinary people in a number of less developed states and
frequently does not need any Marxist global conspiracy theory to explain
it. It is as home-grown as the corruption that has cursed government at the
national and local levels in states in the developed and intermediate world
such as Japan and Russia. The only difference is that in the less developed
world, where the purse to steal from is by definition greatly smaller, the
results are much more severe for the poor.

Equally, diseases such as AIDS, which has wreaked havoc in a number
of third world economies by killing and incapacitating large numbers of

food producers, and as such is becoming a major factor in the exacerbation of global poverty, are present also in the developed world. But the poverty of the less developed states has meant that insufficient funds have been available for educating people about AIDS and the ways in which it can be spread, with the result that the World Health Organisation predicts that by the year 2000 90 per cent of the world's AIDS cases will be in the less developed world.

Finally, one of the factors which has contributed noticeably to continuing global poverty has been inappropriate aid strategies.[14] The whole idea of effective aid is to enable the poor to achieve a position whereby they can support themselves. In rural areas, for example, this can mean providing technical assistance with irrigation and land conservation techniques and the supply of technology that is not useless when it breaks down because it requires expertise and expensive parts that are not available locally. One of the problems of the past twenty years is that much government-to-government aid has been wasted because it has not been provided in this way, and global poverty has remained at a higher level than need have been the case because of this. Some aid in the past has been used by corrupt third world governments to buy support in the politically crucial urban areas and has never reached the rural poor, some has been 'tied' in the sense that it could only be used to buy products from the donor state instead of being targeted at the most pressing needs of the recipient state, and some has simply been spent on inappropriate or badly thought-out projects which have done little to benefit the poor. Various non-governmental relief and developmental organisations such as Oxfam have been pressing developed world governments to ensure that such errors and malpractices do not recur.

Now that the above perspectives and factors have been outlined, it is possible to move on and evaluate some of the alleged solutions to the problem of global poverty which have been offered.

Chapter 7

An end to global poverty?

What are the solutions to the global poverty problem?

In 1974 the then US Secretary of State, Dr Henry Kissinger, made a famous statement that the world had achieved a position whereby it could and should eliminate hunger and malnutrition within ten years. Little seems to have happened since to turn his words from a mere pious statement into hard reality. The question, therefore, is given that there is enough food for everyone on the planet, how might they actually receive it? What are the means by which global poverty might be relieved? As will be shown towards the end of the chapter, there is an important sub-question as well. That asks, 'how might it be possible to ensure that women's poverty, hunger and ill health is given equal attention to that of men's within societies where traditionally they have been treated as second-class citizens?' The first two of the above questions are addressed below.

The liberal remedy

As one might expect on the basis of the preceding discussion, the answers to the question of how might global poverty be relieved are dependent upon one's ideological standpoint. As far as liberals are concerned, everything depends upon the extent to which the conditions deemed necessary for free market economics to be able to operate successfully (set down in the preceding chapter) are met. If they are adhered to rigorously then wealth creation will be maximised and the benefits of this process will trickle down to the poor. However, classic liberalism makes no pretence of distributing wealth on any basis of egalitarian justice – according to people's *needs* – but rewards them in accordance with the value which the market places on their *deeds*. Those who are most decisive in stimulating and maintaining the wealth creation process – the entrepreneurs who are the prime movers in generating the supply of industrial goods and financial and other services – can therefore expect to be paid the most. This, it is argued, is a good thing because it will encourage them to keep on putting in the effort to create yet more wealth and will therefore keep the economy expanding. The corollary of this, of course, is that those who are least decisive, the factory workers, bank clerks, shop assistants and so on, of whom there is a large supply and who can generally be replaced relatively easily without any damage to the productive process, can expect to be paid relatively little. But, liberal economics argues, being paid a relatively low wage is better than not being paid, and once an economy starts developing then the need for such people will give incomes to those who previously had none at all. What is more, some skills will be valued more highly than others in any productive process and those who equip themselves with the skills that are most in demand can expect to be rewarded more than those whose talents are deemed to be less attractive. In addition, a free-market economy in which the virtuous circle is operating to full effect offers everyone within it the chance of bettering themselves if they work hard enough. All of this, liberals argue, creates a better standard of living within an economy than would be available were it to work on socialist or other greatly interventionist principles which, they believe, would merely reduce incentives, constrain growth, and keep incomes down for everyone. For liberals such doctrines as socialism are well-intentioned but impractical, while their own ideology offers the most practical way of helping the poor and everyone else within an economy.

Structuralist remedies

There is a large variety of remedies for the poverty problem advocated by different types of structuralists. All agree that there are elements within liberalism that it is vital to retain if the global economy is to create the wealth that they believe needs to be distributed more fairly. What they disagree on is how much of liberalism should be preserved. At the more modest end of the spectrum some argue merely for an increase in the foreign aid budgets of the developed states, together with such measures as the stabilisation of commodity prices to assist the poorer states which are dependent upon commodity exports, the introduction of effective debt relief measures and the provision of greater access for the poor states to the markets of the developed world. Such measures, it is argued, will help the less developed states feed and provide employment for their people while developing a more secure market environment which should facilitate the long-term expansion of their economies. They should be effective without being so far-reaching that they might damage seriously the growth rates of the wealthier states, a consequence which would affect adversely the popular support or at least tolerance that would be necessary for their long-term implementation.

Others argue that the position of many of the world's poorer states is now so weak that any attempted remedy needs to be drastic and wide-ranging. The two Brandt Reports of the early 1980s, for example, effectively amounted to a global Marshall Plan to massively reduce poverty across the planet.[1] They started from the observation that moral considerations appeared to have been ineffective in persuading the developed states that they had an obligation to act in a truly effective way to deal with the global poverty problem. What the Brandt Commission (an international body chaired by the respected former West German Chancellor Willy Brandt) proposed as an alternative incentive for action was the argument that the implementation of its ideas would boost growth across the world economy as a whole and, while involving high initial costs for the rich world in the short term, would pay off for them in the medium to long term with economic benefits for both the rich and the poor states.

The Brandt proposals included both an emergency programme of action and a wide-ranging series of medium- to long-term measures which, it was argued, would establish the conditions necessary for the emergence of the less developed states as economies which could support adequately their own peoples. The emergency proposals included the promotion of a global food programme with the aim of stimulating world food production in order to begin abolishing hunger, the establishment of a global energy strategy to benefit both producers and consumers and help the poorer states with the severe energy problems that followed from the oil price hikes of the 1970s, the provision of additional financial flows to ensure the stability of poorer states' economies strained by heavy debt burdens and serious problems with their balance of payments, and, finally, the introduction of reforms to give poorer states more say in the running of international financial institutions and to make the conditions under which world trade is conducted more favourable to them. Among other things, the more long-term programme involved a substantial transference of funds and technical assistance from the rich to the poor states, proposals designed to make multinationals strike more generous bargains with less developed states, a requirement that the less developed states in receipt of assistance from the rich states should ensure that the benefits of this flowed to their poorest people to a satisfactory degree, and measures to try and stabilise commodity prices and ensure access of the less developed states' exports to the markets of the developed world.

One of the main purposes of the Brandt proposals was ultimately to boost global demand by creating a new pool of consumers from the previously poor of the third world. Because of the means which they proposed for trying to do this they were frequently labelled as an example of 'global Keynesianism'.[2] (The significance of this with regard to the chances of the proposals being implemented will be examined later on in the chapter.) The idea, very simply, was that as the poor states need adequate education, expertise, investment and market access before they can even begin to grow the kind of industries that will compete and survive in world markets, these things should be provided by the rich states as a matter of priority. Once in place within less developed economies, they would enable the latter to create enough employment opportunities to set in motion the virtuous circle that is at the heart of liberalism, and this would not only alleviate the poverty of the poor states' people and begin to give them an at least minimally decent standard of living, but would also turn them into consumers who would be able to purchase the products of the states that had assisted them as well as those produced by their own and other developing states.

In short, structuralism looks at what it sees to be the continuing failure to solve the global poverty problem of the various varieties of liberalism and neo-mercantilist tendencies that dominate the thinking of developed states and argues that the latter need to be eliminated and the former modified. Such modification should be designed to spread demand more evenly across the globe in such a way that the poor are enabled to at least feed themselves and, hopefully, also become new consumers and thereby boost the opportunities for growth in the world economy. The Brandt Commission argued that only something as wide-ranging as their own plan would be sufficient to maximise the attainment of these aims.

The radical solution

The radical perspective obviously was dealt a severe blow by the collapse of Marxism–Leninism in the vast state where it first took hold as an example to the world, together with the merciless exposure of the failings of the allegedly communist regimes right across what used to be the Eastern bloc. Nevertheless, at the time of writing (1995), over one billion people remained under allegedly Marxist–Leninist rule, mainly in the People's Republic of China and Communism was regaining some popular favour in

Russia as a result of dissillusionment with capitalism. In addition, like the most fervent liberals, the most convinced Marxists would argue that their doctrine's failures have arisen simply because it has never been properly implemented. Had it not been abused by the Soviet Union and the other allegedly Marxist states, then it would have produced the results which Marx predicted for it. For them, therefore, Marxism remains the only viable solution to the problem of global poverty. Liberalism is too motivated by greed for its practitioners ever to agree to the ambitious structuralist programmes of people like the now deceased Willy Brandt and his international commission. The only way forward for the poor of the less developed world is to seize control of the means of production through revolution and to organise society along Marxist lines in order that they can escape from their chains forever. Once it is they, not the capitalist exploiters in charge, distributing wealth on the basis of need rather than greed, then social justice will have been achieved. The problem for such people, however, is how to ensure that such revolutions will remain true to their Marxist aims given the inability of previous Marxist regimes to achieve this, and on this point there are as yet no convincing arguments.

In recent times some Marxist regimes, such as that of China, have shown themselves prepared to accommodate a degree of liberalism to the extent that this might help overcome shortcomings within their centralised economies, and Chinese recipes for solving the problems of the poor in other states presumably would allow for such a limited mixed-market approach. For pure Marxists, however, such preparedness is nothing more than a symptom of their failure to apply and benefit from a correct Marxist approach and introducing elements of liberal greed will merely betray the poor.

A green tint

As pointed out in the chapter on the environment, green parties and green-thinking economists lay great stress on the need to aim for sustainable growth and not just growth for growth's sake. For them, it will be of little benefit for the poor if a growth strategy is found which ends their economic poverty in the short term but which damages or destroys their chances of better health through environmental pollution and degradation and which perhaps even damages the planet's ability to produce the food necessary to sustain future generations. While it is as yet difficult to identify any one comprehensive green strategy for global poverty relief that is both entirely distinct from the above ideologies and as globally prominent as they are, there is a 'green tint' which some of those who follow the latter are applying to their economic prescriptions for such relief.

Finally, solutions alleged to be capable of dealing with most of the causes of global poverty that were treated separately at the end of the previous chapter are offered within one or more of the above ideological prescriptions. The need for more appropriate aid strategies is one of the things that is tackled within the Brandt Report for example. Similarly, the latter would provide the funds necessary for the educative programmes required to bring diseases like AIDS under control within the third world. The one factor that is not covered above, that of war, is tackled in the chapters specifically concerned with it, where a number of strategies for controlling the frequency of its occurrence are discussed.

What are the obstacles in the way of the solutions?

Problems with the liberal solution

There are problems with the liberal solution to global poverty that originate from both within and outside the ideology. An application of the Change Map in its checklist function reveals that these result from the intervention of blocking factors, power, influence, ideology and the competing perceptions of different state elites. Such interventions are detailed and explained concisely below.

First, as pointed out in the previous chapter, the virtuous circle is becoming harder to attain due to the increasing use of labour-saving devices in industry across the globe. Increases in demand no longer automatically mean the type of substantial increases in employment that used to be necessary to meet them in less automated times. This is an example of what the Change Map describes as a blocking factor in the form of modernisation intervening and obstructing the realisation of one of the aims of liberal policies.

Second, as the previous chapter emphasised, there are problems with the notion of trickle-down. The idea of wealth 'trickling down' to the poor depends upon a specific type of economic logic that seems to be inherently flawed. Where there is a large supply of cheap domestic labour employers may feel able to offer such low wages that the 'trickle' may be almost invisible. Such large, cheap supplies occur usually in precisely those conditions which are most prevalent in the less developed world – economic stagnation, decline or backwardness. The conditions themselves are the blocking factors which can provide employers with the opportunity of paying negligible wages and minimising the liberal objective of trickle-down.

Third, multinational corporations, as was noted in Chapter 3, instead of investing their own capital and local profits in poorer states, may choose both to use scarce local capital and to repatriate most of their profits back to their home state, thus doing little to help develop the states which host their plants. This is an example of the way in which aspects of global inter-fusion can act as a blocking factor with regard to liberalism's declared aim of relieving poverty globally.

Fourth, as pointed out in the previous chapter, investors in general often are dubious about risking their funds in third world states, leaving the latter short of the capital they need to launch and support their own economic growth. This is an example of the way in which the economic stagnation or decline of poorer states, together with fears over possible political instabilities such as revolutions, coups and wars, can be blocking factors acting as disincentives to foreign investors.

Fifth, it is difficult for many developing states to help their poor via virtuous circles when their economies are in the vice-like grip of massive foreign debt. This is an example of how the perceptions of desirable economic policy of the governing and business elites of the developed world, as determined by liberal ideology and interests framed by that ideology, ironically can undermine the declared global development aims of liberal policy as applied to the poorer states. Their allegedly ideologically motivated refusal to lift very greatly the poorer states' debt burden is severely damaging the latters' attempts to develop their economies. The fact that the debt problem remains against the wishes of the poorer states is, of course, also an example of the determining role which power and influence can play in the relationships between the elites of different states and groups of states. The elites of the less developed states simply have not been able to muster sufficient influence or economic or military power to be able to persuade or force their developed counterparts to change their debt policies in any substantial way. In addition, where developing states do achieve any significant level of success in manufactured exports to the developed world, they often find pressures growing from threatened interests in the latter for protectionist barriers to be erected against them.

. These are just some of the reasons why liberalism on its own generally has not proved very effective in improving the lot of the absolute poor when it has come up against the real as opposed to the theoretical world. (The qualificatory word 'generally' is used because many liberal economists would claim that the application of liberalism has helped to improve the lot of the absolute poor considerably in states such as the Four Tigers of Asia – Hong Kong, Singapore, Taiwan and Korea. However, the alleged relative success of the Tigers in reducing poverty is overshadowed by a massive failure in most of the other states which have tried or have been forced to try to apply elements of classical liberalism within the less developed world.) It is problems with the liberal prescription like the above which have been crucial in motivating structuralist analysis.

Problems with structuralist solutions

Structuralists have approached the problem of how to persuade developed states' governments within the capitalist liberal economic system to implement their prescriptions from three main angles (although a fourth approach exists also, which is outlined briefly towards the end of the chapter). First, some structuralists have tried to appeal to the moral principles of governments and their electorates. The quote from the English and Welsh Catholic bishops in the previous chapter was an example of such an appeal. Second, some have tried to appeal to the governments of the developed states on the grounds that it is in their economic interests to help the poor, as was the case with the Brandt Reports. Third, governments in less developed parts of the world have in the past tried various means of exerting leverage on the governments of the developed states in order to get them to adopt structuralist measures.[3]

The first type of approach has proved to be largely ineffective to date. To the extent that developed states' governments have taken any notice of it they have tended to reply either that their hands are tied by their electorates, who simply do not see things in terms of the developed world needing to make substantial adjustments to the international economic system in order to help those in the poorer states, or that orthodox liberal prescriptions are likely to be more effective than structuralist ones. The second type of approach has met with similar results to date, together with a well-practised strategy on the part of developed states' governments by which good intentions to act are expressed but reasons continually found for not actually doing anything. Noting the response to the first Brandt Report, Willy Brandt observed in 1981 that 'Official reactions of governments and institutions follow the well known pattern: they agree on many specific points but they argue that in various ways steps are being considered or progress has been made in principle while further study of specifics seems to be required.'[4]

The governments of the poorer states put a great deal of effort into the third of the above approaches during the 1970s in particular, but did not get very far.[5] As early as 1961 many of the less developed southern states managed to establish a united front on the need to reform the way in which international trade was conducted. This unity, together with the increasing numerical strength of the less developed states in the UN General Assembly, persuaded the northern developed states to agree to convene a UN Conference on Trade and Development (UNCTAD) in 1964. In all its years of existence, however, UNCTAD produced only minor improvements in the position of the less developed states of the south. This was despite the apparent opportunity created by the oil price hike of the early 1970s. At that time it looked as if the oil-producing southern states were finally in a strong enough position to use the oil weapon to force the oil-dependent north to make significant concessions on international trade. Furthermore, the then growing northern demand for other vital raw materials of the south suggested that, if the relevant producing states organised themselves in the same way as the oil producers had done in OPEC, they too would be able to exert leverage on the north. The latter took the threat sufficiently seriously to enter into negotiations with the south over its 1974 demand for a New International Economic Order, a structuralist programme which overlapped considerably in its content with the later Brandt Reports.[6]

However, by the late 1970s several things had become clear. First, when it came to the crunch, the oil-producing states were not prepared to use the oil weapon against the north in order to improve the lot of the poorest states. This was partially a function of a second and crucial factor, namely the inability of the south to maintain a sufficiently united front to present an effective threat to the north. A simple application of the Change Map reveals that this was due to significant differences in interests between the governing elites of the various southern states and the fact that, by definition, the poorest states did not possess the power and influence necessary to persuade all of the richer oil producers to follow the policy line on linkages between oil and international trade that they wished to see being implemented. The differences in interests arose from the fact that, for example, the members of OPEC politically had very different regimes and cultures, and ran economies which were at considerably different levels of development. Such differences were if anything even more marked when OPEC members were compared with the rest of the large number of southern states. This latter fact meant that some of the south's governments saw their economic interests *vis-à-vis* the international trading system in very different ways to others, while the wide differences in political ideologies and regime types made it difficult to achieve the kind of warmth in inter-regime relationships that would have been necessary to sustain a united southern position.

Finally, instead of strengthening as many had predicted, demand for and the price of many crucial non-oil raw materials were dropping significantly by the 1980s, undermining the south's hope of using their position as producers to try and threaten to force prices up if the north did not meet their demands. The consequent decline in their economic and bargaining position therefore acted as a blocking factor preventing their exercise of leverage on the north, even had they managed to achieve the unity necessary to make this effective.

The governing elites of the north, on the other hand, for the most part benefiting from and therefore perceiving a common interest in the global economic structures which the most powerful among them had established, were much more united and were able largely to preserve the international economic system in its existing form, arguing that many of the south's structuralist demands would simply make international trade less efficient and therefore benefit nobody. They had the power to do this as a result of their relative economic muscle and unity and the corresponding disunity and lack of muscle of the south. As pointed out earlier in the book, which ideological prescriptions prevail in the global political economic arena tends to be a function of where power lies. Furthermore, as the Four Tigers became increasingly successful exporters to the developed world and began in consequence to threaten entrenched economic and social interests within the latter, new pressures for protectionist measures to be taken against southern imports grew up. Consequently, by the 1990s, the strength of such pressures in the agricultural and traditional manufacturing sectors made it difficult for the north to respond to southern structuralist demands even if it had wanted to.

In short, the obstacles in the way of structuralist solutions to the global poverty problem have become formidable.

Problems with the radical solution

Given the complete collapse of allegedly Marxist–Leninist *one-party* state capitalism as a political force right across the old Soviet Union and its previously dependent Eastern European states, and the subsequent exposure of the massive weaknesses of the Marxist state capitalist economic system that had operated there, together with the unedifyingly brutal political repression carried out by the Beijing Marxist regime in 1989 in front of the television cameras of the world, Marxist solutions to global poverty have a massive and quite possibly irreversible image problem. Even where old communist politicians are reestablishing themselves as a result of the failures of capitalism in Eastern Europe, it is notable that they are doing so as left-of-centre democratic socialists and social democrats, not as *revolutionary* Marxists. In its 'pure' sense, Marxism–Leninism as a force for global change seems to be spent.

How and to what extent might the obstacles to solutions be overcome?

The intention in this section of the chapter is to use the Change Map to show some ways in which the obstacles to at least partially solving the problem of global poverty might be overcome. This does not mean that definitive solutions will result from this exercise – but what it will do will be to show some possible and practical ways in which solutions might be produced, together with something of the level of difficulty or ease required to make them work.

The starting point is the *liberal solution*. The problem with the liberal prescription for the alleviation of the global poverty problem is that, as was noted in the previous section, the theoretical model upon which it is based simply deviates too greatly from the inconvenient realities of the practical world. Among other things, trickle-down frequently does not work in the anticipated manner, competitive forces can be blunted by the carving up of world markets by a few large multinational corporations and price increases and fluctuations brought about by market conditions can help to plunge significant parts of the world economy into debt, as happened with oil in the 1970s, thereafter severely disabling the poorer debtors in their attempts to reach economic take-off. In short, the liberal prescription on its own, while being capable of helping some previously poorer states, as in the case of the Four Tigers, is a clearly inadequate remedy for trying to solve the problem of the very poor on a *global* scale.

At the other end of the political–economic spectrum obviously is *Marxism*. But given that many of those who have in the past acted in the name of Marxism effectively have discredited it in the eyes of those who might otherwise have tried to apply its prescriptions to see what happened, *structuralism* in its various forms seems to be the only alternative to traditional liberalism as a potentially 'marketable' solution to poverty on a global scale. However, as noted above, the obstacles in the way of its adoption by the developed world are formidable.

Nevertheless, if one chooses to adopt a moral position which says that it is wrong for millions of the world's people to be short of food when there is enough in the world for everyone, and that it is wrong for so many children and adults to be dying of preventable diseases when the means to remedy this situation are available, then every effort to surmount such obstacles must be made. Given that tackling them via the types of political leverage outlined previously in this chapter does not seem to be a practical possibility, bearing in mind the failures of the Brandt Commission and UNCTAD, at this stage of the analysis the only alternative would seem to be to find new arguments and/or levers with which to persuade the rich world that it is in its interests to help the poor. To understand what might be possible and what ideas are impractical, it might be useful to consider in a little more detail the obstacles that stand in the way of any attempt to persuade the rich world to provide more assistance to the poor and then refer to the Change Map to see how and to what extent these might be overcome.

First, there is the problem of massive popular ignorance across the rich world (as in all parts of the world) about the details of economic debate. Most people are simply not in a position to make any informed judgement of the relative merits of different economic arguments. While the Brandt Reports aimed at trying to educate people across industrialised states in the economics of their case by using non-technical language in attractively presented paperback books, and organisations such as Oxfam went even further with high-quality, well-presented educational packs accompanied by publicity stunts and a 'Hungry for Change' campaign in the mid-1980s, the simple fact was that they did not get their message across to a sufficiently large number of people to produce effective enough or sustained enough political ripples. To the extent that Brandt's message or the message of the structuralists as a whole did get across, to many ordinary people it seemed simply to say that within the short to medium term they would be asked to accept higher taxes and job losses in traditional industries in order to facilitate the 'adjustment' of the northern economies to help the poorer states' economies take off.

This brings in a second enormous problem with the selling of structuralist prescriptions in the north. Because wealth in developed states is frequently perceived to be distributed on a less than fair basis by many 'ordinary people' within them, their fear is that it is they rather than the rich who would have to bear the brunt of any adjustment costs, and that their standards of living might well decline seriously as a result. Another question that has been asked in sections of the US and European economies that have been hit quite heavily by competition from the manufactured exports of the Four Tigers and Japan is, 'why on earth should we add to our problems of job losses and declining living standards by funding the economies of potential new competitors in order to enable them to take away yet more jobs and security?' Areas of high unemployment in the north frequently have a low quality of life due to high crime rates, poor housing and a high rate of marital breakdown. Who in their right mind would wish to add to all of that?

In other words, the detailed schemes of Brandt, UNCTAD and others for redistributing global wealth and pump-priming the south's economy appear to have been seen as a massive threat by many of those ordinary people in the north who to one extent or another have become aware of them, most particularly because they have believed that such schemes would be a burden to be borne by them while the rich in their own societies remained largely unaffected.[7] For them, to the extent that Brandt's message that the pay-off for northern economic pain in the short to medium term would be a more secure world in the longer term with a higher growth rate across the global economy as a whole – from which everyone would benefit – actually got across, this was too much of an uncertain and long-term prospect to consider. Apart from the fact that for most people it was not possible to judge the economics of Brandt's claims adequately, there was the question of why they should trust the Commission's promises any more than those of their own politicians, which so often proved to be unfounded. Why should they be prepared to enfeeble themselves economically for a Valhalla that might never materialise?

Such problems remain for anyone who might wish to try and sell structuralism in the north. Even were they to succeed in getting across something similar to the Brandt package to most of the electorates of developed states, unless they were able to ensure that any pain which the package might cause would be spread – and be seen to be spread – fairly across their societies, their case would be likely to be lost because of the above fears and most ordinary people's confusion in the economic debate that would follow.

These facts are well-understood by northern governments. For most conservative parties, such as the German Christian Democrats, the US Republicans or the British Conservative Party for example, the idea of spreading the initial domestic burden that a Brandt-style programme would cause fairly across the rich amongst their electorates as well as the relative poor would be too likely to result in them losing the bedrock of their support. Equally, it is the case that many of the varieties of social democratic parties that exist in Western Europe and the USA now believe it is important to attract and retain the support of wealthy middle-class voters. They too would be cautious about attempting to spread any such burden in the way that is necessary in case by doing so they alienated a now vital area of their electoral support.[8] Northern governments are not prepared therefore to try and implement drastic reforms either in the manner in which they distribute resources amongst their own people, or, in the absence of such reforms, in the way in which they deal with the less developed states economically (given the above fears and the knowledge that the latter would result in them being evicted from office at the next election). They make little effort on the whole to ensure that their populations are economically literate enough to consider such issues adequately for themselves and do not appear to be interested in trying to change this situation. On top of this, many in power in the north simply do not believe that a comprehensive structuralist plan such as Brandt would work. They are simply nearer the liberal end of the economic ideological spectrum than the structuralist in terms of the range of economic practices and institutions which they believe would contribute to efficient wealth generation.

All of this makes the prospects for the world's absolute poor, and for those who would wish to help them urgently on the basis of any system of moral beliefs that regards human life as the supreme value, seem desperate. But such a situation could be argued to contain a simple lesson, namely that, as the failure of Brandt demonstrated, to attempt too much at one go ultimately will lead to the achievement of too little to be of any real value. Given the obstacles in the way of comprehensive structuralist proposals at present, they are not a realistic policy option, as many of the less developed states have come to realise. An application of the Change Map shows not only that the balance of elite and popular perceptions in the relatively rich north is actually and potentially weighted heavily against the adoption of comprehensive structuralist plans, for reasons outlined already, but that there are no competing elites across the greater part of the developed world who are in a position of sufficient power or influence to change that situation within the short to medium term, and that equally there are no opportunity factors at work to change it either.

However, while it might be argued that to attempt too much at one go in the manner of Brandt is to risk achieving very little on the basis of the above, it could be argued also that some *more modest but nevertheless highly useful structuralist measures* would stand a much better chance of being implemented than such large-scale schemes *if an effective channel for their promotion could be found*. In short, while it is difficult, for previously mentioned reasons, to obtain any domestic consensus in the developed world around proposals that are likely to be seen as simply expensive means of setting up new competitors to destroy one's own job and living standards, arguably it should be much easier to gain agreement that if the means exist both (a) substantially to reduce hunger and malnutrition globally, and (b) significantly to improve the health of the world's poor, *without greatly increasing unemployment in the developed states*, then these should be deployed on a scale that will facilitate this. This is for the simple reason that such means would threaten far fewer interests at both elite and popular levels in the developed states than comprehensive schemes. For example, it could be argued that it is only the absence of political will at government level that prevents the establishment of truly effective global agricultural production and distribution enhancement programmes, together with global health programmes, at a *relatively* modest cost to the developed world as a whole. Such programmes would require *some* sacrifices on the part of those in the north, and there would be a need to ensure that such sacrifices were distributed in a manner that was seen to be fair and therefore more sustainable within those societies (arguably, it might be easier to do this with the more minor sacrifices that would be required for such relatively modest programmes than with the much greater sacrifices that would be necessary to implement the Brandt proposals). But properly executed, they should not be seen as presenting anything like the short/medium-term threat to the well-being of those societies that might be perceived in the case of a comprehensive Brandt approach. If 'sold' in the right way to the peoples of the developed states, in terms of their ability to produce maximum humanitarian benefit with *relatively* little domestic cost, it is perfectly possible that popular consent for their implementation could be obtained. *How* it might be possible to lever governments into a position where they were prepared to make the necessary effort to sell them in this way is a question that will be addressed shortly. First it is necessary to say a little bit about the kinds of health and agricultural programmes that are being referred to here.

Because such measures would lack the comprehensiveness of more ambitious schemes, they would not be able to remove hunger and malnutrition on the scale that Brandt was intended to do. For one thing, they would not be tackling the problem of how to make poorer societies more successful as export earners in manufactured goods, or of how to improve their market access for such goods. But nevertheless, the scale of the global health and agricultural programmes that is being implied here *would* make significant inroads into the existing level of human suffering and would have the potential for improving the quality of existence and life expectancy for millions. In order to maintain this achievement over the longer term, however, it would be necessary for such measures to include the large-scale alleviation and, preferably, elimination of the third world debt burden. Should this not happen then the pressures to turn land needed for domestic food production over to export crops to pay off debt interest would remain.

Rather than laying down any detailed plan for such schemes here, it is proposed to state simply what needs to be done as *a basic minimum* for the world's absolute poor. The developed world needs to provide, either through the UN or via coordinated bilateral programmes, sufficient funding and technical assistance to enable less developed states to become self-sufficient agricultural producers and to help those that might be unable temporarily to feed their peoples as a result of foreign aggression, civil wars or natural disasters. Equally, sufficient funding needs to be put in place to establish across the less developed world a substantial level of low-cost but effective health education and preventative medicine programmes and to provide for an expansion of the availability of basic medical training, medicines and equipment in every less developed state *that would be sufficient to increase significantly the lifespan and quality of life of rural as well as urban populations*. As pointed out above, in order for such provisions to remain effective over the longer term, measures need to be taken to alleviate and preferably eliminate the massive third world debt burden without crippling the economies of the affected states themselves. In order to achieve this it may well be necessary to write off that debt entirely.

What is also important is that the details of the above-mentioned agricultural and health programmes need to be worked out in partnership with those non-governmental relief and development organisations which have crucial experience of the needs of the poor and of how best to provide assistance to them, and with the governments and people of the intended recipient states themselves.[9] What is also necessary, if such programmes are to be politically sustainable over the longer term, is that adequate safeguards are built into them to minimise theft or misdirection of any resources that might be channelled into the recipient states, together and relatedly with the setting in place by recipient governments of policies that ensure the aid reaches the absolute poor as a priority. Finally, the donor states must establish adequate monitoring facilities to enable them to demonstrate to their electorates that their money is going where it should. Such a provision will be essential to counter the propaganda and 'easy news story' efforts of those in a position to undermine the support for such programmes which it is necessary to build up and retain in northern states.

The reason why any detailed plan is not laid down here is simple – governments already have all the necessary expertise collectively, and in the case of the larger states, individually, to draw up programmes which would achieve the humanitarian objectives set out above. It is not the blueprints of others that are needed therefore, as much as a decision on the part of a sufficient number of governments to act. All that is necessary is that, ideally, at the very least the minimum requirements set out above should be met globally.

Having shown what type and scale of structuralist reforms arguably might be feasible over the short to medium term, it is now necessary to return to the question of how a mechanism might be found in order to secure their introduction at the level of state policy. What might be useful in this regard would be to use the Change Map to help summarise and eliminate those mechanisms for gaining support for structuralism which are *not* likely to be successful and to see, in the process, if it might help suggest those which *might be*.

On the surface, in order to do this the first step is simply to look at the methods which have failed structuralism in the past, understand why they failed and then to draw appropriate lessons which should enable structuralist reformers to avoid repeating the errors contained within them. So, in this regard, when the map is applied to the methods used previously to try and secure the implementation of large-scale structuralist reforms, it can be seen that it was not possible to introduce them via the use of *influence* (one of the methods employed by the Brandt Commission) because the governments of most developed states either did not believe in structuralist economic theory and/or were afraid of the short/medium-term electoral consequences of applying it on any significant scale.[10] Equally the attempt by structuralists to create a *moral imperative* for governments to act failed either because the moral line they projected did not fit in with many politicians' ideas on ethics or because what they proposed was believed to be admirable in ethical terms but impractical in the 'real world'. The attempts to use levers of power domestically on governments via such devices as the 'Hungry for Change' campaign in the UK were unsuccessful for reasons which will be explained at the end of this chapter. Attempts to use levers of power externally on the governments of the developed world via the oil weapon ultimately were similarly ill-fated for the reasons already explained.

From all of this it might be deduced that influence has little *independent* role to play in any practical attempt to promote global structuralism, given that efforts to overcome the developed states' objections (outlined above) to any attempt to introduce significant levels of structuralist reforms seem unlikely to be successful without the accompanying use of power. But power applied externally on developed states equally does not appear to have much prospect of success, given the lessons of the oil experience and the fact that the political, economic and cultural differences which then undermined the attempt by the less developed states to construct an effective united front have not gone away. The 'Hungry for Change' example equally does not provide very much encouragement for the idea that the best approach might be to try and apply pressure on governments internally, one by one, until sufficient changes in policy have been produced across a range of developed states large enough to make global structuralism a realisable prospect. Overall, it only attracted a small degree of interest in the UK, failing to mobilise any real lobby power from within the electorate, and had little impact at governmental level, thereby failing to provide a successful model of action that could be used to the same effect by similar groups in other states.

However, a qualification is necessary here. Most of the above examples relate to attempts to secure acceptance for *comprehensive* structuralist programmes. Therefore one should not presume that all of the methods used necessarily will fail in the case of *less ambitious* structuralist proposals. There is not the space here to examine all of the possible ways in which such methods might be applied to the latter and to then assess their likely chances of success, so one method will be taken and followed through as an example of how the Change Map might be of assistance in thinking about the feasibility of change in the global poverty issue area with regard to less ambitious structuralist proposals.

The method to be applied takes the form of the use of domestic levers of power. In this regard it is important to note that in emphasising the role of power, the Change Map does not stipulate that any one route towards its attempted exercise domestically must be followed. But ideally, given the existing balance of power among political elites across the developed world at party level, one that is not likely to make any significant concessions towards the kinds of structuralist programmes that have been proposed here without strong prodding, what would seem to be the most appropriate 'route' would be the channelling of structuralists' efforts through *interest groups* – more particularly, ready-made, well-placed and *actually or potentially powerful* interest groups whose interests or perceptions of morality are already near enough to structuralism to make them relatively easily fully convertible to its cause. It could be argued that such groups able to call upon much larger constituencies than Oxfam and its global equivalents exist and that they represent a 'route' for the exercise of power whose potential has been exploited only weakly so far.

The groups in question are regarded frequently as the least obvious sources of *effective* lobbying power in many developed states, perhaps because in many cases they have not yet developed a sophisticated enough understanding of how they might legitimately operate in a political context without compromising their (in most but not all cases) non-party political positions, or because they have not been sufficiently successful in practising what they preach in the past. The leaders of the groups concerned are categorised as part of the BTC elite within the appropriate section of the Change Map discussion in Chapter 1, while their memberships fit within the section on the wider population. The groups themselves consist of several of the various numerically significant *mainstream* allegedly Christian religious bodies in the developed states, the Catholic, Methodist, Anglican and Lutheran Christian churches for example. (To avoid complications, those American fundamentalist and evangelical groups which already exercise considerable influence as lobby groups are not included here because of the simple fact that some of the most prominent are seen as being identified much more closely with traditional liberalism than with structuralism.) Politically, they are *potentially* of enormous significance, not only because of the overall size of their membership, but because the need to help the poor is at the heart of their declared belief systems (the same is true of Islam with respect to the importance of the idea of the giving of Zakāt[11]). It has been shown already how the hierarchies of the English and Welsh Catholic churches recently have advocated publicly key aspects of structuralism, although they seem to have concentrated on a hierarchy–government-level approach without very much idea of how to mobilise effectively their church *memberships* behind their position. Furthermore, in a key document laying down Christian ideology, in his Second Letter to the Corinthians, for example, the central Christian thinker St Paul sets out a morality of economic behaviour that, if translated from a personal to a state level, dovetails neatly with key aspects of structuralist thought when he says,

> Our desire is not that others might be relieved while you are hard pressed, but that there might be equality. At the present time your plenty will supply what they need, so that in turn their plenty will supply what you need. Then there will be equality, as it is written: 'He who gathered much did not have too much, and he who gathered little did not have too little.'[12]

However the credibility of such churches has been undermined in the past because many Christians have partially or totally ignored the implications of this aspect of Christian doctrine. The mainstream Christian churches have millions of members across Western Europe, for example. But for the most part their ability to persuade the latter to make their voices heard on the question of world hunger has been only limited. In the United Kingdom, where there are around five million practising mainstream Christians, church leaders and clergy have been quite successful in persuading their members to make private donations to their joint and individual third world relief organisations, and yet greatly ineffective in persuading those same members to lobby their elected representatives for increased foreign aid (targeted at the kind of objectives set out earlier in this section) in the huge numbers that would be required to bring about a substantial change in government policy. There has been a failure also to show those that have lobbied in one way or another how to do this most effectively. That the debate over foreign aid should be so low-key and of such limited interest in much of the developed world where the mainstream churches are prominent could be argued to be an indictment of either the leaders of those Christian churches or the ordinary members of the same – or both. In many cases, the leaders could be much more effective than they are, and given the life-and-death nature of the issue, and its centrality in their own declared belief systems, it could be argued that they need to be encouraged to seek professional help to show them how they might achieve this.

In short, it could be argued strongly that part of the key to changing developed states' government policies towards structuralist prescriptions lies in the business of turning mainstream, numerically significant religious groups' memberships from being merely *potentially* powerful lobbies on such issues into ones that have the skill and organisation to exercise *real* power with regard to the latter. That can be done, theoretically at least, through those in favour of structuralism finding ways to educate or even shame religious leaders into learning the lobbying, communication and motivational skills necessary to do this and generally being prepared to be far more active in persuading their congregations of the need to turn the preaching or 'policy' on poverty of such potentially momentous documents as the New Testament from words into effective action.

This is *one* remedy which an application of the Change Map suggests might be tried. It would be attempting to alter *political elite perceptions of the desirability of a change* in foreign aid policies through persuading part of the *BTC elites*, in the form of the leaders of the mainstream religious faiths of developed states, to in turn persuade their memberships to convert their enormous *potential* lobbying *influence* into *real influence* and electoral *power*. Given that no government is anxious to lose electoral support, it is unlikely that a sizeable lobby would be ignored.

The difficulties in the way of such a strategy would be the conservatism of some religious leaders and their followers and their reluctance to look at new approaches, the inadequate understanding of the need for persuading and motivating their congregations on such matters of some leaders and the mistaken belief on the part of others that such non-party politics is the same as party politics, together with the problems that might be involved in agreeing a commonly advocated *appropriate* (i.e. neither over- nor under-ambitious) set of proposals which could be lobbied for in order to most effectively open up meaningful parliamentary debates and pressurise governments into action. With regard to the latter point, the fact that a particular set of proposals has been advanced here as allegedly practical and realisable does not mean that such disparate groups would automatically see things the same way, even though they might be the best channel through which such proposals could be promoted. None of these difficulties would be easy to overcome, although the latter is probably the one that could be resolved with the least trouble, should it arise. While the Change Map helps to suggest a theoretical way of achieving progress on structuralism, what it does not and cannot do is show precisely how to make such progress easy. Ultimately, everything would be dependent on sufficient numbers of adequately skilled individuals being prepared to help to get the process off the ground – both at the level of those initially lobbying religious leaders for example, and at the level of the leaders themselves.

Given all of these potential difficulties, it might be argued that it is somewhat naive to suggest trying to achieve change through the medium of religious groups. But it might reasonably be asked whether the suggestion is any more naive than, for example, the past emphasis of many Marxist writers on the need for global revolutionary political–economic change led by Marxist 'vanguards' within the capitalist states. At least mainstream religious groups are already in place across most of the developed world, with millions of members in some of the most powerful states such as the USA. This has never been true of Marxism.

But, of course, it is not just religious groups who hold humanitarian values and might be prepared to press more effectively for government policies which would fund the kind of properly constructed health and hunger programmes that are needed to tackle global poverty. Surveys in Britain and elsewhere suggest that humanitarian values are held widely among young people, for example, whether religiously inclined or completely atheist. Religious groups would not find themselves alone if they chose to press more effectively for greater help for the world's absolute poor from the developed world (although how well-organised and channelled any complementary support might be is another question). Neither would political parties which broke the mould and actually showed imagination in presenting the problem of world poverty and the greater contributions their societies could make to alleviating it without crippling themselves, and which put in the effort necessary to make the issue an inspirational one.

Ultimately, the nature of the sacrifices which any individual developed state might be prepared to make to help get measures such as the proposed health and agricultural programmes off the ground would be dependent upon the limits set by the debate on the desirable scale and nature of its contributions to those programmes within it. What is first necessary is that such debates are provoked through channels such as that outlined above and that there are strong advocates, such as effective church lobby groups, at work to try and secure maximum support for such programmes during the course of those debates. What would be particularly crucial would be the success of effectively organised religious and complementary lobbies in *one of the larger* Western economies in persuading their government and its wider electorate to support such programmes. The advocacy of such a government, together with pressure from it on other northern states to shoulder their share of the burden, would greatly accelerate the pace at which a truly global and substantial health and hunger strategy could become a reality.

So, what are needed are the right conditions to generate political elite support for the kinds of structuralist measures discussed here (which might include the transformation of mainstream religious bodies into the powerful groups that potentially they are on poverty issues) and an understanding of the practical limit of what electorates might and might not be prepared to support – and the right people with an awareness both of the requisite skills to make the case for structuralist programmes effectively and of the need to try and coordinate their efforts.

Parts of this list of conditions have been in place in Britain and other major northern states at various times during recent years, but never all at once. (It is important to acknowledge that some of the smaller European states have been much more generous in their aid policies than the larger ones.) In Britain for example, the 'Hungry for Change' campaign of the mid-1980s achieved a relatively high profile and gained the public support of a number of prominent politicians, but asked more than many of the public could understand or would support in terms of the breadth of reforms it suggested, presented a media image of being worthy rather than inspirational with its hunger fasts and associated strategies, and was not backed up by *effective* support from the churches for the reasons mentioned already above.

The conclusion here, therefore, is that real change is possible in the policies of the North which would be of substantial assistance to the world's poor. But it will not occur through any magical political solution originating from within the government elites of the rich states. Individuals committed to the idea of such change need to think of the different ways in which *they* might try and help *create* the conditions for it within their own societies. For example, well-planned individual or group action that persuaded the Christian and Muslim religious leaders in Britain to adopt a more effective strategy for persuading their members to take the trouble to lobby their MPs on behalf of the world's poor would be potentially enormously effective, given that the two faiths represent a sizeable proportion of the British electorate in terms of their practising members.

Governments in most of the developed world have shown conclusively that they are not prepared to make any substantial contribution to solving the problem of global poverty without pressure from their electorates and from interest groups for them to do so. It is up to those committed to tackling the poverty problem to consider ways of acting more effectively therefore, and to have the patience to continue their efforts over the medium to long term that may well be necessary to achieve maximum success. If they fail to do this, then, within the global political economic system as it stands, there would appear to be few other means of helping the millions of people who suffer and die as members of the world's absolute poor. The existing liberal system has played a part (it has not by any means been the whole story[13]) in enabling states such as the Four Tigers (South Korea, Taiwan, Singapore and Hong Kong) to start pulling themselves up into the developed world, but they are relatively only very small drops in an ocean of global poverty and suffering.

Having said all of this, readers might like to use the Change Map to help think about these conclusions and decide for themselves whether they believe there might be other more credible routes for attempting change than the one outlined above. As pointed out previously, there has only been sufficient space to discuss in detail one possible route here. A basic purpose of the map, after all, is to provide a framework which can help to generate as many new avenues of well-structured thought on global issues and the possibility for change as is possible.[14]

Women and development

Last, but certainly not least, if it is to be assumed that everyone has an equal right to relief from poverty and ill health, it is necessary to consider the specific plight of women within the development equation, because until comparatively recently there was a tendency almost to ignore women's needs completely in any attempt to improve the lot of the absolute poor. The essence of the problems facing many women in the less developed world was summarised in the Brandt Report:

> Women participate in development everywhere. But they are not equal participants because very frequently their status prevents them from having equal access to education, training, jobs, land ownership, credit, business opportunities and even to nutritious food and other necessities for survival.[15]

> Women are half of the world's population and of its workforce and do nearly two-thirds of the world's work-hours, yet receive directly only one-tenth of global income.[16]

During pregnancy and childbirth over half of the world's women have no trained help, and two-thirds of pregnant women in poorer countries suffer from anaemia and its associated problems.[17]

Females in poorer countries are also especially at risk during the first five years of life. In some Asian and African countries girls' chances of surviving are considerably lower than those of boys. There are many places where, when food is short, boys (and male adults) receive a much greater share of the family diet. In India, for example, girls are more often affected by the food deficiency disease Kwashiorkor but are less often taken for treatment. The inequality in nutrition and health care in childhood has its effects later on (e.g. without enough protein, calcium and vitamin D bones will not grow as long, strong or hard as they should. Mental development is also affected).[18]

Women are often exploited in factories in the less developed world, as in some cases are both male and female children. Many such factories are used by developed world companies to supply them with low-cost goods. Not only are hours often Dickensian in length, but wages frequently meagre and working conditions dangerous.

While the situation has begun to change in recent years, in the past, despite all of the above sufferings and inequalities, development projects frequently focused on males almost as if women did not exist and in some cases actually succeeded in worsening the workload and health of women.

What all of this means obviously is that if all the world's absolute poor are regarded as having an equal right to relief from their plight, any attempt at promoting economic development and improved health care has to focus on men and women equally within the different cultural contexts of each society. It is particularly important that the specific needs of child-bearers are allotted adequate attention, especially given the fact that the current pre- and post-natal health problems of many mothers can affect adversely their children as well as themselves. This frequently requires a change of attitude in societies where women traditionally have been treated as second-class citizens. The extent to which such changes are possible varies according to the societies in question and the degree of effort which is put into negotiating or driving forwards change by their own governments at both national and local level and also the extent to which aid agencies are able to supply educators and health-care fieldworkers to try and persuade communities to adopt new attitudes and practices. In some societies there is little that can be done without pressure on their governments by those states or organisations which supply them with significant levels of development assistance. There is no magic wand that can be waved instantly because of the scale of the problem, but what aid agencies have demonstrated success-fully so far is that, despite all of the obstacles, change in the role, health and status of women is possible within many communities. They have done this through such diverse means as organising women's cooperatives and the funding of health education programmes targeted specifically at women. One prominent UK-based development agency, for example, is supporting a nationwide women's development programme in Bangladesh. It decided to do this after it concluded from its first-hand observations that women in rural Bangladesh often are 'brutally exploited' and that they are frequently excluded from any active role in their communities. Its programme has been designed to set up a network of women's groups through a process of education and leadership training. The core aims have been to build up rural Bangladeshi women's confidence, to increase their literacy levels, to support their legal rights and to improve educational facilities for their children.[19]

The fact that the work of development agencies has demonstrated convincingly that change for the better in women's position within poorer societies can be achieved, even in the most difficult circumstances where women are treated almost as subhuman, is itself sufficient evidence to dismiss excuses that it is not possible to improve the lot of women in many of the most traditional cultures (the World Bank in particular seems to have taken note of this, and of the crucial importance of women in the devel-opment process, in deciding in August 1995 to offer a small-loans facility specifically for poor women in the less developed world[20]). In some societies the process of change is very difficult and will probably take considerable time, and in the most oppressive it may well indeed prove almost impossible to make more than the most basic progress, but in the eyes of many development agencies such facts should be seen primarily as a challenge to themselves, governments and other interested parties to pursue equal rights in development for both genders as a central goal and not as a reason for giving up on their pursuit.

At the most basic level, development programmes that do not take properly into account half of the people in the communities at which they are aimed, due to discriminatory practices, negate completely the idea that the right to freedom from poverty and ill health should be possessed by all. States that promote or tolerate such programmes within their borders presumably would be relegated to the lowest priority within any expanded global relief programmes which had such a universal goal at their core.

Chapter 8

A second United States?
Integration in Western Europe

Introduction

Historically, to put it mildly, Europe has not been a peaceful continent. The Nazi holocaust was simply the most murderous and horrifying example of a well-established European tradition of the persecution of ethnic minorities. Both the First and Second World Wars started as European conflicts between peoples with a long history of attacking each other in different combinations and numbers. More recently, the Serbs, Croats and Bosnian Muslims in the former Yugoslavia have demonstrated graphically how easily old hatreds and distrusts can still spill over into the worst excesses of barbarism.[1]

Nevertheless, in a very real sense, a large slice of Europe was integrated in key respects such as defence policy, and its constituent states peaceable towards each other (unless one decided to try and leave the fold, as in the case of Czechoslovakia in 1968), during almost half of the twentieth century, right up until 1989. The three Baltic states swallowed by the Soviet Union under the Hitler–Stalin pact, together with most of Eastern Europe – Ukraine, Belarus, Georgia, Poland, East Germany, Hungary, Czechoslovakia, and, to a lesser extent, Romania – were effectively run as one in most key foreign policy matters and in terms of the permitted shape of their economic systems (those states deemed to be within the territorial boundaries of the former USSR were run *completely* as one). The instrument of their union was the Moscow-led communist party system which began to collapse in Eastern Europe during 1989 and which finally vaporised in the failed coup against Gorbachev in August 1991. The problem, of course, was that the union was involuntary, and as communist power disintegrated it fell apart under the pressure of the resentments which the period of oppression had engendered.

So whatever the vices of the Moscow-led system, it did have the great virtue of removing war as an option between the various peoples under its rule, except on the rare occasion when their Soviet master instructed one to invade another. And, while the Cold War that arose out of the creation of the Eastern European empire, and from the general distrust between Stalin and the West after the Second World War, threatened on at least one occasion to lead to the incineration of millions of people, it also had an important role to play in helping cement the new peacefulness of Western Europe. The apparent military might of the perceived Soviet opponent and its Eastern bloc satellites forced most of the Western European states to band together in an alliance under American leadership. They had largely to bury the option of the use of force between themselves as the final resort in any serious clash of interests.

That burying of the force option was greatly reinforced by the process of economic integration that began with the formation of the European Coal and Steel Community in 1951, and then progressed via the creation of the European Economic Community and the European Atomic Energy Community in 1957, and the final unifying of all three in the late 1960s into a single European Community. While one of the fundamental aims of the Community (now the European Union or EU) has always been the containment of German might within an integrationalist framework, it has been concerned also with making Western Europe economically stronger in order to be better able to resist the pressures from 'communism' from both the East and from within itself that it perceived prior to the Gorbachev revolution.

In short, ironically communism had a powerful binding role to play on both sides of the ideological divide, being one of the factors that forced the Western states to like each other (although Greece and Turkey might find 'like' a rather strong word), just as it compelled the Eastern bloc members to be peaceful and fraternal neighbours.

The cosiness of the old order, if anything that is cemented by nuclear weapons can be called 'cosy', was disrupted gradually by the erosion of Yugoslavian federal control over the constituent republics in the years following the death of Marshal Tito in 1980, and most spectacularly, by the rapid evaporation of the Soviet empire between 1989 and 1991.[2] This latter event has changed the agenda in Western Europe almost as much as it has changed that in the East. Germany and the European Union have suddenly had to absorb the old East German Democratic Republic and several other of the old Eastern European states are now queuing for EU membership, although the enormous economic difficulties of some of them probably will make it some time before the EU is prepared to accept them. In addition, the evaporation of Soviet power, and the consequent lessening of US interest and involvement in European affairs (although the Americans still seem to be prepared to take a leadership role where they deem it to be in their interests to do so), saw the EU having to attempt to take on a new dimension as a more coherent political actor during the early 1990s to try and contain and resolve the political and military problems arising in the former Yugoslavia – a role that it may have to repeat elsewhere now that the discipline of the old Eastern bloc alliance system has disappeared. In this respect, the collapse of communist supremacy in the East, while increasing the danger of conflict in that half of the continent both between and within states, possibly may give political integration in the West a boost over the next few years, despite the difficulties of the early 1990s.

Leaving issues of war and peace aside, what all of this means is that while the future of voluntary European integration prior to 1989 was an extremely complex matter for analysis, even when academics' attention was focused almost entirely on the then European Community (EC), that complexity has now been increased enormously. It will take several years to determine how many of the former Soviet European republics will choose to chart a long-term future in a new, freer association within the ruins of the old, now vanished USSR and how many will prefer instead to try (or, given alleged Russian machinations in Georgia, Belarus and elsewhere,[3] be *allowed* to try) and join the EU when or if they become credible candidates for admission.

These possibilities add to the difficulty of trying to assess usefully where the current EU members are going. On the one hand, leaving Eastern Europe on one side for a moment, at present (1995) much of the single market is in place and is serving to liberate previously restricted aspects of trade between member states. On the other hand, as Dinan points out, some serious obstacles have arisen with regard to a number of important single market measures and some states are more conscientious implementers than others. Dinan believes that in the long run the success or failure of the single market will depend on the Commission's ability to resist attempts to erect new trade barriers and the level and quality of state implementation of the market legislation's various provisions.[4] But arguably it will be the success or failure of the firms of individual member states that will be the most crucial factor in determining whether the market will survive the 1990s intact. Industrially weak countries like Greece or Portugal may at some stage be forced to drop out to one extent or another and to introduce new protectionist measures by various means, and such full or partial defections could be a serious blow to hopes for continuing integration within the EU. If they were imitated by other larger states with areas of significant industrial weakness within their economies, such as Britain or Italy, they would have a highly negative impact on the progress of wider economic and monetary union (EMU) and on political union.

Furthermore, this author observed at the time of the signing of the Treaty on European Union that should the provisions of EMU prove over-tough for some states, or, alternatively, prove to be too lax, thereby failing to secure the necessary financial discipline, they could in themselves start to unravel the integration process. In addition, Black Wednesday (16 September 1992, the day on which a particularly virulent EU currency crisis came to a head), when Britain was forced to drop out of the exchange rate mechanism of the European monetary system (a key ingredient within plans for EMU), followed rapidly by Italy, showed vividly how rocky and unstable even existing levels of integration can be. These events were followed by severe difficulties experienced by several other states in trying to remain within the rigorous confines of the mechanism. Even though most of the currencies that had got into difficulties had returned to their old parities by early 1994, the Union had been given a stark lesson as to just how easily its plans could be upset.

On top of all of this, the new situation in Eastern Europe perhaps has been forcing the EU states towards an integrated foreign and security policy before they are ready for it. Contrary to the more optimistic view expressed earlier in the chapter, it could be argued that the consequent strains could greatly damage wider political relations between the member states if they become too severe, and that also would be a considerable blow to the EU's prospects for further integration. Already, the inability to deal effectively with the problems in the former Yugoslavia without the help and involvement also of NATO, the USA and Russia, has produced an observable disillusionment with the Union both among its electorates and a number of its leading politicians.

So, bearing in mind the complicated situation above, how feasible is it to carry out a useful analysis of the prospects for integration in both halves of the European continent? The judgement here is that the situation in the former Soviet Union currently is too fluid and ill-defined, and several Eastern European states' future ability to fulfil all of the EU's formal and informal entrance requirements as yet too uncertain, to make it worth engaging in any detailed attempted predictions as to where they will go politically over the next ten years, and as to how their various future moves might affect the EU. Given the complexity of the situation within the EU itself, as outlined above, any such attempts would create merely an analytical quagmire that revealed little of practical use. It would therefore seem most logical to focus concern here predominantly on the EU, given that real and substantial progress on integration has been and is still being made within it. Reference to Eastern Europe will be made, but it will not form one of the central concerns of the chapter.

However, developments in the EU's legislative and negotiating forums are now occurring so rapidly that any attempt to concentrate on each of their specific implications would be of limited value, given that attitudes on EMU, for example, can change several times within only a few months. What will be done here instead is something of rather more value as far as long-term analytical perspectives are concerned. The focus will be on the underlying trends, forces, ideas, and interests at work in the integration process of which the day-to-day developments that are the concern more properly of journalism form a part. Several main questions will be examined in this chapter and the next. First, what is the EU and how far has integration actually gone within it – what is the real significance of the moves that have occurred so far? Second, what are the main incentives towards further integration? Third, what are the major obstacles to further progress? Fourth, what are the conditions that would be necessary for the incentives to overcome the obstacles? Fifth, would continuing European integration be a benefit or a cost to the global community?

Relevant aspects of the Global Change Map will be applied in answering the second, third and fourth of the above questions, both to show further the utility of the map and in the belief that the analysis will be given extra depth as a consequence.

What is the EU and how far has integration really gone within it?

In one sense, the answer to the question of what the EU is is very easy. It is an organisation in which the member states have agreed to establish a customs union (that is, a body of states which imposes common tariffs on trade with non-member states and which promotes free trade within itself) together with common policies in a number of major fields, including agriculture, regional aid, energy and competition among others. It is also grappling increasingly with the problem of the extent to which it is possible to formulate a common foreign and defence policy, and is committed to the idea of an economic and monetary union. This commitment is likely to remain as a future aspiration even if the timetable set out in the Maastrict Treaty on European Union proves to be impractical within the short term.

It has four main institutions of governance – the Commission, the Council of Ministers, the European Parliament and the European Court of

Justice. The powers and composition of these bodies have been subjected to a number of changes in recent years and no doubt will continue to be so. The observations that are made here relate to the situation as it stood at the end of 1994. The Commission researches and proposes legislative measures, possesses a certain amount of delegated decision-making power on such things as agricultural and competition policy, is responsible for administering the Community, for ensuring that the treaties are adhered to, and for mediating in disputes between member states. It is required also to act as a key engine of European integration, thinking up new ideas and doing its best to keep the existing momentum going. To a considerable extent, its effectiveness in performing these roles at any one time depends upon the character and diplomatic skills of whoever holds the office of President of the Commission, together with the nature of the overall political situation within the member states and the extent to which it favours a Euro-perspective on the part of their governments.

The Council presidency shares some of the above functions with the Commission, most particularly the mediatory and policy-proposing functions, in relation to which gradually it has come to exercise a role of its own. The rules set down in the treaties which govern the EU, and the fact that the Commission has a sizeable body of officials who specialise in researching and framing European policy and legislative proposals, mean that even when the Council effectively proposes policy, it generally refers it to the Commission for further research and refinement before making any final decisions on it. The Council's key power is that it is the ultimate decision-making authority on most matters. While on policies such as agriculture a single state theoretically can block new developments adversely affecting its fundamental national interests, on most single market matters and, under the Maastricht Treaty, on matters relating to some additional policy areas, the Council can make its decisions on the basis of qualified majority voting. As will be seen shortly, this has introduced a genuinely federal element into the Union in so far as even if two of the largest states oppose a particular single market measure, they nevertheless can find themselves obliged to introduce it because they have been outvoted in Brussels.

The European Parliament is directly elected, with each member state being entitled to a number of seats that is proportional roughly to its population size. Germany, for example, with over 79 million people, has 99 seats, while Britain, with 57.5 million people, is allowed 87 seats and the Republic of Ireland, with 3.5 million people, has 15 seats.

The Parliament gradually has been increasing in its powers since the first direct elections were held in 1979. It can make suggestions for new legislation to either or both of the Council and the Commission, and has the right to scrutinise new policy and legislative proposals and offer opinions on them. Under the cooperation procedures first introduced under the Single European Act, and the co-decision procedures introduced by the Maastricht Treaty, the Parliament's powers over EU legislation have been increased significantly. The latter procedure, for example, effectively gives the Parliament a veto over legislation relating to such things as the single market, and aspects of education and training, public health and consumer protection. While the co-decision procedure does not as yet cover every area of EU law, the fact that the Parliament has such powers in reserve has given it greater influence over those aspects of the policy-making process affected by the procedure. It also has joint decision-making powers with the Council on new association agreements with non-Union members and in negotiations with states making applications to join the EU. In addition, the range of matters which now require an absolute majority of MEPs in their favour before they can be passed includes even the role of the European Central Bank.[5]

The Parliament's most significant powers lie in the area of the budget, where it has the last word on allocations for such key items as regional and social policy, although the Council retains the final word on the biggest consumer of EU funds, the Common Agricultural Policy. It also has the right to throw out the entire budget until the Council and Commission produce proposals that are more to its liking, a power that it exercised both in 1980 and in 1985.

The Parliament's influence so far has been restricted by its failure to establish a clear and strong enough identity in the minds of the EU's electorate, and by the fact that MEPs remain rather remote from most voters.

The Council, like the Parliament, is composed of elected politicians (except where the occasional member of the British House of Lords is involved in the former as a minister), although it is only the Members of the European Parliament who are elected by the voters specifically as European representatives. The Council is drawn entirely from the cabinets of the member states, and the voting power of each state is roughly proportional to its size. Commissioners are not elected and are appointed by the member states, with the larger states appointing two commissioners each and the smaller members one each (under the Maastricht Treaty the entire Commission now also has to be approved by the European Parliament before it can be appointed). However, once in office, commissioners are theoretically beyond the control of the states and take an oath of allegiance to Europe rather than their home countries. Decisions within the Commission are taken by a simple majority.

The European Court of Justice has one judge more than the total number of states in the Union, at least one judge being drawn from each of the member states. It ensures that national laws do not conflict with Union laws and settles disputes on EU law between and within member states. It is the highest court on EU law within the Union and can overrule both national legislatures and national courts. It is important in the decision-making process in that its interpretations of disputed sections of Union law and practice can effectively change the rules of the game by which things are done within the EU. While, perhaps sadly, it does not have the power to send politicians to jail, member states are aware that if they ignore its judgements more than occasionally, then there is a danger that the Union will start to fall apart, losing them the benefits for which they joined originally. In addition, under the Maastricht Treaty, the Court may impose fines on those states which fail to comply with its judgements or which fail to implement Union law.[6]

So what is the situation regarding these various institutions overall? While the powers of the European Parliament are undoubtedly growing, and it is now no longer the mere talking-shop that it used to be in its early years, it is clearly still very much the junior partner to the Council and the Commission in decision-making, and so far has been somewhat cautious about using its new veto powers.

After a period of decline in the 1960s and 1970s, the Commission was effectively reborn under Jacques Delors in the second half of the 1980s, and during that period was very much a force to be reckoned with on economic and many political matters. Delors resurrected its status as a body almost equal to one of the big four member states. However, the economic downturn of the early 1990s and the doubt which this fostered about the immediate feasibility of several aspects of the integrative process served to push several EU governments back towards a more inward-looking perspective, which in consequence noticeably reduced the influence of the Commission. Furthermore the popular backlash against Maastricht (one of the Commission's most treasured projects) in a number of states produced an additional reduction in its influence. Nevertheless, it still retains a role at the heart of the policy-making process on the key issues of the single market and economic, monetary and political union, albeit a less ambitious one than in its heyday of the late 1980s.

The Council's last word on most matters by definition makes it the primary decision-making body. However, it relies on the Commission to help act as an engine of progress within the Union by researching and proposing new ideas, finding compromises and generally contributing the energy and commitment that is necessary if the EU is not to stagnate when the Council runs into the doldrums. (As pointed out earlier, the Commission's effectiveness in performing these roles depends considerably on whoever holds its presidency at a particular time.) Progress on integration was at its most impressive in the late 1980s and early 1990s at those moments when the presidency of the Commission and that of the Council acted in harness to try and drive the Community (as it was then called) forwards. In this sense, even while the Council is the supreme body, effective decision-making is very much dependent upon a good partnership between itself and the Commission.

So, now that the role of the various major institutions has been explained, how far has integration really gone within the EU? Stanley Hoffman has described the Union's political system as 'an elaborate set of networks, closely linked in some ways, partially decomposed in others'.[7] In practice, the Union is a mixture of a federal decision-making authority capable of binding all of its members to its decisions by force of law and of taking majority votes on some matters, and a purely cooperative intergovernmental bargaining forum, within which the last word on whether or not to participate in a particular initiative rests with the individual state governments whose fundamental interests it affects. The nature of the federal authority that exists within the EU currently is very different to and rather more limited than that which governs other major federal unions, such as the USA, and involves a very different view of the role which states should play in relation to the centre. None of the three Union presidencies (those of the Commission, Council and Parliament), for example, not even that of the Council, has the right to veto the legislative proposals advanced by representatives of the member states, whereas the US President has such power. It is largely the representatives of the states alone who can exercise the right of veto, although the European Parliament is now beginning to share in this power also.

Ultimately, it is the defence and foreign affairs fields which are likely to ensure that even if, for example, the presidency of the Council in future should be modified so that it begins to resemble much more closely the US model of a federal presidency in terms of its powers, the EU does not grow into a US-style federal state, in which such key policy areas effectively can become the sole prerogative of a strong presidency. This is for the simple reason that foreign and defence policy goes so deeply to the heart of national sovereignty in some long-established states such as Britain, one of the largest actors within the Union, that they probably will feel unable to forgo their right of veto on such matters, even if they decide to avoid using it as far as possible. An interesting example which shows something of the extent to which this is the case is provided by the following extract from a description of EU foreign ministers' discussions of what to do about the 1990/1 crisis resulting from Iraq's invasion of Kuwait:

'Until Christmas the 12 kept to a common line in support of UN and American policy on the Gulf. Things started to come apart at the meeting of foreign ministers in Luxembourg on January 4th, when it seemed that James Baker [then heading the US State Department] and Tariq Aziz [representing Iraq] would never meet. France wanted EC foreign ministers to talk to Mr Aziz anyway. It also wanted to offer Iraq "linkage" between withdrawal from Kuwait and a general Middle East peace conference, meaning an international attempt to settle the Israel–Palestine issue. Britain and Holland vetoed both ideas.

At one point the Dutch minister, Hans Van den Broek, argued so vigorously against acting independently of the Americans that a furious Roland Dumas, the French minister, snapped: "If the EC had majority voting on foreign policy you would be outvoted." Douglas Hurd, Britain's foreign secretary, replied coldly: "That is exactly why Britain wants to maintain unanimity." '8

Nevertheless, there are increasing pressures on the member states to try and formulate effective common policies in the fields of defence and foreign affairs on a *cooperative* basis, given a growing realisation that if they do not do this, then even the major European states are likely to have serious difficulties in influencing such core international developments as the consequences of the disintegration of the Soviet Union and Yugoslavia. In other words, while there is little prospect within the short to medium term of introducing majority voting on significant foreign and defence matters, the growing pressures of global politics may prove strong enough to force the member states to compromise sufficiently to produce coherent EU defence/foreign policies on major international issues within an intergovernmental context as a matter of normal practice.

On the basis of first impressions, therefore, what looks likely to emerge out of the present situation and the trends that are visible within it is a new kind of actor, which is both to a significant extent a federal union (considerably more so than at present if economic and monetary union succeeds to any great degree), while simultaneously remaining a collection of states with the capacity for some unilateral international action, albeit with much reduced independence, particularly on economic matters.

However, as will be seen below, there are a variety of crucial considerations which may prevent all of this from occurring. For example, as pointed out earlier, whether EU integration progresses further or starts to unravel is liable to be significantly dependent on such things as the success or failure of the single market. Furthermore, the growing need to try and produce common foreign and defence policies could work two ways and, instead of bringing about increased cooperation, may actually undermine the Union. For example, the serious difficulties which the then European Community experienced in trying to achieve an effective and co-ordinated foreign policy over the Gulf and the former Yugoslavia in the early 1990s suggest that the significant differences in the external interests of the member states carry the potential risk of causing such major disagreements in the future that these in themselves could cause the Union to split apart. Equally, as will be seen shortly, potentially there are deep pitfalls which lie in the way of significant further steps towards economic and monetary integration. In addition, both the popular backlash against the Maastricht Treaty prior to its final ratification and the continuing failure of the European Parliament to educate the electorate as to its powers and relationship to them, illustrate vividly the shallow roots which the elite-driven integration process has laid down so far. Unless significant steps are taken to change this situation, the EU could become dangerously vulnerable to popular disaffection in the future.

Finally, to reiterate the point made above, if the EU does succeed in achieving significant further progress in integration, what will emerge is likely to be something rather different to federal states as they traditionally have been known.

For non-European readers who might have found any of the above a little bit baffling there are two excellent foundational readers to which they can turn for further elaboration in the form of Desmond Dinan's *Ever Closer Union* (London, Macmillan, 1994) and Neill Nugent's *The Government and Politics of the European Union* (London, Macmillan, 1993).

What are the main incentives towards further integration?

The present European Union is the result of the merger of three predecessor organisations, the European Coal and Steel Community, established in 1951, and the European Economic Community and the European Atomic Community, both set up by the Treaty of Rome in 1957. A fourth organisation, the Western European Union defence alliance, now appears to be being drawn into it.

In order fully to understand the incentives that currently are at work in the EU integrative process it is necessary first to have an understanding of those that have been influential in the past. This is because some of the key factors at work currently have long historical roots, and cannot be understood adequately without some knowledge of those roots. It is essential also to apply the Change Map in the analysis that follows, in order to try and identify as broad a range of crucial factors relevant to the integrative process as possible.

The map might first prompt an examination of elite perceptions. A core concern for the ruling political and administrative elites of states like France in particular in the establishment of the earlier communities was the containment of Germany as a military power. Given past unhappy European experiences with German military might (in France's case, involving three massive invasions in eighty years) this was understandable. The concern first was to integrate German coal and steel production into a European framework, so that at the very least, its neighbours would have an early warning if attempts were made to divert it towards a potentially aggressive military build-up. Second, there was also a strong hope among many of the governmental elites of the original six member states (and of some of their administrative elites) that if the Western European economies could be made more interdependent it would become difficult and economically unfeasible for them (Germany included) to consider going to war against each other.

These were not the only factors initially fuelling European integration. Governmental elite perceptions in both the original six member states and the United States suggested that there was a need to secure a firm economic recovery if it was going to be possible to support credible countermeasures against the perceived threat from the Soviet Union and its then Eastern European allies. A common market policy seemed to be one way of achieving this, in that in offering the prospect of tariff removal, it promised lower costs for European firms, resulting in greater profitability, and thereby in increased economic growth prospects. In addition, as Europe lay in the shadow of the newly emerged military superstates of the USSR and the USA, there was a growing realisation among the political elites of the original six that integration may well be the only way by which Western Europe could regain a position of real influence in the world. In both of these senses, therefore, the original six states felt integration to be very strongly in their interests.

There were also reasons for some degree of integration specific to each of the original six member states – France, West Germany (East Germany was a separate entity firmly in the Soviet orbit after the Second World War and remained as such until reunification in 1990), Italy, Belgium, the

Netherlands and Luxembourg. The Coal and Steel Community offered particular economic benefits for the Belgian coal industry for example. For some key early post-Second World War French governmental leaders such as de Gaulle (who became President in 1958), 'integration' under France's leadership offered a unique opportunity for increasing French power and influence in continental Europe – provided Britain could be kept out of the communities. For the governmental elites of Germany and Italy, both of which had been tainted by aggressive Fascist regimes during the Second World War, membership of the various European communities offered a useful route back towards full political respectability.

The economic success of the early communities coincided with better economic conditions generally in the West, reinforcing the psychological effect of the former in politicians' and populations' minds. This first helped to persuade the member states of the value of expanding the scope of economic integration by setting up the European Economic Community in addition to the European Coal and Steel Community. It then spurred the newly created EEC onwards in integrating much of its agricultural production into a single managed market during the 1960s. Despite the costly and controversial nature of the policy, its very creation and survival showed that integration at the European level was possible in even the most difficult areas of states' economies.

To return to the Change Map, both interests and ideologies can be seen to have been at work in the above developments. The common liberal element in the economic ideologies of the original six member states persuaded them of the value of the particular type of economic communities they were trying to set up, while the apparent success of the ECSC suggested that further integration was in the interests of the governmental political elites (in so far as they identified economic success with likely future success at the polls) and in the interests of business elites and those of the wider population.

Opportunity factors were at work also in the form of the economic growth that was attributed to the integration process initially under the ECSC and then under the EEC. This arguably helped persuade the governmental political elites of the desirability of further economic integration. On top of this, fortune took a hand, given that the growth produced by these communities was helped by a general upturn in the world economy and the effects of United States economic policy towards both Europe and the world at the time. Had the Americans been less favourable towards the Europeans via Marshall Aid and subsequent policy, then their economic record might have been rather different.

The American attitude in turn was affected by ideology in so far as an

important section of the US governing political elite saw it as vital to reconstruct rapidly the economy of Western Europe on liberal capitalist lines if
the spread of communism was to be prevented and if Europe was to be
preserved as a market for US goods. That ideological perspective clearly
made it in the interests of the US governing and business elites to help the
Europeans.

However, despite the rapid and successful removal of formal tariffs
on industrial goods, progress in achieving a truly single market in non-
agricultural produce was slow due to the continued widespread use of
non-tariff barriers to trade, such as differing national technical and safety
standards for particular products. Growing fierce competition from Japan
and other more newly emergent Asian economic actors in the 1980s,
together with the continuing threat of American competition, was one of
the reasons which finally persuaded the European Community, as it had
been known since the late 1960s, to put the achievement of a full single
market in goods and services on the express track (the economic reasoning
behind this decision will be explained more fully later on in this chapter).
There were also a variety of specifically political reasons that were relevant,
as Dinan explains.[9] The fear of being left far behind in the global economic
race which helped motivate this move is still a significant force behind
proposals for further integration, which, some key European politicians have
argued, will make the EU stronger and more able to stand up against the
competition. The truly efficient working of a single market, they contend,
requires additional economic and monetary integration and, in order to deal
administratively and democratically with such additions, further political
integration will be needed as well.

To return to the Change Map, the fear referred to in the above paragraph
clearly was a manifestation of an imperative at work at the heart of EC
thinking. There was a strong feeling that the Community had no choice but
to find an effective response to the growing external competition, and to the
increasing flow of investment funds out of the EC states to competitor states,
if it was to survive as a major economic force.[10]

The concern with keeping Germany in check, given its expansionist
past, remains a significant factor behind the desire for further EU integration
among the governmental elites in states such as France and Belgium,
especially now that East and West Germany are unified. Given that the
united Germany potentially is an elephant that could trample over Western
Europe should it fall into less benign hands than those of the current
mainstream political parties, then such concern is perhaps understandable.
Equally, their awareness of such worries continues to persuade German
governments of the need to tread carefully in Europe, not least because of

their recent memory of the US Bush administration making it plain in private after the fall of the Berlin Wall that it shared some of the French and Belgian concerns over unification.

Such awareness was greatly reinforced in 1991 by the hostile reactions in both Yugoslavia and the USA to the idea of German participation in any EU peace-keeping military operation in Croatia. It is one of the main reasons why German governments so far have remained in favour of further European integration. They have calculated that if they continue to pursue German interests in a cooperative European context, and show a strong commitment to furthering the integrative/cooperative process within the EU, they have the possibility of achieving those interests without the strongly negative reactions from their neighbours and the USA which might well result from their 'throwing their weight around' unilaterally.

So, to bring in the Change Map again, the above discussion demonstrates how interests have affected the perceptions of both the French and German governments of the desirability of further integration. The intervention of fortune, in the form of the new situation in Europe following the collapse of communism across the continent (that was almost completely unanticipated at the time of its occurrence by most major commentators and analysts), has created additional incentives for integration. There has been an awareness that the political situation across parts of Eastern Europe and the territory of the former Soviet Union could become very unstable and that no one European state on its own is capable of responding effectively to consequent economic and security problems. This has forced the EU states to think seriously about incorporating a military dimension within the Union by absorbing the Western European Union defence organisation, which presently is closely linked to NATO, and to which many EU states belong. The Maastricht Treaty greatly tightened WEU–EU links, for example. An added incentive for such a move is the realisation that, in the post-Cold War era, as evidenced by the war in the former Yugoslavia, there is no *guarantee* that the United States will commit ground troops for combat or even peacekeeping purposes in European war zones. Overall, the various revolutions and convulsions in the East since 1989 have forced defence integration on to the EU agenda whether many of the member states like it or not, and it is significant that during September 1991 the then EC issued instructions to the WEU, despite it not yet being part of the Community, and the instructions were followed immediately. Ultimately, however, any integrative arrangements over defence are likely to take the less than completely federal form outlined earlier in this chapter for the reasons explained there. In addition, the extent to which an imperative develops behind them is likely to be dependent on the extent to which the USA continues its partial withdrawal from Europe and upon the stability or otherwise of the former Soviet Union and Eastern Europe over the next few years.

Having said that all of the above have been or are factors working in favour of integration, one should of course be aware that they do not affect all states equally. Italy, for example, both at the popular level and at the levels of business and political elites, traditionally has been much more in favour of far-reaching integration than the United Kingdom,[11] although whether that inclination will remain in the event of the massive sea changes in Italian politics that have followed the end of the Cold War is not entirely certain. Furthermore, the political and administrative elites in some states are strongly in favour of further integration in some policy areas but not in others which are favoured by neighbouring states, while in others the enthusiasm for a particular aspect of integration can vary within a single month in response to related and electorally significant issues at home. What is important is simply that the strong pressures for further integration outlined above exist and that, while they have different impacts upon the individual states, and within them, upon the internal elite and popular perceptions and attitudes that are crucial in shaping their attitudes on policy, their cumulative effect upon all such states looks likely to continue taking the integrative process forwards, if only gradually (providing the political elites of those states do not forget to persuade their electorates of the desirability of this).

Finally, it is perhaps useful to consider briefly the integrative process and the incentives for further progress which exist within it from the perspective of integration theory. The most widely adopted approach has been neo-functionalism, a term which sounds extremely complex but which refers to a set of ideas which are straightforward in essence. It would be misleading to say that there is a single neofunctionalist view, for there are in practice several. What it is intended to do here is to consider one approach which fits under the neofunctionalist umbrella, but which is whittled down to some of its bare essentials for the purposes of this study. (A short list of neo-functionalist theorists can be found in the reference notes at the end of the book for those wishing to examine the perspective in more detail.)[12]

This argues that once it becomes realised that certain basic technical and/or economic functions are better performed in an international co-operative forum and that forum is both set up and seen to be successful, there is a strong chance that such forums will be tried for additional technical and economic functions. If they also are seen to be successful, then more functions will be handled in this manner and so on. If this cumulative development occurs in a regional context, then ultimately it will lead to a considerable degree of economic integration within the region in question.

The further integration proceeds towards the hearts of states' economies, then the further will it impinge also on the political decision-making processes which regulate the central economic issues. The problems this creates will force politicians to have to start discussing them on an inter-state basis, which gradually leads also to a process of political integration in order to manage the economic integration that is already occurring. In addition, as economic and political power begins to shift to a new, integrated centre, then the interests and loyalties of politicians will be transferred increasingly to that centre. There is, in other words, a spill-over from the economic into the political arena.

It could be argued convincingly that perspectives like this offer a useful insight into what has been occurring with regard to the single market. As the single market programme has progressed further and further into the hearts of the EU member states' economies, due to the growth of the belief that the successful working of the former requires real progress towards economic and monetary union, the states have been forced to consider a simultaneous extension of political integration in order to manage the new economic developments. So the key implication of the kind of neo-functionalism outlined above is that as long as the incentive remains for further integration within the economic heart of the Union, an incentive for further political integration will be created also, which will be extinguished only when the member states believe the political institutions are adequate for managing the integrated areas of the EU economy satisfactorily.

What it is important to realise, however, is that this kind of neofunctional-ism does not claim that integration is inevitable, but only that it will continue to occur if states perceive its demonstrated effects to be sufficiently desirable. It is important to remember also that even strong incentives for integration can be partially or completely neutralised by the character of particular political leaders in a powerful position to influence EU developments, as was the case with Charles de Gaulle of France in the mid- and late 1960s. The influence of business and other elites in the form of powerful interest groups also should not be forgotten. While they can be a significant force pushing integration forwards when they find such a course of action to be in their interests, they can also create powerful blockages within EU programmes. It could be argued, for example, that the opposition of farmers' groups to reform of the Common Agricultural Policy (CAP) in recent years has brought about some unravelling of the integration that previously had been one of the policy's chief claims to virtue.

So, arguably, the type of neofunctionalist perspective outlined above is a useful means of trying to understand the integrative process that has occurred so far, together with the fundamental nature of the incentives for further political integration, providing the limits of its explanatory powers are borne in mind. It will be noted also that there is nothing within it that on its own makes it incompatible with the Change Map.

What are the main obstacles in the way of further integration?

As has been made clear both in the discussion of neofunctionalism above and in references to the single market, further substantial progress in European integration is not inevitable. In addition, as will be seen below, it is quite possible even that the progress which has been achieved so far could be reversed within the future.

The single market is so important here that it requires some elaboration. The reasoning behind the fundamental point that it can either make or break the prospects for economic and monetary union, and ultimately some form of political union, needs to be examined.

First of all, it is necessary to look at the economic logic behind the enthusiasm for the completion of the single market that developed during the second half of the 1980s and very early 1990s. In doing so, it is important to realise that not all states are equally attracted to all the threads of the arguments for it, several being keen on some but cautious and even worried about others.

The starting point for the '1992' single market programme, as it became known, was the fact that while the common market had been successful in removing tariffs in intra-community trade, by the mid-1980s it still had left untouched many non-tariff barriers to trade (NTBs), such as time-consuming frontier paperwork procedures which slowed the movement of goods from one member state to another, preferential treatment for home states' companies in national procurement policies, the lack of harmonisation of indirect taxation, variations in safety and technical regulations and standards across the Community, state subsidising of industries and so on. These barriers were believed to be an impediment to economic growth within the EU. They made goods more expensive than they need be and therefore kept consumption at a lower level than it would be in a community free of NTBs. Because consumption was lower, fewer people were required for production of goods and services. The result was a higher level of un-employment than would otherwise have been the case, which further encouraged 'underconsumption' and the economies of member states could not operate at their full potential level because of this. This factor in turn was a discouragement to investors.

However, free marketeers[13] argued that the removal of NTBs would reverse this situation, the consequent cheapness of goods encouraging consumption, increased consumption creating new employment and spending-power, which in turn would encourage investment. With sound economic management a virtuous circle would be created, whereby each new creation of employment would increase consumption, which would encourage investment, which in turn would create new opportunities for employment and so on.

Another positive aspect of the removal of NTBs was seen as being the subjecting of the less efficient European industries (which previously they had protected) to a new bracing 'cold shower' of competition, which would force them to increase efficiency and cut costs and prices, thereby contributing to the wealth and growth creation process described above. It was believed that the removal of such protections of inefficient firms as state subsidies would lead to a situation which would truly be one of the survival of the fittest. Without protection, those inefficient firms that failed to reform themselves would go to the wall and production would be concentrated in the hands of the efficient.

Economies of scale also were seen as being important. These may be defined here simply as the economic advantages of large-scale production, and can be created in several ways. For example, when faced with a choice of raw materials suppliers, a large-scale producer whose order is financially very valuable to such suppliers should be able to negotiate a much better price than a small firm whose purchases are relatively insignificant. Cheaper raw materials enable large firms to cut costs and either increase their profits or lower their prices to consumers (they might well choose to do both of these things). A lowering of prices should again contribute to an increase in economic growth in the manner described above, providing demand for the product in question is expandable (elastic) enough. Alternatively, new industrial plant for production is frequently very expensive. A large-scale producer which markets its products successfully is able to pay off the costs of such plant much more quickly than a smaller-scale producer. This allows it to cut the costs of production much more quickly, and thereby to bring down the prices of its goods much more rapidly, in the process stimulating growth in the manner already described.

The 1992 process was supposed to make such economies of scale significantly more realisable through its creation of an enormous truly single market from which large-scale producers would be able to reap considerable benefits. For example, instead of having to produce different telecommunications equipment to comply with the standards of the various member states, as had previously been the case, companies would now be able simply to produce equipment to a standard which would be acceptable right across the Community. This would enable them to cut down on the number of different types of manufacturing plant they required to produce the equipment and to aim single products at much bigger markets. Such savings on plant costs and the increase in single-product market size could be translated into higher profits and/or lower prices. Such economies of scale were seen as being a good thing not just because of the hoped-for contributions to economic growth, but also with regard to the Community's ability to stand up to competition from Japan and the other new Asian industrial powers, and from the United States. It was believed that the attractive prospect of the new economies of scale being opened up would encourage cross-border mergers between EU companies, resulting in the creation of new organisations which would be large enough to generate the scale of research and development funds which are now necessary for effectively competing with the large Japanese and American corporations.

Finally, in theory, competition from the most efficient states is supposed to force the less efficient to improve their performance, thereby encouraging economic convergence within the Community.

This is necessarily a concise summation of the various arguments that have been advanced in favour of the single market programme, and it leaves out some important considerations with regard to both capital movements and the freedom of movement of labour. However, such omissions have been made simply because there is now more than enough material above to examine the major ways in which the single market is liable to work for or against further integration.

It is useful to begin by looking at the different impacts which the single market (SM) process may have on the stronger and the weaker of the member states. The first problem, critics of the SM scheme argue, is that the idea that greater competition from the more efficient economies will force the less efficient to become more efficient also is fatally flawed. The headstart which the more efficient larger firms of the most successful states have with regard to research and development, and the sheer scale of the resources available to a number of them, will, sooner or later, simply drown their smaller and more backward competitors in states such as Greece and Portugal. Over the next few years, those states with weak economies will find that these are significantly further weakened as a result of the removal of the non-tariff barriers which previously offered them some degree of protection, and that even the doubling in size of the EU's regional and social funds that was proposed under the 1992 programme ultimately will not be enough to help bail them out from the consequences.

Equally, even some of the largest states could find themselves in deep trouble. Both the United Kingdom and Italy have regions which have been for some time, or have become, industrial deserts. Their distance from the most profitable markets, together with a variety of other factors,[14] has left them without much in the way of manufacturing industry (and much of the service industry that has developed within them is relatively worthless because of the poor wages that it pays to the majority of those it employs), and should that industry which does operate from them prove unequal to the increased competition over the next few years, then their devastation will be complete. The electoral consequences could be considerable for the governments affected, so the argument runs, and this could well force them to have to totally or partially withdraw from the Union. To bring in the Change Map again, opportunity factors in the form of greatly accelerating economic decline would be in danger of persuading governments and their electorates that they would be better off outside the EU.

There is another argument, however, which contends that even if such economic disasters did occur, the reaction of the affected governments would be determined not necessarily by initial domestic dissatisfaction, but by the response from the EU. It is possible, for example, that the political elites of the richer states might perceive that their interests required them to keep everyone on board the Union if at all possible. If, therefore, such a perception forced the richer states to agree to help bail out their weaker fellow states, through allowing them to introduce a high level of special protective measures until their economies became strong enough to stand up to the others, or through substantially increasing regional and social assistance, then the economically troubled states might well feel they had something that would satisfy their electorates and which thereby would enable them to maintain a long-term commitment to the single market.

Queries also have been raised against the claim that even if some areas suffer, the overall result of the SM will be a European Union with an enhanced growth rate. Going back to the idea of the virtuous circle, mentioned above, some have pointed to the decreasing need of industry for humans in the productive process as a result of robotisation and new technology in general.[15] Others have argued that the many multinationals operating in the EU will continue the existing trend of moving jobs to low-wage economies in Asia and Eastern Europe. The implications of all of this are that increased consumption resulting from lower prices will not necessarily create many new jobs within the Union itself. This in turn might mean that unless taxation and social welfare systems transfer significant levels of the new profits to the unemployed, then there will be an inbuilt ceiling on both consumption power and growth within the Union for those firms that rely predominantly on the single market. Equally, the benefits of growth might be much more narrowly distributed than some have anticipated. The combined effects of these possible negative outcomes, should they occur in the 'real world', will be that both the single market and the idea of European integration will become much less popular and firmly rooted in European society than they otherwise might have done, leaving the new Europe on even more vulnerable and insecure foundations than those which have resulted from the rumpus over Maastricht. To return to the Change Map and its emphasis on the importance of popular perceptions, this could mean that further significant integration would be impossible, or even that the EU could start slowly to unravel as political elites tried to untangle themselves from something which they believed had become an electoral liability.

In addition, doubts also have been raised with regard to the claim that the economies of scale resulting from the rush of cross-border mergers that initially was precipitated by the single market process will in themselves help to lower prices and boost efficiency and growth over the next few years. While the EU has a coherent policy in place to try and deal with monopolies and restrictive practices,[16] it has little power to cope directly with the fact that when firms merge to create a new super-large company which is not quite big enough to be a monopoly, they simultaneously reduce the competition within their markets by so doing. When mergers are as widespread as they have become, it can be contended that what results is a significant overall lowering of the level of competition within the EU which may not only negate key benefits of the economies of scale involved, but also lead to a lowering of efficiency in comparison to the pre-existing situation. Just as more competition is said to stimulate efficiency, less reduces it.

Others argue that such criticisms miss the point that one of the main economic problems facing the EU is competition from the new Asian economic powers and the USA, and that European firms need to be larger in order to match the resources of Japanese and American corporations. Providing the EU does not simply become Fortress Europe at some stage and shut out such strong foreign rivals through high tariff walls, their presence in the European economy as competitors will be more than enough to keep the new merged EU firms on their toes. So, according to this line of argument, the single market, with its encouragement of cross-border mergers, should enhance both the EU's key industries' chances of survival and their wealth creation capability and thereby ultimately help make the idea of European integration something that has and retains popular support.

One of the most serious problems that has been raised with regard to the single market process concerns the tradition of providing a high level of subsidies to industry in several states. There is a belief among a number of economists that states with a strong tradition of subsidising and protecting key industries will continue to do so despite claiming to be implementing the spirit as well as the letter of the single market programme. They will find it almost impossible electorally to dismantle their subsidy systems completely, although they might well devise more subtle means of their application to give them reduced visibility.

The worst of all worlds for the EU would be one in which not only do subsidies continue in visible or invisible forms, but in which they are surreptitiously increased as a means of compensating for the removal of other forms of protection. The effect of such practices obviously would be to leave states such as Britain, which under recent Conservative governments has been vigorously reducing state financial assistance to its industry, at a considerable disadvantage in the market-place. The consequence of this, in terms of lost production and jobs within those states that 'play by the rules', ultimately could be a level of bitterness and disillusion with the single market idea, not only within the wider electorate, but quite possibly across all elite levels, which would be strong enough to halt or at very least severely stall the integrative process, or even lead to a situation in which Britain and other affected states retaliated in a subsidy 'war'. The consequences of this latter eventuality would either be to bring the Union to its senses and force it to work out some kind of compromise, or to destroy the potential for its continuation as an economic and political force.

The Change Map's section on economic factors suggests that the global level of analysis potentially is often of enormous importance, and indeed, it can be argued that the state of the global economy over the first few years of the single market's existence as a substantially completed entity will be crucial. As has been noted already, if during the first decade of its existence the programme works as it is supposed to do and gradually or even rapidly leads to the inefficient, high-cost producers being taken over or pushed out of business by the more efficient, then there is likely to be considerable unemployment in some parts of the EU which can be directly attributed to it as opposed to other possible causes. The theory behind the single market project argues that this problem will be resolved because new jobs will be created by the economic growth created by the 'take-over' of the EU's economy by the most efficient firms.

However, if psychological factors, such as a general lack of confidence in the economic future on the part of potential consumers, lead to a situation of continuing global or European recession at the time when the single market creates such unemployment, then that is likely to mean that many of the new jobs would not arise until well into the medium or even the long term. In more politically explosive states than Britain, such a situation could lead not only to disillusion with the EU, but to a level of political unrest which could force their governments to consider partial or total withdrawal from the Union. It could also create the conditions for the rise to power of the neo-Fascists in Italy or of other right-wing nationalist groups across Europe, an eventuality which might in itself lead to the demise of the EU. (In terms of the Change Map, economic stagnation would have triggered a substantial level of popular disillusionment, which in turn would have triggered a switch in ideological allegiance, which in turn would have a highly negative impact on the prospects for change in the form of further European integration.)

On the other hand, should the EU be lucky, and the regional and global economy head into a period of sustained economic growth during the rest of the 1990s, then the single market programme could well benefit from association in the eyes of both the wider electorates of the EU and its various elites and thereby help to cement the European commitment to integration.

The activities of powerful interest groups, in the form of some trade unions or lobbies led by members of the business elites of the EU, might also be important. Should some national industries feel themselves to be under unacceptable levels of pressure from the single market, then governments might well find themselves being heavily lobbied for some form of protection or partial suspension of their adherence to the offending parts of the single market programme.

However, important as it undoubtedly is, the single market is not the only factor likely to affect the success or failure of the EU's integrative agenda. To move into the Change Map's 'ideologies' and 'government personnel changes' sections (see the opportunity factors box for the latter), one should remember also the importance of the political balance within the Community. A single highly nationalistic and formidably assertive Margaret Thatcher in a state which, despite being large, and despite the domestic rhetoric, was clearly continuing to wane in power in the eyes of many influential European politicians, was unable to do very much of real substance to hold back the integrative process. However, had there been simultaneously a Thatcher equivalent in Germany, France or Italy, then the Community would have been in deep trouble. It is unlikely that economic and monetary union or further political integration would still be on the EU's agenda in any meaningful form. Equally, to use the crude device of a Thatcher currency, given the predominant position of the German economy, a single German Thatcher would be equivalent at the very least to one and a half British, Italian or French Thatchers in her ability to draw firmly in the reins of the integrative process. In short, it is always possible that future personnel changes and ideological shifts within EU governments could throw a very large spanner in the works of European integration.

In addition, there is the unknown quantity of EMU. Several negative things are a possibility here. Just to take one example, some economists and politicians argue that the economic logic behind fixed exchange rates and ultimately a single currency is badly flawed.[17] They claim that such measures could seriously damage some economies by depriving them of what they believe to be the essential tool of independent currency manipulation. Even while full monetary independence for most EU states is now something of a lost cause due to the dominant, somewhat elephantine position of the German mark in setting the trend in currency matters within Europe, some degree of independent manipulation still would be possible outside an EMU. This might provide valuable help in cushioning economies such as Britain's during periods of weakness. So, this line of argument contends, far from benefiting from moving towards a monetary union, states such as Britain could find themselves with problems they could otherwise have avoided, and this could help to create popular disillusion with the idea of European integration within their borders. The economic benefits which Britain obtained as a result of having to drop out of the exchange rate mechanism of the EMS during September 1992 frequently are cited here.

So, the political balance – in the sense of both ideologies and personalities – and the effect which such factors as the consequences of moving towards an EMU might have on popular perceptions of the desirability of further integration could well be crucial to the Union's success or failure.

There is, in addition, the question of Germany. As previously emphasised, during almost the entire existence of the various European communities now incorporated within the EU, German governments have found membership valuable because of the way in which it enables them to pursue national goals in a cooperative context which removes the suspicions of – and possible backlashes from – others. However, if the united Germany eventually overcomes its difficulties and realises the enormous economic potential that lies within it, then it will become an economic superpower. In such a situation, bearing in mind the role of economic growth as an opportunity factor in the Change Map, German politicians might well feel that the position of Germany has become so powerful that they need no longer worry so much about the sensibilities of others concerning their actions and therefore choose to go it alone. Their withdrawal would seriously weaken the Union in every sense initially. However, the fears which such a withdrawal would be likely to cause might well act as a strong pressure on the remaining states to press ahead with integration in order to try and counterbalance their German neighbour more effectively.

Another possibility is that a German superstate may decide to stay in the EU providing the others accepted its leadership role. What would suffer then would be the previous vision of an integrated Europe in which the four largest states would roughly balance each other, preventing the predominance of any one or two (although in practice France and Germany frequently have formed a dominant partnership). At the very least, a stronger Germany would be in an enormously powerful bargaining position within the Union's institutions, and the problem of how to deal with this situation could divert valuable energy away from the integrative process. Economic growth in Germany, therefore, could prove to be an extremely potent opportunity factor which changes the existing course of European integration greatly.

Finally, even if the EU escapes or survives all of the above problems, there is the question of the likely impact of Eastern Europe and the former Soviet Union on its institutions over the next few years. The post-Tito wars in the former Yugoslavia already could be argued to have acted as a negative opportunity factor (or blocking factor) for European integration and to have placed considerable strain on the EU's cooperative foreign policy procedures. They have served not only to reduce what confidence there had been among EU political and administrative elites concerning the potential for effective cooperation on major issues, but also have caused the EU to be portrayed as largely ineffectual as a peace-keeper/promoter to the electorates across the Union. It is not yet clear whether the damage done to the idea of an integrated Europe, both at the popular and political/ administrative elite levels, by the initial failure to coordinate a truly effective response has in fact been outweighed by the simultaneous kick which was given towards the inclusion of a defence dimension within the Union.

What is clear is that there are many potentially serious instabilities of a political, economic and military nature in both Eastern Europe and the former Soviet Union which could strain the EU's attempts to try and coordinate its foreign policy to breaking point. To bring in the role of fortune, should the above instabilities so combine as to produce several crises in quick succession before the Union has had time to develop and consolidate its common foreign policy-making capability adequately, then it may well find itself with an equally quickly produced list of embarrassing failures. There is always the danger that the acrimony resulting could spill over into other areas of EU policy and do serious damage to the future prospects for the entire integrative process.

Another danger could arise if the Union feels pressured to grant early membership to some of the Eastern European states as a means of trying to stabilise the situation in that part of the continent. Should the force of events mean that such admissions occur before it is clear that there is likely to be a long-term commitment to the Western Europeans' broad view of integration on the part of the new members, then considerable political difficulties could be created within the Union in the future. From the perspective of the Change Map, such an eventuality, which could well have highly negative consequences for the European integration process, would be directly traceable back to opportunity factors in the form of the revolutionary changes that swept Eastern Europe in the wake of Gorbachev's *glasnost* and *perestroika* policies and the failed coup of August 1991 in the former Soviet Union.

So, to return to our analysis in Chapter 1, it can be seen that the Change Map provides a potent checklist for helping identify the wide range of factors that potentially may play a significant role in determining how far European integration is able to advance in the future. Such factors as ideologies (as in the case of nationalism with regard to people like Margaret Thatcher, for example), interests (as in the case of Germany's interests in either going it alone or remaining within the cooperative context of the EU), imperatives (as with regard to the belief of some within the French elite that it is essential to keep Germany within the EU), and power factors (as in the impact which a German superstate might have on the future direction of integration) have all been shown to be of importance. The potential role of a variety of opportunity factors and fortune has also been illustrated, together with that of the perceptions of the desirability or otherwise of goals which may change the course of the integrative process which are held at the popular and various elite levels. It is a combination of an as yet indeterminable number of these factors that will be crucial in deciding how much additional progress towards European integration can be achieved.

What has been shown also is that the potential obstacles that lie in the way of further significant European integration are numerous and in some cases formidable. It is one of the purposes of the next chapter to investigate the chances of such obstacles being overcome.

Chapter 9

The future of European integration

Introduction

This chapter examines two questions concerned with the future of European integration which lead on directly from those discussed in Chapter 8. The first asks to what extent the incentives towards further integration are likely to overcome the obstacles that stand in its way and the second asks whether continuing European integration would be a benefit or a cost to the global community.

To what extent are the incentives towards further integration likely to overcome the obstacles?

One of the results of sustained and largely unsuccessful attempts to produce a scientifically predictive theory of international relations in the 1960s and early 1970s was the demonstration of just how many complicating factors there are in international affairs to make the life of the would-be crystal ball-gazer a difficult one. To give a short but potent indication of the obstacles in the way of forecasting developments in global politics, it can be noted that some factors of core relevance to predictions, such as political will or the loyalty of armies, are too intangible to measure, while the emotional and often irrational elements that potentially can be present within all human behaviour mean that the actions of political leaders are simply not predictable in the manner of a chemical reaction between sulphuric acid and iron oxide. However, if no attempt were made to try and anticipate the future, governments would be left with no choice but to be continuously reactive and totally devoid of initiative in the global arena. Accordingly, what can be done (and what is done by the more sophisticated governments) is to draw up likely scenarios for particular foreign policy issues and to try and anticipate what might happen within them. As a result, if one or more such scenarios becomes a reality, then the government concerned should be able to react in a much more rapid and coherent manner than would otherwise be possible. Even if only part of a scenario is realised, as is frequently the case, to have thought that part out in advance means that the government concerned should be in a much better position to try and formulate effective policy than would otherwise be the case.

It is this highly qualified kind of 'what if' thinking that is useful in trying to anticipate what might happen within the European Union. For example, in attempting to answer the question of whether or not the Union will succeed in establishing a common defence policy, a scenario can be drawn up which splits the world in and around the EU into several different segments and which looks at what might be likely developments affecting the defence policies of member states within each. This kind of approach is perhaps the most practical way of trying to answer various aspects of the question posed at the beginning of this section. It will be used here to analyse the extent to which the obstacles in the way of two key aspects of proposed further integration – a common defence policy and EMU – might be overcome by the incentives in their favour.

Scenario I: an examination of the possibility of the emergence of an EU common defence policy

At the highest level, it might be noted that the Gorbachev revolution and the years of state capitalist mismanagement preceding it, together with the final collapse of the Soviet Union, has left only one military superpower with the unity and economic resources necessary to play the role of *global* policeman.

However, it might also be observed that the collapse of the Soviet Union as a mortal enemy has greatly reduced the incentives for the United States to remain militarily 'on the ground' in Europe. There is a strong possibility that the current signs that the USA has decided to, as far as possible, strictly limit any involvement of its military forces in the lesser squabbles within Europe (while the USA was the first to shoot Bosnian Serb aircraft out of the sky and played a central and rigorous role in the August/September 1995 air strikes on the Bosnian Serbs, it continued to adhere to its position that it would not provide ground troops until a peace accord had been signed) will be confirmed over the longer term, *providing there is no reemergence of a perceived threat from Russia*, especially given the pressures on the US economy of ever-increasing competition from Japan and the new Pacific states. Such a limitation worries some European strategists because while the use of air–power – which seems to be the maximum extent to which the USA will commit itself militarily to conflicts like Bosnia prior to the signing of a peace agreement – can be spectacularly successful, they believe that on its own it is too unreliable in its effects to provide a *guarantee* for peace-keeping or peacemaking purposes. As a result, European memories of the horrific results of a continent without an effective war preventer in the period immediately prior to the era of American military domination in the West may well act as a strong propellant forcing the EU to put aside its unhappy experience in trying to forge an effective common foreign policy on the former Yugoslavia during the early to mid-1990s and to thrash out a clearly defined defence and peace-keeping role for itself.

In terms of the Change Map, one might back up this projection as follows. The revolutions which overturned the communist order in Eastern Europe and the Soviet Union acted as an opportunity factor which greatly changed US elite and popular perceptions of the world, and which, *at the time of writing*, appears to have produced a revised security view in which American military involvement in Europe no longer seems to be as important to Washington as previously. Equally, another opportunity factor, in the form of concern about some sectors of the US economy subject to strong competitive pressures from Asia, has raised the importance of the New Pacific perspective in the US view of the world, producing a partial re-orientation of outlook away from Europe.[1] Western European governments have became concerned about this – and probably will become even more concerned if such a reorientation continues – because of their awareness of Europe's warlike past prior to the US presence and of the destabilisation of the Balkans that occurred as a result of the break-up of Yugoslavia.

EU governments' perceptions of the effects of past and present wars, therefore, have turned the major change which appears to be taking place in US policy towards Europe into an opportunity factor which is persuading the European Union to think more seriously than previously about the need to be prepared to take on a defence role should the availability of US ground forces continue to be subject to current restrictions.

The Eastern European segment would seem to confirm the likelihood of the already visible pressures in this direction which emerged during the Yugoslavian crisis growing considerably stronger if such restrictions remain in place after US and NATO forces withdraw from Bosnia. The bitterness generated during the Balkan ethnic wars means that it is not at all certain that any peace between the warring factions will be a stable one. It is also far from clear as yet that *all* of the regimes which ultimately emerge from the present economic and political uncertainties in the rest of the East will be benevolent and peace-loving ones. There is always the danger, as Hitler and Stalin and some lesser European luminaries illustrated earlier in the century, that a 'strong man' (or woman) will emerge in one or more of the more economically embattled states as the people's misguided answer to what they perceive as chaos. 'Strong' leaders frequently and notoriously prove susceptible to the temptation to use military force in their own states and sometimes against others. In addition, there are a number of ethnic and territorial questions which could in future prove to be sources of dispute in non-Yugoslavian Eastern Europe. The Russian core of the old Soviet Union still has the nuclear forces of a superpower and a nightmare at the back of the minds of some strategists is that it could be drawn into future conflicts in Eastern Europe should instability there spread beyond the former Yugoslavia, quite possibly even against its will. With the forces at its command still likely to be enormously powerful even after the continuing process of arms control and disarmament, this is not a possibility which the EU states would wish to see realised.

In consequence, if the risk of this happening becomes more widely perceived, the pressures on the EU to get its act together as an integrated and effective peace-keeper capable of damping down Eastern European conflicts before such dangers become serious – should current restrictions on the availability of US ground forces continue – should grow considerably. The memories of the destructiveness of past European wars, the fear that Russia might once again become a permanent military presence in Eastern Europe and the knowledge that any future war involving the use of nuclear weapons would be catastrophic, would combine to turn the US intention to limit its European military role into a powerful opportunity factor pushing towards a common EU defence policy.

In the EU segment of this scenario, while states such as Italy in the recent past have been strongly in favour of a common Union defence policy, others such as neutral Ireland, or Conservative-governed Britain, which, prior to the unhappy Clinton–Major relationship, much preferred the idea of the United States as its major military ally to what it considered to be the relatively unreliable and even naive Europeans, are much more reserved about the idea. However, unless the American decide to reverse their policy of restricted military involvement in post-Cold War Europe, both the British and the Irish will have little choice but to accept the reality that an effective EU defence policy is the only viable means of filling the gaps in Europe's security framework and of trying to ensure the kind of continental stability that fits in with their preferred policy objectives.

In short, the various segments of the above scenario suggest that there is a strong possibility of a common European defence policy emerging during the medium term – outside or within the NATO framework – *providing* the assumptions within them correspond to reality. For the reasons outlined in the last chapter, the procedures by which such a policy is run are likely to be intergovernmental rather than supranational (for the purposes of this discussion supranational policies are those that can be decided on in circumstances where at least two of the big states can be outvoted). Despite the obstacles to a common policy of the caution of the British and others, and of the difficulty of reconciling the, in some cases, very different interests of member states in defence and foreign policy matters,[2] the stakes set within the framework of the scenario at first sight look strong enough to outweigh the reluctance to achieve progress of some member governments.[3]

However, a strong cautionary note ought to be added to this judgement. First, while German troops were becoming established in the former Yugoslavia in a non-controversial field hospital role in July 1995, memories of Nazi atrocities during the Second World War continue to make it difficult to deploy German fighting forces across much of Europe. To a lesser extent, Italy also has the same problem in areas where Mussolini's inept army left its sometimes brutal mark. In addition, Britain has been made extremely cautious about becoming involved in partisan fashion in anything which smacks of civil war due to its recent, long-drawn-out and costly military involvement in Northern Ireland. In short, if a common defence policy does emerge, there will be definite limits to the range of options which it can cover because of these factors. On the other hand, the fact that the Rapid Reaction Force established in Bosnia during the summer of 1995 involved detailed cooperation between French, British and German troops in a context in which the USA proved unwilling to assist with its own ground forces demonstrated – symbolically at least – the potential for the future.

Having said all of the above, it should be noted that the prospects for an EU common defence policy might become rather different if one considers an additional scenario which might be developed from existing trends. The cooling of US Congressional attitudes towards Russia which occurred after the strong reassertion of a Russian sphere of influence in Eastern Europe and the row over the discovery of a Russian 'mole' at the top of the US intelligence services (both events occurred in February 1994), demonstrated how fragile US–Russian good relations are. That fragility means that at any time there might be such a deterioration in those relations as a result of a series of misunderstandings, or the increasing influence of conservatives and nationalists over Russian foreign policy, for example, that the USA decides that it is necessary to become more assertive again in protecting its remaining and not inconsiderable political and economic interests in

Europe. Such a decision could well spur on dramatically the reinvigoration of NATO that began to occur during and after August/September 1995 and reduce the need for a separate European Union defence initiative.

With regard to the Change Map, such a modification of American policy would be the result of US political and administrative elites becoming convinced that Russian interests posed a threat to American interests once more and that they therefore required the USA to take a prudent and deterrent/defensive attitude towards the Russian state. It might also be the consequence of opportunity factors in the form of government personnel changes in Russia, which result in the further lessening of the influence of the Yeltsinite reformers and the previously mentioned growth in influence of conservatives and nationalists over foreign policy, and which thereby increase the scope for American mistrust of Russian intentions. Fortune of course might well also play a role in, for example, creating the grounds for misunderstandings between the two sides.

Scenario II: the single market and the EMU

Another scenario might concern itself with the likelihood of the *substantially completed* single market (so referred to because it did not prove possible to introduce all of the measures necessary for its completion by the beginning of 1993, leaving a number of key issues for further discussion) remaining intact and acting as the springboard from which the final stages of EMU can be launched successfully, whether or not this happens within the existing Maastricht timetable. Again, the world inside and around the EU can be split into segments.

At the global level, the Union is faced with a challenge from Japan and the other new Asian economic powers that a number of its key industries have been having difficulty in countering. This is on top of the long-established strong competition from the United States in such areas as computer manufacturing. The belief that the bigger, supposedly more efficient companies which the run-up to the 1992/3 deadline spawned are Europe's best chance of surviving the foreign economic challenge, and that they need the single market to succeed, currently remains influential among some crucial sections of the political, administrative and BTC elites in a number of key EU states. In addition, as George points out,[4] EU governments are aware of the importance of the single market in attracting investment which might otherwise go to other areas of the world.

Furthermore, even if this and other aspects of the single market process prove to be a disappointment, the single market and EMU have the status of the EU states' only 'big ideas' for dealing with the external pressures currently facing them. For this reason, if nothing else, the Union is likely to try and keep as much of the single market in place as it can, even if the member states feel disappointed by its results. This is likely to be the case until a new 'big idea' comes forward to rescue them from the ruins of the old. The relative stagnation of some key sectors of the EU economies as compared to the corresponding sectors of the economies of New Pacific states, such as Japan, therefore has been acting as an opportunity factor which first of all helped create the single market, and which now is helping to preserve it.

At the EU level, it has been seen already how some states' strong attachment to subsidies, or the fact that states such as Greece and Portugal ultimately are likely to suffer badly from increased economic competition from the likes of Germany, may create a real danger of the single market falling apart. However, the fear of economic devastation by Japan and its Pacific neighbours is likely to act as a strong pressure on the EU to find compromises to get it out of such difficulties. The Common Agricultural Policy would seem to provide a working model for the EU's ability to hold a key policy together through crisis-initiated reform and against all the odds.[5] Whatever else may be said of the Union, it has a long and proven track record of being able to open a parachute after having slipped over the edge of cliff tops.

In short, the above scenario – again, always providing the conditions set down within its framework hold – would seem to suggest that, despite all the potential obstacles, the common fear of external economic threats is strong enough to hold the single market together, even though it may undergo considerable amendments during the horse-trading that may well be necessary for its survival. At the moment, the EU's governing political elites simply do not have any viable 'big' alternatives on their agendas through which they might try and deliver the economic results necessary to keep their electorates happy. In terms of the Change Map, their position is shaped by perceived interests (such as the need to retain, through appropriate economic policies, enough popular support to be re-elected) determined within a particular and limited market-dominated economic ideological framework, which in turn makes the preservation of the single market seem to be an imperative when it is combined with the common perception of strong external economic threats.

Whether the single market's survival will provide a sufficient springboard to help launch the final stage of EMU is a different question however. This brings in such crucial factors as the state of the global economy during the substantially completed single market's first few years, as outlined in the last chapter. If at least the last two or so of these crucial early years coincide with an upturn in the global economy and the single market becomes associated in popular and elite minds with a noticeably better standard of living, the economic growth which occurs may well act as an opportunity factor which persuades political, administrative and BTC elites, together with the wider public, that there are economic advantages in taking the market to what many economists argue is its logical conclusion, which is economic and monetary union.

If, on the other hand, it is undermined by simultaneous long-term global recession, and, in a worst-case scenario, only survives as a result of major surgery and one or more somewhat acrimonious resuscitations, then its public image will not be a good one, and the omens for the further integrative steps that are supposed to lead on from it may well not be favourable.

At the time of writing, two years into the substantial completion of the single market, significant parts of the Union are still suffering from the lingering ill effects of recession with little visible popular enthusiasm for the single market or any other aspect of the EU. It remains to be seen whether or not the Union's economy will pull itself back up into a renewed relatively strong growth phase during the remainder of the decade.

So, the above analysis of the likelihood of the survival of the substantially completed single market helping lead to EMU points in at least two directions without giving a clear indication as to which will be the most likely outcome. This is simply because there is not enough information available at the time of writing to provide a reasonably 'safe' prediction. This is a common problem in attempts to anticipate the future in international relations. However, to return to the point made at the beginning of this section, such an analysis at least enables us to think through a few of the most likely circumstances in which real progress on the EMU timetable might be achieved, and *some* of those in which it is most likely to fail to be realised.

This analysis, of course, can be taken considerably further. For example, it is worth considering also the specific conditions which have been laid down for progress to the final stage of an EMU. These require the member states to remain within extremely tight limits with regard to their budget deficits, interest and inflation rates, and currency fluctuations. In order to be able to manage this a considerable degree of convergence between the member states' economies is required, with the weaker coming close to the performance of the stronger. For the latter to occur, the single market would have to prove successful in helping to stimulate the weaker economies to become more efficient. However, it was pointed out in the initial discussion of the single market that it could cause severe damage to the weaker economies. Alternatively, it is possible that it could simply have very little in the way of either a positive or a negative effect. Either of these outcomes could be compensated for by assistance from the EU's regional and social funds and other measures. However, domestic electoral consent for the extra contributions that would be necessary to finance the increases in the size of these funds that would be required if such compensation were to be effective might well be absent, particularly in Germany, where there are already substantial domestic economic development problems in the eastern *Länder* (states). In terms of the Change Map, popular perceptions of German interests may well lead the German government to conclude that it would not be viable electorally to divert funds that their voters feel are needed at home to helping other states. So this possibility may well prevent full EMU from being established.

Equally, should the necessary increased contributions be supplied, then their size might well cause the budgets of the main providing states to fall outside the limits of the EMU's convergence criteria, further undermining its chances of success (always assuming they were to succeed in remaining within the limits in the first place).

There is a considerable gap between the weaker and the stronger EU economies still.[6] In the light of this, the above considerations suggest that it would be extremely difficult to construct a credible scenario showing how EMU might be attained for all of the EU states within the short timetable originally set by the Union if the single market failed to have a rapid effect in stimulating massive growth within the weaker economies. At the time of writing there is no sign of such massive growth occurring, and even if significant growth *was* to begin, then it is highly doubtful that it could occur at the phenomenal rate that would be necessary to help bring about sufficient convergence across the EU for EMU to prove a workable goal for all of the Union's states within the existing short timetable. The current gap between the weak and the relatively strong is simply too great.

The above scenarios therefore suggest that the final stage of EMU is highly unlikely to commence within the original deadline set for it as far as the economically weaker states are concerned, although they do not preclude the stronger states from moving forwards on their own if they wish to. This conclusion is further reinforced when one considers that a number of intractable internal factors specific to some individual states would need to be resolved before the various EMU convergence limits could be met by those states. Italy, for example, would have to sort itself out politically before it could even begin to tackle the problem of its massive budget deficit. The political 'sorting out' of Italy is something that frequently during the twentieth century has seemed beyond the capacity of mortal man or woman. (However, it would be an unwise analyst who ruled out completely the possibility of fortune taking a role here. Time alone will be the test in this regard.)

Whether or not any of the above scenarios will prove to offer accurate guides to the possibilities of the future is a judgement that will have to await relevant developments. But at the very least they do provide a useful means of trying to answer a significant part of the question set at the beginning of this section, albeit in some cases in a highly qualified manner. It is not possible here to cover all of the possible obstacles and incentives relating to the integration process, but the preceding demonstration of how the Change Map and the scenario method might be used provides undergraduate readers with a means for trying to answer questions relating to those obstacles/incentives not examined here for themselves.

It is now necessary to move on to the second and final question to be examined here on the future of the European Union.

Would continuing European integration be a benefit or a cost to the global community?

Given that this is a book concerned with global as well as regional change, it is important to look not just at the EU itself, but also at what the likely effects of any successful and substantial further European integration might be on the rest of the planet. The analysis begins by examining one of the world's most pressing problems.

The impact of further European integration on the world's poorest people

On the negative side of the equation, some have pointed out that predominantly regional organisations, by definition, tend to detract from the greater well-being of the world around. They are in many respects aimed at maximising regional objectives over and above global ones. This is all very well, they say, but some global problems are so pressing that they should be given precedence over all regional concerns. For example, there is a massive discrepancy in living standards between the hundreds of millions of desperately poor in the less developed world and most of the people who make up the relatively small populations of the rich developed world. From the point of view of the world as a whole, what is needed urgently is a global framework which addresses directly and starts to remove the lethal poverty of the underdeveloped states. In these circumstances, the priority given to the desire to further EU integration on the part of some of its members is almost an obscenity. A super-integrated regional club of relatively rich states, predominantly obsessed with increasing their own wealth, is hardly going to help resolve the massive imbalance in the living standards of the rich and the desperately poor states, and is simply one more self-concerned distraction from the need for such a global framework.

Pro-integrationists within the EU would respond that it has been helping the less developed world for many years already, and that an economically more fully integrated Europe would be more successful at the vital business of wealth creation and thus able to increase its aid and trade concessions even further.

It is possible to respond to this line of argument by accusing the EU of being somewhat hypocritical in its aid policies, using them as a mask to conceal virtual neocolonialism. Despite its supposed commitment to free trade, it could be pointed out, the EU also has strong protectionist tendencies where its own interests are concerned. For example, the EU's main aid and trade policy towards the less developed states (or, to be more precise, those less developed states which previously were European colonies), that conducted under the Lomé Conventions, appears on the surface to be very generous, with 99.5 per cent of the industrial exports of the states concerned being allowed into the Union without tariffs or quotas. But in practice, apart from the fact that the less developed states involved have very few industrial products which can compete with those of the EU, whenever a competitive threat to EU products is presented by the less developed states, the Union has preferred generally to negotiate an export restraint agreement to protect its own market.[7] It also enforces strict rules of origin on the exports of the less developed states, which make it difficult for them to export goods produced within their borders by US and Japanese multinationals, and, in consequence, to attract investment from such firms.

The effect of all of this, critics argue, is to keep the less developed states in a semi-colonial, dependent position relative to the European states, several of which are their former colonial masters. The intention, it is argued, is to make sure new industrial competitors do not arise in the poorer states concerned, and a more integrated Union which was also more prosperous would simply be in a stronger position to maintain this unfair regime.

In addition, the size of the aid funds available under the Lomé Conventions has been criticised consistently for being far too small to deal with the huge scale of the problems faced by the less developed states. Some might accuse the Union of using them as bait to keep the Lomé states within the regime and to thereby ensure that they will remain underdeveloped in the manner described above. The size of the funds, it could be argued, is just enough to retain the poorer states' interest without being large enough to make any real impact on their problems.

Defenders of the EU point out that in the past it has provided more aid under the European Development Fund (part of the Lomé regime) than it has done to its own member states through the regional and social funds. They also point to the fact that the increase in the aid budget under the current Lomé agreement has been greater than recent increases in all other government aid budgets around the world.[8] Critics reply that such arguments are simply attempts to disguise the fact that, despite the Lomé arrangements, the economic gap between the poor states involved and the Union has widened and is continuing to widen. For them, a more integrated EU which turned the benefits of integration into more wealth would simply continue to widen the gap between itself and the poor.

Others criticise the Union on rather different grounds than some of the above. They do not see the EU's Lomé policies as part of a neo-colonialist conspiracy. While agreeing that the member states' governments are simply doing the minimum they think to be necessary to help the poorer states without raising awkward questions at home, they offer much more mundane explanations for such behaviour. Governments are accused either of being concerned primarily with domestic matters and of having little real interest in far-away people who are not going to be voting for or against them in the next election, or of not really believing in the value or effectiveness of aid or preferential and concessional trade as means of helping with economic development.[9]

Politicians to whom the latter charge looks in danger of sticking tend to reply that the main problems poorer states face are caused by bad economic management at home, not lack of assistance from abroad, and that to throw money at them is simply to waste it. Critics of their position frequently either argue that they could do more to ensure that the recipient states use the money effectively, or that they simply do not understand the economics of trade, aid and development. Whatever the truth of the matter, so long as the EU governments tend to see aid and trade in such an under-committed manner, so it is argued, then any further integration and economic growth of the Union will be of little benefit to the poorer states covered by the Lomé regime. The statements of the EU about the positive nature of the Lomé Conventions are regarded as mere propaganda designed to hide what is in reality a rather minimalist approach.

So, overall, the judgement is split. There are those who see existing EU aid as being of real worth, despite its small size relative to the problems that need to be addressed. They see a further integration under the single market and an EMU as being likely to benefit the poorer African, Caribbean and Pacific states covered by Lomé, if such an eventuality succeeds in producing more wealth in the way many anticipate, because more funds will thereby become available for disbursement. Then there are those who see further European integration as being of no real benefit to the Lomé states. For the latter, existing assistance is much too small in relation to the scale of their problems and there is little evidence around at the moment to suggest that it is not likely to remain so, with or without further integration. There are no visible signs of strong and irresistible pressures at work on politicians to force them to change their attitudes. Furthermore, there is a growing lobby within the EU for the diverting of more Union aid towards Eastern Europe.[10]

There are, one could argue, three things at the heart of the problem of the Union's development assistance policy, if one were to agree that there is a problem. The first concerns the economic philosophy which governs much of EU policy currently. This is a strain of liberal capitalism which is declaredly *laissez-faire* in its commitment to the single market and its outlook on the world economy in general. Public funds are regarded as a dubious way of securing economic growth by the British Conservatives in particular, and it is notable, for example, that the size of the EU's planned internal regional and social aid budgets has been judged by many economists to be likely to fall far short of the needs arising as a result of the impact of the single market. Union external aid policy could be seen as being to some extent a victim of this outlook. (Curiously, the Union has a split personality, with strong elements of interventionism surviving with regard to agricultural policy and the domestic industrial subsidy policies of some states.) If this philosophy changes and moves back in a more interventionist direction during the next few years, then an EU that is both more integrated, and, if well-managed, wealthier as a result, is much more likely to improve the level of 'interventionist' assistance it provides to the poorer states.

But, bearing in mind the Change Map, what kinds of things might make such a change occur? Wishful thinking on the part of those on the centre-left clearly will not. Such a change might arise, paradoxically, for reasons of self-interest. Just as the Union moved to the right and centre-right during the 1980s in the wake of popular disillusionment with the left and centre-left, the holes in the remedies to its economic problems which rightist perspectives have offered may well act as opportunity factors causing EU electorates to switch back in the opposite direction within the foreseeable future, resulting in the election of left-of-centre governments across the Union.

A move in a more Keynesian direction with an emphasis on the importance of pump-priming (or boosting demand), for example, might even cause the partial resurrection of the Brandt Reports,[11] although this probably would be something of an outside prospect unless the move towards Keynesianism was very pronounced. The reports argued strongly that until the poorer states are developed economically, and thereby able not only to become successful as producers of industrial goods and services, but also to offer the existing rich states huge new markets of consumers to expand into, then the rich will be missing out on the potential for significant economic benefits which could greatly reduce current tendencies towards periodic stagnation and consequent electoral dissatisfaction within their own political economies. In order to bring about such development and the mutual benefits that would go with it, substantial transfers of resources from the rich to the poor states would have to occur, among other things, and newly industrialising states would be allowed to protect their infant industries until they were strong enough to stand up to foreign competition.

To sum up, in terms of the Change Map, something as basic as initially self-interest-driven changes in electoral attitudes in favour of more interventionist government and a *significant* shift in the ideological balance within the political parties of key members of the EU could precipitate such a Brandtian resurrection. It is unlikely that the EU would be prepared to implement very many of the Brandt proposals unless the USA and Japan agreed to help carry the medium- to long-term burden of so doing, but, centre-left critics of current policy would argue, even a partial implementation of the Brandt programme would be a considerable improvement on that policy.

The second factor of relevance here is the attitude of electorates specifically on global poverty questions rather than simply on the question of interventionism. Should they start to exert more pressure on EU governments to help the poorer states, then, to put it cynically, the strong desire of politicians to remain in office is likely to persuade them to respond positively with changes in their trade and aid assistance policies. To be realistic, the omens for such increased pressure would appear to be poor. While one-off consciousness-raisers, such as Bob Geldof's concert for the starving in the mid-1980s, have succeeded in putting aid on to the popular agenda, it has not yet proved possible to keep up sufficient interest over the longer term to sustain real pressure on EU governments such as the British Conservative administrations of Major and Thatcher.

The third and final problematical factor at the heart of the EU's development assistance policy takes the form of pressures from sections of the popular electorate and industry for protection against foreign competition. As noted earlier, these can seriously undermine attempts to assist the world's poorer states, given that political elites with an eye on the next election can prove very susceptible to such pressures. Arguably, the only effective way of reducing the latter is the achievement of a level of economic growth that is sufficient to reduce people's fears of unemployment by providing alternative jobs should their existing ones be lost. In such circumstances, economic growth can act as a crucial opportunity factor which changes popular attitudes on protectionism, even if it might have less of an impact on manufacturers' lobby groups.

With regard to the first two of the above factors, a method is demonstrated in the second of the global poverty chapters which shows one way in which it might be possible to increase electoral pressure on governments for the alleviation of the plight of the world's poor sufficiently to bring about change. If such a method fails or simply is not tried, then one suspects that the only really effective instrument of change as far as the first factor is concerned will be the kind of self-interest-driven shifts in the overall political balance and ideological thinking referred to above with regard to the Brandt proposals. Such shifts are most likely to occur if enough of the major EU states run into economic problems, and encounter consequent adverse reactions from their electorates, which jointly are sufficiently serious to, for example, force their political elites to start rethinking their own economic philosophies, and, quite probably, because of the size and influence of such states, the philosophy of the Union as a whole. In such a situation, the economic state of the Union would be a powerful opportunity factor operating in favour of significant change.

So, in the final analysis, things yet again may be crucially dependent upon the single market. If ultimately it is perceived to be successful as a wealth generator, then this will probably spell bad news for the poorer states in terms of their hopes for any radical changes in the philosophy behind Union development assistance policy. An important stimulus to the rethinking of economic policy will have been neutralised by the single market project's good fortune, and the most they might hope for would be the kind of small increases in aid that would result from, for example, the replacement of the Conservatives by Labour in Britain. However, if ultimately the single market sank into serious trouble or even failed, while this would not offer any guarantee of a rethink that would resurrect Brandt-style proposals, it would at least increase the possibilities of such an eventuality. On the other hand, it could also cause the EU itself to collapse.

Moving away from foreign aid policy, two other areas which often are identified as posing or potentially posing serious problems for the rest of the world are the already frequently mentioned single market policy and the Common Agricultural Policy.

The impact of further European integration on global agriculture and the EU's relations with other agricultural producers

The frequent friction which the protectionist nature of the Common Agricultural Policy has caused in recent years, with both developed and underdeveloped agricultural producers outside the Union, has threatened on a number of occasions to undermine the movement towards international liberalisation of trade that has been conducted via the 'Uruguay Round' of the General Agreement on Tariffs and Trade negotiations. It has threatened on several occasions also to help cause a trade war between the EU, the United States and others.

However, at least as far as the USA is concerned, the GATT global free trade deal of December 1993 dealt with a number of its main complaints about EU agricultural policy and under a 'peace agreement' the Americans have agreed not to attack the CAP for nine years, starting from the day on which the treaty was signed. Other of the world's food producers are not so satisfied with the concessions which the EU made under the GATT deal, however.

So, what would happen to the CAP if the EU became more integrated? Would this make it any more or less damaging to the rest of the world? The most important clue lies hidden within the negotiations which led to the setting up of the substantially completed single market. In agreeing to advance the latter on the grounds of the crucial economic benefits which significant sections of the political and BTC elites across the then EC believed it would bring, the member states recognised that it would have costs in terms of unemployment and bankruptcies as the inefficient were put out of business. As previously explained, there was a worry that such costs might endanger the continued existence of the single market if some attempt to deal with them was not made. Accordingly, the member states agreed to double the size of the regional and social policies of the EU by the end of 1992 to help cushion badly hit areas against the impact of such costs. This initiative was one of the reasons why member states decided that their attempts to control and reduce agricultural spending earlier in the 1980s would have to be increased greatly. They had an urgent need to find room for a doubling of social and regional spending within the EU budget.

There is a fear now that, over the next few years, demands for further significant increases in financial assistance may grow substantially from weaker regions of the Union adversely affected by the single market, such as Greece, Portugal, southern Italy, western Ireland and northern Britain, or from states which are unable to even begin approaching the convergence conditions for EMU. As the member states are in many cases unenthusiastic about greatly increasing the size of the Union budget, one of the only viable alternative ways to help fund the size of the regional and social policies necessary to tackle such problems is going to be through making further inroads into the slice of around 50 per cent of the overall EU budget which agriculture still accounts for.

Sooner or later, therefore, if the single market and the need for the economic convergence which is required for EMU do indeed make increasingly heavy demands upon the Union's regional and social policies, this might well lead to a cut-back in financial support for domestic agricultural production which may just be big enough to offer farmers outside the EU a chance of significantly improved access to its market.

However, the agricultural lobby in a number of EU states is still strong and likely to remain strong. This fact will limit the extent to which the Union can go in cutting back on agricultural spending. Nevertheless, the type of 'intermediate'-level cut-back implied above would probably be feasible if the member states felt they had no other alternative (and if those with sizeable farming lobbies were free of imminent elections) and were therefore prepared to stand firm against opposition from farmers, and it might still be of real benefit to non-EU farming interests. In this sense at least, if the Union continues to progress towards further integration via the single market and EMU, then the end result as far as agricultural policy is concerned just might be of more benefit to the rest of the world than the situation of recent years.

Should the CAP be cut back in such a way, then, in terms of the Change Map, one might argue that the perceived interest of many of the governing political elites and significant sections of the industrial BTC elites[12] of the EU states in furthering both the single market and EMU would have played a crucial role in changing the CAP at the expense of the agricultural lobby. Furthermore, the promise of the economic growth which the single market and EMU ultimately are supposed to bring presumably would have acted as an opportunity factor helping to change political elite attitudes in agriculturally important states such as France, as was the case at the end of the 1980s. The importance which French governments have attached to the single market and EMU as means of keeping Germany 'harnessed' within the EU also would presumably have acted as an opportunity factor in this regard. The fact that French farmers still wield considerable power within French politics therefore would have been *partially* neutralised by their government's (and other EU governments') belief that such factors as key aspects of single market policy are important enough to their future prospects of remaining in office – or even to the security of their state – to make the political risks involved in limited sacrifices of farming interests worthwhile.

The impact of the continuing development of the single market on the rest of the world

Moving the focus now on to what used to be referred to as '1992', the main worries that have been raised concerning possible negative impacts of the single market on the rest of the world centre around the idea that it might lead ultimately to a Fortress Europe mentality which would shut out the goods and services of non-EU states through a high protective tariff wall. The purposes of the single market are, after all, critics argue, to enable the EU to stand up to foreign competition more effectively and to boost internal trade. In doing these things, it is all too easy to succumb to the temptation to become self-reliant as far as possible and to shut out much of the economically and socially painful inconvenience of low-cost competition from elsewhere. Such fears were particularly noticeable in the USA and Japan during the late 1980s. The consequence of Fortress Europe would be to restrict the growth of world trade by limiting the overall size of the world market for goods and services.

However, such fears may well prove largely even if not entirely ungrounded. If the single market continues to progress towards the removal of as many non-tariff barriers as is practicable, and if part or all of the EMU is implemented, then the economic logic of firms merging within Europe in order to reap bigger economies of scale within the new relatively unrestricted market might become inescapable. Indeed, a significant number of mergers have occurred already. As pointed out in the previous chapter, in recent years, in some quarters of the EU, it has begun to be feared that such mergers could so reduce competition that many of the anticipated benefits of the single market would be put at risk. There is therefore a strong argument for allowing non-EU firms easy access to Union markets in order to keep the new EU giants on their toes. At the same time, however, should Japan continue to make substantial inroads into European markets, there is a real possibility that the Union will decide that there is a difference between keeping its firms on their toes and knocking them off them, and erect some kind of strong Fortress Europe against those imports which are causing most damage to European industries, while leaving alone those imports which are judged to be a positive stimulus to competition within the EU. In this regard the Commission has negotiated already with Japan an agreement which restricts motor vehicle imports from that state until the end of the century.[13]

Concluding comments

Some of the most strongly positive arguments for further European integration point to the stabilising effect it might well have within Europe as a whole. Even if the EU did not expand the number of its member states very greatly, if the single market and any further economic integration following on from it produces the greater wealth it is supposed to, then the Union's ability to provide stabilising economic assistance to Eastern Europe and the former Soviet Union would be increased. Equally, if it convinced most or even all the Eastern European states that it was prepared genuinely to admit them when it judged them to be ready, and that it was prepared to countenance the financial burden that would be involved, then this might well give it valuable influence over their willingness to be both peaceful internally and externally and non-authoritarian in the regulation of their own societies. (Such influence is already at work in some Eastern European states.)

Furthermore, once the Eastern European states (other than the now defunct East Germany) start to gain entry to the EU, its fundamental idea that economic integration helps make it too expensive for states to go to war with each other may well work to guarantee peace in the Eastern part of the continent. This is a possibility that is discussed further in the second of the chapters on war.

Should integration progress as far as an effective common defence policy that is independent of NATO, then even if many of the Eastern European states remain outside the EU, it will have the potential to act as a powerful policeman in the region. With the combined strength of the armed forces of (possibly) Germany,[14] France, Italy and Britain, the Union also would have the potential to take on a global policeman role if necessary, and to act as something of a counterbalance to the conventional military strength of the United States, Russia and Japan,[15] should the latter also choose to expand its forces in line with its economic potential to do so.

Those who see the United States as having had too much military and political influence over world affairs in recent years would see this as a good thing. Those who fear that the Europeans might act in their bad old traditions, and use any combined power for neocolonialist purposes, would be rather less supportive of the idea of a European global policeman. Equally, there are those who view the idea of another major military power as potentially destabilising, causing ultimately a dangerous rivalry between the EU states, the USA, Russia and possibly Japan. (Such a worry would of course be greatly lessened if the EU decided to construct its common defence policy within NATO rather than outside it, as France proposed in December 1995.)

The problem with military power is that in itself, it tells one nothing of how it might be used. Everything depends upon the humanity or aggressiveness of those who control it. Accordingly, all that can be said about the idea of a new European military power is that whether or not it would be a good thing for the rest of the world would depend entirely upon the political complexion of the EU leadership in charge of it.

This last observation holds the key to all speculation about how beneficial or otherwise a substantially further integrated Europe might be for the rest of the world. It will be the personalities in charge of the EU in the future, together with the prevailing political–ideological balance, that will most crucially decide whether such things as aid policy under the Lomé Conventions become more or less beneficial to the less developed states, or whether the single market turns into a Fortress Europe or something that benefits the world as well as the EU.

While again presenting the reader with no crystal ball with which to gaze into the future, what has been done here, among other things, has been to explain some of the circumstances in which further substantial European integration might be seen as benefiting the rest of the world, and some of those in which it might be seen predominantly as a cost. To re-emphasise the above point, however, which of these possible costs and benefits becomes a reality will be determined by the personalities and political forces that predominate within the power structures of the Union over the next few years. Which of the latter do in fact predominate in turn will be determined by which of the variables from the Change Map are influential during the period in question and the particular ways in which they interact.

Once again, available space has permitted only a limited, predominantly illustrative examination of the Change Map's relevance to the subject matter of this chapter. Readers might care to try and extend the application of the framework to additional questions which interest them concerning the EU.

Chapter 10

Global rivalries
and the causes of war

Introduction

Possibly as many as twenty million people have been killed as a result of military action since the end of the Second World War. One estimate of the number of war-related deaths during the whole of the twentieth century puts the total at 110 million.[1] During the 1990s Europe, which for over forty years had been frozen in a largely stable, terror-inspired peace, once more has been witness to a series of bitter and bloody conflicts at its heart in the Balkans. In Africa, in the early part of the decade, Somalia was ripped apart by an armed internal power struggle that caused starvation on a scale that is beyond the power of the pen to describe adequately, while afterwards, in Rwanda the 'ethnic cleansing' that accompanied the civil war there resulted in an almost unimaginable six-figure death toll. These are but a few of the brutal conflicts to which the 1990s have been host. War and the mayhem it unleashes clearly is a part of the human tragedy that is as resilient and dominant now as it was during the time of the ancients. Equally, it is one of the greatest of all threats to the health, well-being and survival of humankind.

This and the next chapter will bring together a representative sample of the various key ideas that have been advanced on the subject of the causes of war. The discussion will be led by the following questions, each of which will be given a chapter to itself: (1) what are the causes of war? (2) to what extent can war be eliminated? The Change Map will be brought in and applied where necessary with regard to the second of these questions.

Before any meaningful progress can be made in providing answers to the above questions, it is necessary of course to set down the understanding of war that will be used in the analysis which follows. In short, war is defined here as organised violence between political units which are either state governments or which aspire to establish, or to be, state governments.[2]

This means that wars can be conducted between states, or between states and guerrilla or terrorist organisations, or between guerrilla or terrorist organisations, providing the latter two groups meet the criteria laid down in the above definition.

It is not necessary to have a formal legal declaration of military hostilities before a war can be said to exist. Argentina and Britain did not declare war on each other in 1982, for example, but there was no doubt on the part either of their governments, or the rest of the world, that the conflict in which they were engaged was a war.

Clearly, there has to be a minimum level of violence before a conflict is deemed to be a war. One or two attacks by one state upon another, followed by a complete withdrawal, would more appropriately be described as raids, conducted for the purpose of reprisal, warning or whatever. If, however, the two sides became locked in a conflict which could only be ended by the defeat of one of them, the exhaustion of both, or the signing of a peace agreement, then clearly a state of war would exist.

What are the causes of war? An introduction

There has been a long quest in the study of war to try and identify a single primary cause from which all other causes derive. Indeed, if this could be done, the task of eliminating war would be simplified dramatically, providing the primary cause in question could be controlled or removed in some way.

One of the main candidates over many centuries for the title of primary cause has been human nature. However, there has been a variety of contrasting views on the usefulness or otherwise of focusing on it as a cause of war, with, as will be seen below, the 'pessimists' at one extreme and the most fervent 'optimists' at the other. Furthermore and relatedly, the debate over precisely how human nature should be conceptualised has been an enormously complex one. It is not possible to represent adequately the complexity of either of these two debates within the inevitable constraints of the present study, so what will be done is to use a shorthand method of classifying some of the main, broad schools of thought on human nature as it relates to war in order that something of the flavour of the said debates can be conveyed meaningfully within a single chapter, even if their full details have to be simplified. Finally, there have been hotly contested arguments within political theory as to just precisely what thinkers like Hobbes or Marx believed concerning human nature. This is another reason why the above-mentioned schools of thought are presented in broad-brush terms rather than through the alleged views of particular thinkers. To wade into such debates here would detract from the main point of the chapter by entangling the discussion in the distraction of controversies that are secondary to its primary purpose. This is an approach that will not entirely satisfy those who understandably would wish to see examples of relevant theorists cited for each school referred to. But the allocation of major writers such as Hobbes or Marx, for example, to one school of thought or another could not be attempted without becoming bogged down in debates whose complexity is the proper concern of specialist texts on political theory rather than introductory discussions of international relations.

The shorthand method employed here involves the use of the terms *optimists*, *pessimists*, *conversionists* and *non-violent persuasionists* to indicate four important ways of thinking about human nature and about human behaviour. Kenneth Waltz, in his useful analysis in *Man, the State and War*, uses the first two of these terms, but in a partially different way to that employed here (his book will be looked at in brief detail shortly).[3]

For the purposes of this discussion *optimists* are people who believe that it is possible to remove violence from the world entirely on the basis of humankind being *naturally* non-violent.

Pessimists are those who believe that ultimately war can only be removed from or at least controlled within human affairs if violence or the threat of violence is itself employed either on its own, or in combination with other means, to stop and deter people from attacking each other.

Conversionists are effectively a second kind of optimist and believe that human nature is flawed by a tendency to use violence but can be converted to a state in which people become naturally non-violent.

Non-violent persuasionists are those who believe, like the conversionists, that human nature is flawed by a tendency towards the use of violence, but that the latter can be removed from human behaviour without the need for either the use or threat of coercion, or for any conversion to a state of being *naturally* non-violent, but on the basis solely of an appeal to self-interest. Whereas people who have become peaceful as a result of being or having become *naturally* non-violent should not need supplying with frequent reminders of the need to be non-aggressive, those who have become peaceful on the basis purely of a demonstrated self-interest in their so doing may well require constant reinforcement of their perceptions that non-violence is in their interest, given the constantly changing nature of human relationships at the state and interstate level.

In the sense that will be used in the analysis which follows, therefore, optimistic views start either from the assumption that human beings are fundamentally peaceful but are misled by influences external to themselves or, in the conversionist case, that they are fundamentally flawed in the sense of having an inbuilt tendency towards violence but are capable of being converted to an unflawed state. For the first kind of optimist, therefore, it is relevant external influences and not human nature that need to be concentrated on if war is to be avoided. For the second kind, the important thing is to discover the means by which the flaws in human nature which encourage war can be removed.

Pessimists believe that factors leading to a tendency to resort to war are built into the nature of either some or all human beings in every generation and that war can only be prevented by the threat of coercion from national or international bodies.

If one is convinced by the arguments of the first of the above kinds of optimists, that human beings are naturally peaceful and, by implication, can be converted from competitive to cooperative behaviour on a universal scale because of this, then, if one is interested in abolishing war, one will most probably be arguing that there is no justification for the continuation of the kind of interstate rivalry that has so often led to death and misery for human beings in the past. One will be aiming to discover and implement as urgently as possible the means by which human beings can be led permanently away from the corruption of warlike ideas and influences and enabled to follow only the peaceful instincts that one believes are at the heart of their nature. Equally, if one is a non-violent persuasionist, then one's main concern will be to find the most persuasive non-violent way of proving to governments that their selfish interests can be more profitably served by permanent peace rather than a periodic resort to war. Conversionists, on the other hand, will be anxious to experiment with ways of eradicating what they believe to be the flaws in human nature which cause war and to then implement any method that looks likely to be successful should they discover it.

If however one is persuaded of the pessimists' side of the argument, then different conclusions will be arrived at. One 'deeply pessimistic' view of the world, for example, argues that greedy and ruthless leaders will always appear within human society. The evidence of the past establishes this. Unless something like Hobbes's Leviathan (a mighty, common power, which he sees as the only rational – although not necessarily the best – response to humankind's natural state of the war of each against the other, and which will be strong enough to restrain all by its awesome nature)[4] can be constructed at the international level – in modern terms a United Nations which would be strong enough to act as a global government with the necessary military power to enforce lasting peace – then there will always be those who will be prepared to attack others if the outcome of so doing appears to be worthwhile gain. Such people will not be persuaded by *arguments* that their selfish interests are best served by peaceful behaviour in all circumstances in any context other than that of a force-wielding Leviathan.

For most deep pessimists, therefore, human nature means that until a global Leviathan appears, balance of power policies (these will be explained in the next chapter) are the only means of maintaining values like peace, independence or basic survival. Attempts to downgrade the balance of power in whatever form it is utilised, without a guarantee of it being replaced by a Leviathan, would be criminal folly.

For others, however, even a Leviathan would be an uncertain guarantee of peace. Rousseau, for example, believed that 'the tragedy of international society is that it is in everyone's social interest to have a commonly agreed sovereign power, but it is in the interests of each individual state to flout that authority when it is to its advantage'.[5]

There are of course additional variations on the above-mentioned sample viewpoints from within each of the broad schools of thought, and it is not claimed that the preceding selection is an exhaustive list of the possibilities. One set of very distinctive variations that needs to be mentioned before moving on takes the form of feminist writings on the causes of war. These are interesting because they are concerned not just with human nature and behaviour in their broadest sense but with the importance of gender differences in trying to explain violent behaviour. One feminist line of thought, for example,

> involves celebrations of a 'female principle' as ontologically given and superior to its dark opposite, masculinism. . . . The evils of the social world are traced in a free-flowing conduit from masculinism to environmental destruction, nuclear energy, wars, militarism, and states. In utopian evocations of 'cultural feminism', women are enjoined to create separate communities to free themselves from the male surround and to create a 'space' based on the values they embrace. An essentially Manichean vision, the discourse of feminism's beautiful souls contrasts images of 'caring' and 'connected' females in opposition to 'callous' and 'disconnected' males.[6]

Another more loosely formulated feminist perspective, while not setting women up as saints in opposition to male sinners, does see women as having a useful educative role to play with regard to a pacifism that derives from their maternal instincts.[7] As such it would seem to fit most closely into an optimistic or a conversionist perspective, depending upon the particular views on the sources of violent behaviour which individual authors within it hold. Its supporters tend not to have a simplistic view of there being any easy conversion of others to their views.[8]

There is also a feminist view which believes that men tend more to violence than women but that this is a result of long-established societal power structures and cultural factors rather than human nature. These have often forced women into submissive roles and in turn have limited the extent to which men have had to take note of basic family concerns like the welfare of children when considering using and participating in war. Culturally derived role models such as the warrior male have encouraged men to see violence as something acceptable. Adherents of different varieties of this view can be slotted into any of the previously outlined broad-brush schools of thought, depending upon their individual beliefs concerning the underlying sources of violent behaviour and the 'convertibility' or otherwise of humankind. For example, those who believe violent tendencies to be equally built into everyone's nature, irrespective of gender, once the behavioural distortions caused by culture and societal power structures are removed, would fit neatly into the pessimistic perspective.

The first of the above feminist perspectives would seem to be the most problematic in terms of finding a slot into which it can fit, in so far as it seems to hold a pessimistic view of one half of humanity and an optimistic view of the other. However, given that there would seem to be so many exceptions to its gender-derived division of humans into the peaceful and the warlike, from 'Warrior Queens' such as Zenobia of Palmyra (who for a time managed to seize control of Egypt, Syria and most of Asia Minor from the Romans), Boudicca (who is believed to have killed 70 000 Romans in Britain before her eventual defeat) and Margaret Thatcher (who revelled in leading her country to victory in the 1982 Falklands/Malvinas War and who was nicknamed the 'Iron Lady' by the Soviets), to the many males who have been alongside women at the heart of modern pacifist movements, perhaps this is a view that need not be taken as having too much 'real world' relevance.

Overall, while the above is only a sample of feminist thinking on gender and war, what might be fairly said of most views of human nature within the feminist perspective – whether they be expressed explicitly or implicitly – is that they can be slotted fairly easily into one or other of the previously outlined broad-brush schools of thought for the limited purposes of this discussion. However, it should be remembered that the feminist thinking to which they are attached does add an extra dimension to the debate on the causes of war and would need to be taken into detailed account in a more comprehensive investigation of those causes than is appropriate for the purposes of this chapter.

Among modern writers who are on the side of those opposing the idea that human nature holds the sole or primary key to understanding conflictual behaviour, Kenneth Waltz, in one of the most accessible overviews of the origins of wars, *Man, the State and War* (New York, Columbia University Press, 1959), argues that a concentration on the role of the nature of humankind can lead the scholar up something of a blind alley.

His case is simply that just as human nature leads to the declaration of war, it leads also to periods of peace.[9] Just as human beings are capable of acts of unimaginable brutality, they are capable also of acts of great charity and self-sacrifice. At root, therefore, all arguments about human nature tell us is that it is in that nature to be both peaceful and violent. This does not in itself get us very far in trying to understand either the precise causes of specific wars or how the peaceful side of human nature can conquer its violent counterpart. Indeed, the core of the problem, he argues, is that 'human nature is so complex that it can justify every hypothesis we may entertain'.[10]

What, he contends, is most worthless if scholars are concerned with finding ways of curtailing war, is a concentration on the idea that human nature is fixed. This is because 'The assumption of a fixed human nature, in terms of which all else must be understood, itself helps to shift attention away from human nature – because human nature, by the terms of the assumption, cannot be changed, whereas social–political institutions can be.'[11]

Nevertheless, whether it is believed that human nature is fixed or otherwise, the ideas we accept or reject about it will affect our overall belief in how easy or how difficult it is to tackle other causes of war which might be argued to derive from it, or to have little or nothing to do with it. Waltz indeed argues ultimately that it would be wrong to ignore human nature (and that it would be equally wrong to ignore human behaviour, the two concepts together forming his first 'image' of international relations), because he sees it as being linked to other causes of war which cannot be fully understood without considering it, even if it would be foolish to focus an analyst's attention on human nature (and behaviour) to the exclusion of everything else. He identifies three levels (which he describes as 'images') at which it might be useful to study the causes of war. The first of these is human nature/behaviour, the second is the internal structure of states, and the third is the international anarchy within which states operate. 'The third image describes the framework of world politics, but without the first and second images there can be no knowledge of the forces that determine policy; the first and second images describe the forces in world politics, but without the third image it is impossible to assess their importance or predict their results.'[12]

It is, according to Waltz, important that we bear in mind the interrelated nature of these three images or levels when trying to understand why wars occur and how they might be prevented.

Now, remembering Waltz's arguments, it would be useful to provide an indication of the wide variety of ideas that past and present analysts have advanced concerning war causality across his three levels and to advance some thoughts concerning their utility. This process will in turn provide some further basis for judging the accuracy or otherwise of the claims of those who argue that human nature should be the primary focus of concern when trying to understand why wars break out.

A selective journey through ideas on the causes of war

Before beginning this part of the discussion one thing should be understood clearly. The brief empirical examples that are used within it are intended primarily to illustrate the ways in which particular potential causes of war might be alleged to operate in the 'real world'. There is not the space to develop such examples fully here and it is not claimed that they offer any definitive explanations of 'reality'. Their function, as stated, is predominantly an illustrative one.

One of the most frequently suggested causes of war has been economic factors. At their most basic level they take the form of the simple desire for treasure. One of the explanations for the outbreak of the 1991 Gulf War that was most popular with press and other pundits at the time, for example, was the Iraqi regime's deteriorating domestic economic situation. It was commonly argued that its small and ill-defended neighbour, Kuwait, offered an irresistible temptation to the aggressive government of Saddam Hussein because of its fabulous oil wealth, the means by which Iraq's economic problems could be relieved dramatically at a stroke.

But economic factors can have a rather more subtle impact as well. They have been argued to have played a major indirect role in causing the Second World War for example. It was the economic collapse that occurred during the democratic Weimar Republic in Germany that is alleged to have helped create the conditions in which Hitler was able to establish his preeminence during the early 1930s. Desperate for a way out of economic chaos, many German citizens, including crucial sections of German industry, were prepared to support the economic remedies and strong government which the Nazis appeared to offer. Had Hitler not achieved the supreme leadership of the German state, an accomplishment that was significantly assisted by the actual or tacit support of many of those who wanted a way out from an economic nightmare, then, it has been argued often, it is much less likely that Germany would have started and pursued so risky a venture as the Second World War.[13]

However, it is important to remember that even if this analysis is correct, it would be difficult to claim that economic factors on their own caused the outbreak of the war. Arguably, such factors as Hitler's ruthless and aggressive personality and political tactics, his megalomania,[14] the failure of Britain, France or the United States to take any effective measures to control Nazi ambitions before the German war machine became too powerful to stop without a major conflict, and the long-established traditions of authoritarianism in the German state from which Weimar then seemed like a temporary aberration, all have to be taken into account in trying to understand why the war occurred at the time it did. This list of possible causes is only a selection from the many that might and have been advanced.

Another way in which economic factors have been alleged to play a role in causing wars has been through imperialism. One of the most influential of the modern theories of imperialism has been that of V.I. Lenin. In the early twentieth century Lenin argued that imperialism was the product of and indeed the highest stage of monopoly capitalism. The driving force at its centre was the capitalist ethos. This produced several consequences in the behaviour of capitalist imperialist powers. First, there was the obsession with the search for the highest rate of return on capital. At the most advanced stage of monopoly capitalism, some of the capitalist economies had become oversaturated with capital due to the backward state of agriculture and inequalities in the distribution of wealth and income within them. This caused the rate of return on surplus capital to be relatively poor. However, by definition, no such oversaturation existed in the less developed areas of the world, where wages were low and land cheap, so new capital invested in them produced a much higher rate of return. Capitalists consequently competed with one another for control of such less developed areas and the profitable investment opportunities which they offered. Leninists argued that an additional incentive for capitalist imperialism was the desire to gain and control access to the richest sources of raw materials. Such control allowed capitalists to secure the raw materials they needed most cheaply and therefore to obtain a high rate of profit on the manufactured goods which such raw materials were used to manufacture.

Ultimately, in Lenin's view, the world would be divided up completely between the capitalist states. One of the only ways to secure further supplies of cheap raw materials or access to additional high-return investment opportunities would be through one capitalist state seizing the colonies of another. Because uneven development is a feature of capitalism, some states initially acquired more colonies than others, and as new competitors arose Lenin argued that in a fully divided world they would resort to war as the only way to gain some of those colonies for themselves. For Leninists, the profit motive at the heart of capitalism would make such seizures inevitable, leading directly to war. For them, therefore, capitalist imperialism was a major cause of war.[15]

Leninist theory ran into severe problems when the capitalist states started to give their colonies independence in the second half of the twentieth century. Such acts pulled the rug out from under its assertion that colonial rivalry and consequent war were inevitable features of the highest stage of monopoly capitalism. It seemed now that capitalism had developed means of informal control of the less developed world while giving it nominal independence. It appeared also that the capitalist international system could run successfully without wars between its major powers to secure access to cheap raw materials and areas of high investment return. However, a number of writers, both Marxist and non-Marxist, have asked whether such coexistence will continue as some of the key raw materials upon which modern industrial economies depend begin to run out.[16] Additional criticisms of Leninist theory have been examined already in Chapter 6.

Capitalism as a potential cause of war is a relatively new phenomenon. Much older as alleged causes are the frequently related phenomena of ethnic and religious rivalry. Their potency has been most recently demonstrated in the Balkans, with the vicious battle over the future of Bosnia between Serbian Orthodox, Croatian Catholic and Bosnian Muslim forces. However, the barbarity of the proceedings would seem to have little to do with religions which proclaim themselves to be preoccupied with the love of God and of one's neighbour. What the three creeds have become in the specific context of the Balkans is part of the self-identity of each of the ethnic groupings to which they are attached, and as such they have been mutated into measures of intergroup differences.[17]

To best understand ethnic rivalry one has to remember that, fundamentally, ethnic groups are the means by which people who feel themselves to be sufficiently similar in racial origin, custom, practice and interest band together in the hope of creating a social group which will tolerate and even promote their own values, interests and aspirations and which might offer some protection of the same. The formation of such groups simultaneously creates a collective memory from which aspirations can develop and within which historical grievances can be preserved and nurtured. A good example of this latter fact is the Armenian community within the United States, which still remembers the Turkish atrocities against Armenians at the beginning of the twentieth century. Equally the Serbs still remember the slaughter of thousands of their number by the Croatian fascist puppet state during the Second World War. Such memories mean that old disputes frequently do not die and can remain a potential cause of war, as has been most certainly the case with regard to the Serbs during recent history.

Equally, ethnic groups tend frequently to be the means through which crucial interests or aspirations are pursued. War can result where those interests or aspirations clash seriously with those of other ethnic groups. It is always possible, of course, that such clashes might be resolved through peaceful negotiation. Whether or not they go as far as actually causing war can depend on a variety of factors. For example, the existence of the collective memories mentioned above might prevent the possibility of the peaceful resolution of a clash of interest between two ethnic/religious groups because of the continuing deep mistrust which they engender. Equally, if substantial economic interests are at stake, greed on the part of one or both of the groups might prevent the reaching of any peaceful compromise. This demonstrates neatly the way in which frequently it is not any one factor which appears to cause a war but rather the interaction between several.

Territorial disputes also have a long-established claim as being causes of war. The Falklands/Malvinas conflict of 1982 between Britain and Argentina, for example, arose from Argentina's long-standing assertion that it, not Britain, was the rightful owner of the islands and their dependencies. However, given the long preexistence of the claim without it having caused any armed conflict between the two states, it clearly could not have been the sole cause of the war that erupted in 1982. A variety of other factors have been identified by analysts as having played a role. For some the key to the immediate cause of the war lay in the domestic predicaments of the Argentine and British leaders, General Galtieri and Mrs Thatcher. The economic policies of both governments were highly unpopular domestically and their perceived failure was being laid squarely at the feet of the two leaders. In the past wars frequently have been used to distract domestic opinion from problems at home, and this, many alleged at the time, was what was happening in the preparedness of the two governments to use military force to try and resolve the dispute.[18]

Attractive as this explanation for the immediate cause of the war is, however, other factors might be claimed to have been equally important. For example, it was argued that the British simply misperceived a number of strong signals that the Argentines were preparing for an invasion and in consequence failed to take any credible deterrent action before the event. Had they done so then the Argentine junta might well have thought twice before continuing with its invasion plan.[19]

Equally, the then British government has been accused of sending a number of misleading signals to the Argentines which persuaded them that the British reaction to an invasion might be loud in words but lacking in military substance.[20] Finally, going back to the beginning of this chapter, it is of course possible to say that the most fundamental cause of the conflict was the periodical tendency to resort to violence that has been manifest in human nature and/or behaviour throughout the recorded history of civilisations. As Waltz emphasises, however, such a claim would not help us very much with an understanding of precisely why the Falklands War broke out at the time it did unless it was considered in tandem with the range of additional causal factors that have been discussed above.

In short, the Falklands/Malvinas example illustrates again just how complex the causality even of a single conflict might be, with the interaction of several factors quite probably being required before a serious dispute is turned into a full-blown war.

Even basic natural resources like water can be a cause of war. In August 1995, for example, *The Economist* summarised the possible future water situation as follows:

'"Wars of the next century will be over water." This latest warning . . . comes from the World Bank, the largest international investor in water projects. The saving grace, says Ismail Serageldin, the Bank's environment vice-president, would be if this universal natural resource were to assume its proper place as an economically valued and traded commodity.

So is the world running out of the stuff? . . . The answer is that there is no global water crisis but many severe local water crises. These are crises of under-investment, of political conflict over rivers that cross national boundaries, and of plain idiotic water management.

The Middle East is the likeliest crucible for future water wars. A long-term settlement between Israel and its neighbours will depend at least as much on fair allocation of water as of land. Egypt fears appropriation of the Nile's waters – on which its 60m people are entirely dependent – by upstream Sudan and Ethiopia. Iraq and Syria watch and wait as Turkey builds dams in the headwaters of the Euphrates. Elsewhere, India angers downstream Bangladesh by diverting to its fields the sparse dry-season flow of the Ganges, with a barrage built on the border. Slovakia and Hungary are at loggerheads over a huge hydroelectric dam on the Danube, which is on the border between them.'[21]

One claim that frequently has been made is that a serious perceived unevenness or disequilibrium in the distribution of power between large states can be a major cause of war.[22] Pessimists who see greed and the desire to use force continuously lurking beneath the surface of international relations argue that to allow significant power imbalances to arise or to be perceived to arise is to put temptation in the path of the devil. Those states which believe themselves to be in a strong position as a result may well choose to push demands and disputes to the point of war if they believe they can prevail without too great a cost. Had a more even distribution of perceived power been maintained, however, then the same temptation would not have arisen.

One example which might be used to back up this claim is Saddam Hussein's decision to wage war on Iran in 1980 after the successful revolution there of Ayatollah Khomeini. While Iran under the Shah had become a regional superpower, his demise appears to have led the Iraqi leader to presume that the Iranian army would be too disorganised and disoriented after the revolution to be able to mount any effective resistance to his forces. A long and bloody war therefore might be argued to have arisen out of a perceived power imbalance. However, if the validity of this claim was accepted, it would still have to be shown precisely *why* Saddam wished to take advantage of the perceived power imbalance if some of the most fundamental causes of the war are to be understood.

The Falklands/Malvinas War of 1982 could be argued to be another good example. The British Conservative government's prior announcement of its intention to greatly cut down on its ability to mount naval operations of the specific type necessary to defend the Falklands/Malvinas has been argued to have persuaded the Argentine junta that the balance of power in the South Atlantic was shifting decisively in their favour and that an invasion of the islands could be mounted safely.[23] Their mistake was in forcing the British to reverse their decision instead of waiting for them to implement it. In attempting to understand fully the reasons for the outbreak of the Falklands/Malvinas conflict, however, even if such a perceived power disequilibrium was accepted as being important, one would still need to understand the motives which persuaded the Argentine government to try and take advantage of it.

However, the very belief that war can be prevented through the maintenance of a perceived equilibrium is questionable for the simple reason that 'balancing' power is much more difficult than it sounds. There are, for example, serious problems that arise when attempts are made to calculate power in any precise sense and some of these will be explained in the next chapter.

Because power is difficult to calculate, states frequently have tended to err on the side of caution and to arm themselves to a greater degree than experts might believe necessary in order to achieve a satisfactory balance. (This is one explanation that has been offered as to how the USA and the USSR managed to end up with over 50 000 nuclear warheads between them during the Cold War.) By acting in this way, they are in effect taking out an insurance policy in case they have got their calculations wrong. Such behaviour can cause problems, because one state seeing another's excess armaments can worry that the surplus is one designed to facilitate a successful attack on itself, and therefore feel it necessary to try and deploy more powerful armed forces than its neighbour for the purposes of deterrence and self-protection. Once it has done this, its neighbour in turn can worry in case the resulting increase in power is intended to facilitate an attack on itself, and therefore further increase its own military power, leading to a counter-response and so on. The problems of calculating power, in other words, can lead to a situation in which the pursuit of a 'safe' balance of power increases great power rivalries via arms races.[24] Such arms races have a tendency to increase tensions among the participating parties for the simple reason that, as has been shown above, the motives behind them are highly ambiguous. Attempts to maintain peace through the pursuit of balance of power policies, therefore, can increase the chances of war through provoking arms races, which in turn can dangerously increase tension levels.[25]

There is a perplexing variety of additional ideas on the causes of war. Some have wondered, for example, whether the particular way in which some cultures have developed has built warlike tendencies into their centres. The European example most frequently cited is Germany, the idea being that authoritarian, militarist values lurk under the surface of German society as a result of an enduring collective cultural warrior psyche built up by the German rulers of earlier times.[26] Some writers have concentrated even on something as exotic as the business cycle in order to try and discover whether there is a relationship between its progress and the incidence of war.[27]

There is also the role of perception. Human beings act not necessarily in response to the world as it might be seen objectively, but in accordance with their image of it. What they perceive about particular problems, people, states and so on is determined by such things as their intelligence, the amount of relevant information which filters through to them, the influence on their thinking of their culture and the way matters are viewed within it, and the values inculcated by the family and educational backgrounds in which they have been brought up. The implication of several of the above factors, therefore, is that the 'real world' is filtered through the baggage of values and prejudices that is built into our heads from our childhood onwards. Even the 'hard' natural sciences are subject to this process. That there is widespread agreement on a particular scientific theory which appears to be verifiable by scientific experimentation is not in itself proof that that theory is a portrayal of objective reality. All we can say is that the theory appears valid in terms of the criteria that have been established for its verification. The problem is that those criteria are simply a result of human perception of what are useful measures of validity. There is no objective assurance that, in making their choice, the fallible subjective judgements of the scientists involved have got it right.

It is within the framework of these limitations that the leaders of governments have to make judgements concerning such things as the intentions of other states, the effectiveness of the military power of both their own and other states, and the value of peaceful as opposed to violent solutions to the problems confronting them. The most difficult and obvious problem they have is the lack of the ability to see inside the heads of the leaders of the states they deal with and therefore to know beyond doubt their real intentions. Their every act, therefore, is based upon subjective assessments of the purposes of the governments of other states, backed up by the frequently fallible reports of their intelligence agencies.

The importance of all of this for the purposes of this study is that many wars have been alleged to have broken out because of the gap between policy-makers' images of the world and the reality that subsequently was shown apparently to exist. A key reason that is often advanced for Hitler's suicidal decision to wage war on the then Soviet Union, for example, is the utterly contemptuous image he had of the Slavic peoples as warriors or any other kind of human being which he regarded as commendable.[28] The former British Prime Minister Anthony Eden is believed to have orchestrated a short and ultimately futile war against Egypt in 1956 because, among other things, mistakenly he believed its leader, Gamul Abdul Nasser, to be another Hitler.[29] The earlier-mentioned argument that Saddam Hussein's decision to wage war on Iran after its Islamic revolution was taken in the mistaken belief that inner turmoil would make it a 'soft touch' is another good example of a war resulting allegedly from a discrepancy between the real world and policy-makers' images of it. But again, in order fully to understand the reasons for the outbreak of each of the above wars, one would need to examine the other causes which have been alleged to have been involved.

Overall, thinking back to the beginning of this chapter, one might suggest that the causes of all wars must include the tendency towards the use of violence that history suggests seems to be built into human nature or at least the learned behaviour of many individuals. The tendency to resort to war is a recorded feature of human behaviour from biblical times to the present and it would seem pointless to deny its relevance or importance here. However, if such a conclusion is accepted, then, as Waltz points out (and as has been emphasised at relevant points in this discussion), it must be remembered that this aspect of human nature or behaviour does not explain why a particular war breaks out at a specific moment in time and it cannot throw any light on why the Gulf War erupted in 1991 and not 1992 or 1990. Arguably, given the large number of potential causes of war that have been identified here at the individual, state and international levels, the best way of trying to understand why any war broke out is to think in terms of the interrelationship between factors occurring within Waltz's three images or levels of analysis. Such a strategy guards against the danger of attributing too much importance to factors which, while being important on one level, may be relatively insignificant if other levels are taken into account as well. Or to put it another way, it protects the analyst against the danger of oversimplifying the subject of international relations which frequently is in itself almost a definition of complexity. It should also help to explain why any particular war broke out at one moment in time and not another.

Chapter 11

The control of war

Introduction

The first half of the 1990s was notable for the way in which three of the world's most important potential war prevention 'mechanisms' were, in the eyes of many, greatly discredited by their failure to do their job. This was seen to be the result of a mixture of alleged indecisiveness, poor judgement, ignorance, short-sighted self-interest or pure hypocrisy on the part of the major powers. NATO, the European Union and the United Nations, in the view of some strategists, together (or, in the case of NATO, on its own) probably could have stopped the murderous Balkan wars at their outset. The destruction which NATO and the UN finally unleashed on the Bosnian Serbs in late August 1995 would seem to emphasise their possession of the necessary capability to have done this. Yet, at the beginning of the Balkan conflict, all proved unable to get their act together to prevent the mass slaughter and ethnic cleansing that confirmed for the entire world to see that humanity in Europe was still capable of descending below the level of the beasts. Their collective failure, despite their having such an awesome amount of potential military and economic power, would seem to both provoke and emphasise the importance of the question of to just what extent *is* it feasible to prevent the potential causes of war identified in the last chapter from turning into actual conflicts. Are there ways of succeeding tomorrow where the major powers of today so manifestly failed? It is this question which will form the focus for the discussion below. The Change Map will be brought in where relevant to provide an added dimension to the analysis. (Some of the reasons behind the major powers' policies on intervention referred to above will be examined during the course of Chapter 12.)

To what extent can war be eliminated?

The question of to what extent war can be eliminated *completely* from international society is taken as the starting point of the discussion which follows. The view which one holds on this question is influenced by one's perception of human nature and behaviour and of the importance of such factors as ideologies, cultures/societies and global-level rivalries.

For example, as Kegley and Witkopf point out, many optimists have contended that warlike behaviour is a learned trait rather than a part of humankind's biological nature.[1] People wage war because they are misled by misguided traditions, ideologies, leaders or thinkers. By implication, therefore, violent behaviour can be *un-learned* and war thereby eliminated. There is a wide variety of optimistic prescriptions for the ending of war and the discussion which follows contains only a small sample of such views.

One optimistic strategy is to address the ways in which people are socialised within family groupings and educational institutions. The idea is that parents and teachers across national societies should be educated in ways of bringing up the children under their control to be violence-free – a new generation of people who will display only their 'natural' non-violence and non-aggressiveness in their behaviour, desires and beliefs.

However, there are several problems with this approach, even if it were to be accepted that people are naturally non-violent. First, as far as state school-level education is concerned, many existing governments, seeing advantages in the use of violence against other states in certain situations, would be unwilling to help produce a generation of young adults who would not be prepared to serve in the armed forces. Second, existing indicators of public opinion show that sizeable numbers of people in states such as the USA or Britain believe there are circumstances in which the threat to use force, or its actual use, by the state is a necessity and that to educate their children as total pacifists would be wrong.[2] In addition, as was argued in the previous chapter with regard to ethnic groupings, old enmities can be deeply engrained in some cultures. Where this is the case it could be argued strongly that it is likely that any education-for-peace initiative within them would arrive stillborn. Finally, the violent crime rates of people with parenting responsibilities in the United States, Russia, Italy and other states suggest a sizeable minority of parents has already become too brutalised by the societies within which they live to be much interested in 'educating' the aggression out of their children. Schools in turn frequently find that they enrol pupils who already have been so far socialised into violent behaviour, or simply the approval of violent behaviour, within their family backgrounds that there is little they can do to change the situation. On these grounds, it might be contended, educating for peace is a positive idea but one with limited potential. While it is always possible that, to the extent that it is a strategy that could be employed successfully in some schools or societies and so on, it might be able to help reduce the incidence of violence in human behaviour, it is not in itself capable of eliminating war from international relations.

Other optimists have argued that people can best be led to their real, peaceful selves through a simple process of practically demonstrating that mistrust can be reduced to the point where armies are no longer needed. For some, such a process starts from the assumption that weapons and armed forces themselves generate both distrust and the temptation for their use. In order to change this situation, these undesirable characteristics of the military need to be acknowledged fully at interstate level. Once this has been done governments, prompted by their peoples, should agree to undertake graduated, step-by-careful-step, controlled and verified general and comprehensive disarmament[3] in order to remove armed forces and their weapons as a cause of distrust and war, and indeed, by so doing, the means by which any further wars could be fought. Once this has been accomplished, the naturally peaceful nature of humankind will thereafter be the determining force behind all international relations. Because of verification and control measures, the process should not involve any substantial degree of risk for the parties to such a disarmament agreement and it is up to the world's people therefore to make their voices heard on the matter.

However, while limited arms reductions have been achieved within, for example, the context of the INF and START nuclear arms negotiations between the United States and the former Soviet Union, there is as yet no indication that general and comprehensive disarmament is feasible within the foreseeable future. The simple, main reason for this is that few if any governments seem to be in the slightest bit interested in promoting it genuinely as a policy objective and most perceive little in the way of popular pressure for them to do so. Indeed, in several regions of the world, the level of armaments held by key local powers is increasing rather than decreasing, while simultaneously the necessary ingredients for the making of nuclear weapons are being offered for sale on the global 'black market'. Even when or if the START reduction processes are complete, the United States and Russia will still have several thousand nuclear warheads between them. There is also the argument that weapons are as much of a symptom as a cause of warlike tendencies, and that as such they therefore can only be eliminated completely after the other causes have first been removed.[4]

As pointed out in the last chapter, there are also conversionist optimists who argue that humankind is fundamentally flawed but that it can be converted to an unflawed state. Traditionally, one of the most common ways through which it has been claimed that this can be done has been through conversion to a particular set of religious or moral beliefs. Roman Catholicism, for example, has at its heart the idea that people are flawed by original sin, which is seen as the sin inherited by all humankind from the time of the fall of the first human beings as portrayed allegorically within the Bible. Far from being permanently flawed, that religion sees humanity as capable of being redeemed by the saving power of God's grace – if individuals are prepared to respond to the latter. However, while it is able to claim that many people would appear to have done this, most particularly its saints and martyrs, it remains the case that large numbers of the world's people do not seem to be interested very much, if at all, in the idea of God. Given that Catholicism has been around for nearly two thousand years without converting enough people to a spiritual state in which they are so perfect that lethal violence becomes unthinkable, which is what the example of Christ would seem to be all about, then while it might be able to claim to be capable of improving the behaviour of some human beings, on the basis of existing evidence it does not offer a feasible route towards world peace. To put it in religious terms, throughout history, for one reason or another, too many people seem to have preferred, and to continue frequently to prefer, sin to grace for universal peace to be attained through such a conversion route. Indeed, theologians within that church would point out that the fact that it holds that God gives all individuals free choice as to whether to accept or reject him means in itself that the extent of any conversion to perfect peacefulness that might occur is unlikely ever to be universal. For them, those who in the name of Catholicism have said that it might be have been talking of a mere theoretical possibility with only remote chances of realisation. In addition, the issue of the Catholic view of peace and war was complicated during the early church by the development of just war theories by some theologians within it, which some saw and continue to see as going against the teaching and example of Christ.

Many other conversionist views have religious or moral bases also, and all have similar problems in terms of their apparent potential – or lack of it – for success in achieving the scale of conversions that would be necessary to produce universal peace. That does not in itself mean, of course, that they might not successfully help to reduce the *incidence* of war within the international system.

This is only a small representative sample of the views that have been advanced within the optimistic and conversionist perspectives, but one thing is clear and that is that these perspectives as a whole have had scant success in eliminating war from the international system and appear to have little immediately foreseeable chance of changing this situation.

But what of the views of the pessimists? From earlier discussions within this book it is apparent that for many 'deep pessimists', unless an international Leviathan can be constructed, war will remain a permanent feature of human society, with only the balance of power as an in any way effective means of reducing its incidence. So what would a Leviathan look like in a global context and what are the chances of it being attained?

For Hobbesians, a global Leviathan would result from the planet's politicians deciding that their survival could be better ensured through a social contract in which they surrendered power to a world government in return for it providing protection for themselves and their states. In an age in which nuclear weapons are continuing to spread, such an idea might seem very attractive.

Another means of achieving world government is through the conquest of the globe by a single empire. However, this has proved impossible in the past and even proved to be beyond the prowess of such militarily highly effective organisations as the Roman Empire at its peak.

World government would, at a stroke, remove great power rivalry and the wars which frequently result from it – and would neutralise all the other causes of war which were identified on various of Waltz's three levels in the previous chapter and which are advanced elsewhere within the literature. So just how feasible is its achievement? The strongest clue, many argue, is provided by the United Nations, a global organisation established as one of the consequences of the Second World War, with international peace-keeping prominent among its primary responsibilities. Contrary to its original objectives, the UN has no permanent forces of its own. When it wishes to mount any kind of military operation it has to rely upon funds and *ad hoc* forces donated by member states.[5] Most crucially, however, the war between Iraq and the USA and its allies demonstrated that whenever military might is required to enforce the UN's will upon a military power of any significance, everything depends upon the preparedness of the largest powers to supply the necessary personnel and hardware. The Iraq–USA war demonstrated also that it is quite likely that under such circumstances the great power or powers concerned will choose to retain their own command over such forces, given the scale of their commitment that is likely to be required.

What this means in practice, of course, is that the UN can only be effective in major peace and war issues when it suits the interests of the great powers to make it so. The Iraqi invasion of Kuwait could not have been reversed without the determination of the United States to use massive military force, as the political ineffectiveness of the economic sanctions applied to Iraq prior to and after the Gulf War helped demonstrate.

In short, no progress has been made since the establishment of the UN in turning it into a world government, even in the limited sphere of security matters. Each of the five permanent members of the Security Council has a veto over the Council's decisions still. Its effectiveness at all times is dependent upon great-power agreement. There are no visible trends in international politics suggesting that any of this is likely to change within the foreseeable future and there is no absolute guarantee of great-power agreement on anything that comes before the Council. For example, ideologically, the People's Republic of China, one of the key Council members, is in significant respects diametrically opposed to the others. Furthermore, even while Russia now has ceased to be a one party allegedly Marxist state, the complicated internal debates currently occurring within its own political system concerning arms-exporting policy and protectionism, among other things, suggest that the long-standing liberal capitalist members would be unwise to presume Russian agreement on all major issues of war and peace in future. That damaging differences can arise has been demonstrated already by the experience of the Balkan wars, as pointed out at the beginning of the chapter.

Given that the UN is the only global decision-making body that the great powers have been prepared to create and support with regard to peace and security matters, therefore, there does not appear to be any 'real world' evidence that a global government is feasible. To understand the most fundamental reasons why the latter is the case, then, bringing in the Change Map, it is necessary simply to look at the interests of the great powers. For example, some of the key economic interests of the European Union, which has two member states with seats on the Security Council and which is likely to retain at least one into the long-term future, clash considerably with those of both the USA and Japan. Such clashes, of which there are many among the regional great powers as well as those at the top of the global tree, are a severe obstacle to the creation of the enormous degree of trust which would be necessary for states to surrender power to a global authority. In addition, as has already been mentioned, purely at the level of the crucial Security Council, the Chinese retain a declared commitment to Marxism–Leninism and would not wish to be subjugated to a body likely to be dominated by representatives from the liberal capitalist powers. World government has not arisen so far simply because many states' basic interests clash to too great a degree for them to be prepared to entrust their fate to an organisation which would include members drawn from their political and economic competitors.

However, an argument against the apparent impracticality of the idea of world government might be advanced on the basis of the experience of the European Union, an organisation composed of states who, in most cases, a little over fifty years ago were at war with or occupied by one another. It now boasts that it has established a substantially integrated agricultural policy, and has made impressive progress towards the completion of a single market in industrial goods and financial services, together with having taken the first struggling steps towards full economic and monetary union and a common defence policy. Where the EU has gone on a regional level, some argue, why should the community of states not follow on a world level? After all, one of the founding principles of the EU was the creation of a union so intimate that a future war between any of its members would be unthinkable.

The argument against the EU being a model which, with the requisite amount of political will, could be extrapolated to the global level focuses upon its competitive ethos. One of the major reasons why its members remain committed to it now is because they believe it is the only way in which they can compete on an equal footing with the economic giants of Japan and the United States. The EU has little to do with any idea of a model for a potential world government. It is in key respects simply a means of making its members more effective practitioners of the old tradition of great-power rivalry. At the moment it is doing this with regard primarily to economic matters, but it is increasingly trying to develop an independent role for itself in global politics and has an ambition, on the part of some of its members, of extending this to the military realm as well in the future.

However, as has been pointed out already, not all of those who are outside the conversionists' camp and who see human nature as flawed by a tendency towards the use of violence see world government as a necessary prerequisite for the achievement of a lasting international peace. One perspective within the camp of the non-violent persuasionists, for example, argues that while 'deep pessimists' may be right in their diagnosis of humanity's violent tendencies, it is always possible that world leaders as a whole could be converted to the practice exclusively of peaceful relations, without any form of coercion being necessary to facilitate this, by a convincing demonstration that the best way to secure all ends, *good or bad*, is through non-violent means. Self-interest, in other words, could be used to keep the tendency towards violence under control. In this respect it is argued that, on the basis of its past record, force can be shown convincingly to be a highly unpredictable policy instrument that has such a strong chance of backfiring on the instigator that it is not worth considering using it.[6] The baleful experience of even such an enormous military power as the USA in Vietnam is cited in this regard, and rather than pointing to the US victory in the Gulf War, exponents of this view point to extreme American caution now in contemplating involvement in the much messier conflicts that are the norm in international relations, such as the war in the Balkans. In addition, where the use of force is successful, that success can often be only short-lived. The awesome rise and rapid disappearance of Hitler's Third Reich is cited as an example here. The costs of its use also can be a severe drain on the strength even of successful users and can lead to a lowering of their status in the international 'league table'. The experience of Great Britain in the Second World War can be used as an example of this. The British entered the war as one of the key arbiters of global affairs. They lost a quarter of their national wealth in fighting the war, and within twenty-five years of its end had shrunk to a mainly regional power.

So, exponents of this view argue, all that is needed is for their case to be put across to governments sufficiently strongly and they will see the logic of refraining from the use of force. Their own selfish interests will lead them to prefer peaceful means of securing their policy objectives.

There are several problems with this perspective. First, it assumes that there will be no gamblers among world leaders, people who would not be put off by a calculated risk of the use of force backfiring on them, whereas history has shown international politics to be full of such individuals. Hitler gambled militarily on several occasions and won, which persuaded him to carry the process further. Saddam Hussein gambled on several things prior to and during the Gulf War, most particularly on being able to stir up the Arab peoples to such an extent that the international coalition against him would run into severe problems. For some, as Clausewitz implies, gambling can be compulsive.[7]

Second, it assumes that all governmental leaders are rational. This again is contradicted by the historical record. For example, some believe that British Prime Minister Eden's ability to think rationally was temporarily in some doubt at the time when he plotted the 1956 war against Egypt's Gamul Abdul Nasser. His alleged condition was said to be due to medication which he was taking for a debilitating ailment at the time.[8] The sanity of more than one government leader has been believed to have been adversely affected by venereal disease. In modern times Stalin was clearly a paranoiac by the end of his life. Equally, some psychologists have diagnosed Hitler as having been a psychopath.

A third problem is that even if it were to be assumed that all leaders are rational, the question then arises as to whether or not they share the same view of what is rational. A rationality that starts from a religious view that the loss of human life in the cause of a 'just war' is virtuous and guarantees the slain a place in heaven is going to foster a different perspective on military conflict from one which says that human life is sacred and its shedding should at all costs be avoided. In other words, just because people think rationally does not mean that they will conclude that war is undesirable, even if it does carry a high risk of defeat and the mass slaughter of one's own side.[9] What are crucial are the values which underpin any given process of thought.

Finally, thinking back to the discussion towards the end of the previous chapter, there is also the possibility of the misunderstandings that can arise through simple misperception complicating any attempt to try and establish peace through this route.

In short, it may well be possible to persuade some leaders of states that war is a complete waste of time and effort, but the above arguments, in combination with the evidence of history, suggest that there will always be those who will remain unconvinced. Furthermore, the existence of a global black market in armaments means that states' leaders are not the only people who have to be persuaded out of warlike behaviour – if they have access to the necessary funds, terrorist and revolutionary groups can now arm themselves in a major way and are capable of starting their own wars independently of states. This complicates an already complex picture even more for those trying to promote non-violent persuasionism, especially when it is considered that some groups are hardly even heard of before their first bombs go off and a conflict begins, and that it can be difficult to find out who their leaders are, never mind talk to them in order to try and extol the virtues of peaceful behaviour.

However, if there appears to be little chance of war being eliminated *completely* through the attempted establishment of world government or any other of the sample means discussed here, what are the prospects at least for reducing the frequency of its occurrence? It has been noted already that some of the routes towards peace promotion mentioned above might have some utility in reducing the incidence of military conflict. Are there additional strategies that might be tried as means, for example, of securing a substantial reduction in the *tensions* which often lead to war? If such a reduction *can* be achieved might it not be a useful way of preventing some wars?

Here, the picture is very different. Institutions like the European Union and the United Nations take on a rather different light. The cooperative framework of the EU, for example, can be seen to play a valuable role in helping ensure that all the European regional great powers bar Russia collaborate rather than compete with one another militarily within the continent of Europe. In terms of the Change Map, the common and/or complementary economic, political and security interests which key sections of the political, BTC and administrative elites of the member states perceive in the preservation of such a framework are crucial in ensuring its continuation. Such perceptions are in turn the result of a variety of opportunity factors and their consequences which have made the idea of European integration to one extent or another a desirable goal for such groups. For older elite members they include the sobering memory of the Second World War and the desire to avoid another major European conflict, while for many politicians and business people they include the apparent logic and inevitability of greater integration as a result of the process of global interfusion, the belief that such integration is an important way out from Western Europe's continuing economic decline relative to Japan and the USA, and modernisation.

At the global level also the EU is important, in so far as it helps stabilise a region of the world which twice this century has sucked almost the entire planet into grossly destructive wars. In this sense, the then EC's non-successful role in attempting to stabilise the situation in Yugoslavia during the crucial period of 1991/2 and thereafter could be argued to be a relatively minor failure in comparison with its gradual but continuing progress in drawing the states of much of Europe together into a peaceful, closely integrated relationship. Should the USA pull out from Europe completely during the next few years, then that might well create an imperative for the construction of a truly effective common foreign and defence policy *that is strong enough to overcome the differences of interest that have bedevilled policy on the former Yugoslavia*, given that no one Western European state on its own is powerful enough militarily to keep the peace across Europe or balance the potential military might of Russia, should the latter become a threat again at some stage. Such a common policy in itself should in theory be a powerful stabilising factor within Europe – providing it is not seen as threatening by Russia. Should it not appear, of course, then, in the absence of a US military presence, the consequences for Europe ultimately could be disastrous.

So elite perceptions, interests, opportunity factors and imperatives can all be seen to be important with regard to the creation and maintenance of the actual and possible tension reduction roles of the EU. It should be remembered also that, as was demonstrated powerfully during the member states' attempts to secure ratification of the Maastricht Treaty, the governing political elites ultimately are dependent upon the consent of the majority of their electorates with regard to anything that is popularly perceived to be a significant development within the Union.

The EU has important actual and potential war prevention functions across much of Europe. While there is no immediate sign of 'full-blown'

EU-equivalent organisations springing up in other regions of the world which frequently have been torn apart by war, such as Africa or the Middle East (at most there.are only some partial equivalents), the very fact that any major European war could have destructive implications for the whole planet makes the tension-reducing role of the EU of enormous significance in global politics.

Of at least equal significance has been the arms control process involving the world's largest nuclear powers, the USA and the (former) Soviet Union. For the purposes of this book arms control shall be taken to mean an agreed restraint on, or reduction in, arms deployments, the motives underlying which *can include* the facilitation of the achievement of the elimination of all conventional and/or nuclear weapons from the territories of the parties to an arms control agreement in the medium or long term, should future circumstances permit this, but which does not have such a process of comprehensive elimination as its *immediate primary* purpose. This qualification is important because it avoids confusion between arms control and disarmament when arms reductions are being considered. Disarmament is most usefully described as a process of weapons abolition which has as its immediate primary purpose the elimination, or the facilitation of the elimination, of all conventional and/or nuclear weapons from the territories of the parties to a disarmament agreement, preferably within an agreed timescale.

Even such precise definitions, however, have problems when attempts are made to transfer them to the 'real world' in so far as the parties to an arms control agreement can *claim* for public consumption that their primary purpose is to facilitate disarmament while in reality their immediate main motives are otherwise. Without a considerable amount of evidence to back up the claimed priority of such an ambition, however, analysts tend generally to assume it to be of secondary importance to other more immediately obvious motives, of an economic or tension-reducing nature for example.

In 1987 the governments of the then two superpowers signed what still is not fully recognised as the most significant arms control agreement of the twentieth century, the INF treaty. Its significance lies not only in its formal historic breaking of the Soviet taboo over on-site inspection,[10] but in the fact that it is the treaty which showed that nuclear weapons can actually be destroyed and not simply restricted to agreed ceilings, as previously had been the case.

The continuing arms control process between the USA and the successors to the Soviet state is a major force for tension reduction in global politics. While the original onset of nuclear arms control during the later stages of the Cold War was dependent on diplomacy first reducing tension to a level where it could become an acceptable policy goal for the political elites involved, once it had started it became widely recognised as a means for tension reduction in its own right (via the mutual reduction in threat perceptions which it fostered), even if the degree to which it reduced or controlled tensions was seen to vary considerably in accordance with changeable political and diplomatic circumstances.

In terms of the Change Map, one might note that arms control has been the result of the interaction of a number of factors. The INF and succeeding arms control agreements have been in the interests of the Soviet Union and its successors, for example, because the nosedive which their economies have experienced during and since the 1980s has made it vital to cut military expenditure in order to try and free the scarce economic resources involved for rather more productive purposes in the domestic and, theoretically at least, the export-led economy. Equally, however, it could be argued that arms control has been in the economic interests of the USA as well, given the budgetary problems that Reagan's arms build-up caused in the 1980s. It also has been seen to have been in the political–security interests of both former Cold War sides because it made the potentially disastrous nuclear relationship between them more manageable and stable. The process has been helped significantly by opportunity factors also, two of which have been especially important. First, the sustained and skilful peaceful overtures that followed the arrival of the Soviet Gorbachev regime during the second half of the 1980s allowed the then US governing elite, and crucial sections of the American electorate that supported it, to change their perceptions of the then Soviet Union from that of an 'evil empire' to one of a state that genuinely was seeking to improve relations with the USA. Second, the collapse of the Soviet Union, both as an ideological competitor and as a state, following the attempted coup in August 1991, further greatly lessened the American threat perception of Russia and encouraged it to continue to pursue arms reductions with both it and the other nuclear states that emerged from the ruins of the USSR. These are only some of the interests and opportunity factors that have been relevant in promoting arms control, but their identification illustrates usefully how the interaction of such factors can make tension reduction possible even in the case of what was the biggest and most potentially dangerous arms race in history.

It must be remembered also that while the UN has disappointed those who saw it as a potential future world government, it has provided a useful forum for great power tension control in the form of the Security Council. The great powers, the USA, China, Russia, and what must increasingly in future major crises be seen as the EU's two representatives, Britain and France (their own power has shrunk too much for them to be able to justify continued seats in any other way into the twenty-first century), have in the Council a permanent face-to-face negotiating forum for use in trying to keep under control their reactions to crises as they occur around the globe.

There is also the role that has been and might be played by balance of power theories in reducing the incidence of war, together with that of several nuclear weapons policies that have been derived from or affected by them. One of the latter, mutually assured destruction (MAD), the nuclear deterrence doctrine that underpinned superpower relations at the height of the Cold War, was based on the assumption that if both states knew that to attack the other would be guaranteed to bring down unimaginable destruction upon themselves, then they would be persuaded of the value of maintaining peaceful relations despite being ideologically hostile to each other. In terms of the Change Map, under conditions of MAD, in other words, it was believed by advocates of nuclear deterrence theory that the maintenance of peace would become an imperative for the states involved.

A second such policy, arms control, frequently has been subject to enormous pressures from within the negotiating superpowers to ensure that agreements produce particular balances of power desired by interested parties. It will not be outlined here as it has been explained already.

The basic idea of the balance of power itself has been examined to an extent in the previous chapter and will be explained more fully in the next section, where its usefulness as a war preventer, together with that of the above mentioned nuclear policies derived from or affected by it, will be evaluated also.

Finally, when states actually come close to the point of conflict, economic and political sanctions increasingly have come to be offered as alternatives to war. For example, economic sanctions were tried against Iraq by the United Nations before the US-led coalition decided to resort to violence. So far, the strategies which can underly sanctions, of trying to make it in the economic interests of target states to avoid war and comply with the targeter's demands, for example, often have not proved to be particularly successful. Some regimes are impervious to the sufferings that economic sanctions can impose on their peoples as long as they can continue to supply their own needs from the global black market. In other cases, states which are subject to sanctions are able to secure continuing supplies of prohibited goods from other states that are prepared to break the sanctions openly or secretly. Equally, sanctions frequently take time to really bite and, as in the case of the 1991 Gulf War, the patience of one or more potential combatants can run out before they work, leading to the outbreak of military hostilities. However, their effectiveness should not be ruled out completely. During early August 1995, for example, it was reasonable to speculate that the Serbian government held back from intervening on the side of Croatian Serbs (when they were subjected to a massive attack from Croatian government forces) because of its anxiety to persuade the West to lift the crippling sanctions that had been imposed on it after its previous military adventures in the former Yugoslavia.

Clearly then, even if it is not possible to prevent *all* wars, there is a substantial array of methods which are or might be used to try and prevent wars between particular states and groups of states breaking out. Those mentioned above are but a selection from the possibilities. It is intended now to ask a fundamentally important question about these, namely are there some methods of war prevention which are more successful than others?

Are there some methods of war prevention which are more successful than others?

A number of people have attributed to nuclear deterrence the fact that the superpowers did not go to war during the forty-plus years of the Cold War.[11] As their evidence, they cite the huge ideological gulf between the two states during the period and the enormous extent to which their interests clashed. In previous periods of history, prior to the creation of nuclear weapons, they claim, such things would have made a war between great powers so diametrically opposed to each other inevitable. The forms of nuclear deterrence which the superpowers practised during this period therefore implicitly are held up as the supreme form of war prevention. Some have even argued that if nuclear weapons spread into all regional power balances, creating a series of little nuclear balances, then the special deterrence magic involved would create a largely peaceful world.[12] The knowledge that the other side could inflict massive nuclear destruction upon it would prevent another nuclear weapon state from embarking upon a war no matter how many reasons it might have for wishing to do so. Peace would be brought about through the employment of the ultimate imperative.

However, there are several problems with the above. The most crucial is that serious differences in ideologies and interests do not necessarily mean states will go to war with each other. This undermines the case of those who try and claim that nuclear deterrence has been 'proved' to work. For example, the economic and human cost to the Soviet Union of the Second

World War was enormous. An estimated forty million of its people were killed and its economy was set back severely. Given that the memory of this disastrous cost remained strong throughout the Cold War, it is not unreasonable to suppose that the Soviets had no intention whatsoever of engaging in another massive war – non-nuclear or nuclear – unless it was forced on them by a US attack.

Similarly, as long as the USSR did not attack the territory of the United States or Western Europe, it is difficult to envisage the USA wishing to engage directly in a war with a political system that, during the early 1940s, had shown itself able to emerge as a formidable fighting 'machine' despite huge, nuclear war-scale population losses and which rose to such a level of military prowess at the end of the Second World War that some strategists concluded it could probably have crushed Nazi Germany without any assistance from America or Britain.

What all of this means, of course, is that it might well have been the fact that neither superpower wanted to go to war with the other, with or without nuclear deterrence, rather than nuclear deterrence itself, that prevented a Third World War. The fact that each engaged in an arms build-up against the other could be argued simply to have been the result of their desire to guarantee the best defence and deterrence possible in an atmosphere of grave mutual mistrust, rather than signifying any intention on the part of either side to try and manoeuvre itself into a position where it could successfully wage an aggressive war. That each feared the other is beyond doubt. Whether either ever wished to start a war with the other is greatly open to question.

The difficulty in trying to prove that nuclear deterrence was successful in preventing a superpower war, therefore, is that the matter could only be tested convincingly by re-running the Cold War without nuclear weapons and seeing what happened. In consequence, the status of nuclear deterrence as an imperative is as yet unproven, and it would be dangerous to rely on it alone as a war prevention strategy on the basis of existing evidence. As mentioned in the previous section, there are some regimes for whom huge losses of civilian life might be acceptable on, for example, religious grounds.

Nuclear deterrence as practised by the superpowers was often described as a special form of balance of power theory – the balance of terror. The balance of power itself in its various forms, the most influential of which have been the balance of power as a power *equality* relationship (in which attempts are made to establish a power equilibrium within which it is theoretically pointless to go to war, given that the power of one state or alliance is supposed to cancel out the power of another), and as a *predominance* relationship (in which one state or alliance keeps the peace through having dominance over its opponent), has had a long history as a means of trying to prevent conflict. In terms of the Change Map it involves the simple notion of states trying to prevent other states employing war as a means of bringing about change through highly specific uses of the concept of power. Some argue that while it has always broken down in the end, no matter which version of it has been employed, it has nevertheless brought periods of peace which otherwise could not have been obtained. A useful example of how the balance of power is continuing to play a role in great-power thinking about war prevention, despite the end of the Cold War, is provided below. Taken from an article published in July 1995, it shows also how balance of power strategies can interact with other, non-military strategies:

'China is becoming a problem. The United States, the European Union and their Asian and Pacific allies are growing increasingly concerned at the rising power of this regional colossus, whose economy and military strength is expanding every year.

While no country wants to pick a fight with China, government officials and independent analysts are openly wondering whether the West and its partners may need to adopt a policy of "containment" similar to that which was designed to keep the former Soviet Union in check during the Cold War.

"We cannot predict what kind of power China will be in the 21st century," Winston Lord, the US Assistant Secretary of State for East Asian and Pacific affairs, told a congressional hearing last week. "God forbid, we may have to turn, with others, to a policy of containment. I would hope not. We're trying to prevent that."

Apprehension about China's intentions is so acute that it is playing an ever larger role in Western policy towards Russia. Desperate to avoid a Moscow–Peking alliance, the West is adopting a more conciliatory stance towards Russia – to the point where certain once-sacrosanct goals, such as the incorporation of central and eastern European countries into NATO, are now being quietly put to one side.

While a formal Russian–Chinese military pact is highly unlikely, there is little doubt that the two countries have a warmer relationship now than at any time since the 1950s. The Chinese premier, Li Peng, recently visited Moscow and joined President Boris Yeltsin in declaring that the governments of Russia and China would no longer tolerate lectures from the West on how to behave at home and abroad.

The Russian–Chinese friendship has been cemented by Russian

arms sales to China, including fighter planes, which have assisted Peking's military build-up and caused considerable alarm in the Asia–Pacific region. . . .

An Australian government defence policy statement, published last December, said, "Over the next decade China is likely to be the most powerful new influence on the strategic affairs of our wider region. The relative peace in Asia may not last."

. . . The US has not yet abandoned its hope of binding a reforming, prosperous China into a global web of commercial and political ties, but .the strategy is beginning to wear thin. . . .

While the transfer of Hong Kong from British to Chinese rule in 1997 could result in a major local upheaval, an equally serious problem is Peking's claim to virtually the whole of the South China Sea as part of Chinese territorial waters. The Chinese navy recently moved into Mischief Reef, one of the Spratly Islands, a chain off the Vietnamese coast whose sovereignty is disputed among Brunei, Malaysia, the Philippines, Taiwan and Vietnam as well as China.

In responding to Chinese pressure, the US is using a mixture of military and diplomatic initiatives. The Pentagon released a report in February that affirmed the US intention to keep about 100,000 troops in the East Asian arena for the foreseeable future. The US is also poised to re-establish full diplomatic relations with Vietnam, a traditional rival to China.

. . . the most striking aspect of the West's response to China's increasing power is the way that it has convinced Western governments of the need for an accommodation with Russia. Any doubts Western leaders entertain about Mr Yeltsin's semi-authoritarian political system have been pushed aside in the belief that, now of all times, the West needs a co-operative Russia. . . .

The wooing of Russia does not yet amount to a policy of containment towards China. But there is much pessimism in Western capitals over whether China will modify its behaviour in coming years so that containment becomes unnecessary.'[13]

Despite the continued use of balance of power thinking by the major powers, as demonstrated above, its critics have argued that balance of power policies have helped cause more wars than they have prevented. The previous chapter offered some relevant thoughts in this regard. As was claimed to be the case there, it would seem that the heart of the problem with such policies is that they are centred on the idea of measuring and balancing (or 'containing') something which simply *cannot* be measured accurately. This means that those who place their faith in 'power balances' to preserve peace are trusting in something that is inherently unreliable and potentially unstable. Power, as has been seen already, comprises both tangible and intangible elements. It is all too easy to underestimate such intangible elements as the will of an opponent to resist, as Iraq found out when attacking Iran. Equally, there can be severe problems in measuring things accurately even where tangible factors are concerned. For example, on paper, one state may appear to have a superior military capability to another. But those who risk trusting what they see on paper frequently find that whether one's weapons systems are more effective than one's opponents' is something that can only be tested adequately in battle. If one is encouraged to believe that power can be measured therefore, as happens within balance of power alliance systems, then, given the above, it is all too easy for the potential aggressors being 'balanced against' to get things wrong and believe that they have or have acquired a power advantage which makes a successful attack on their opponents feasible. A strong case can be made for saying that history is littered with examples that prove the strength of this point. Perhaps the most spectacular recent example was Hitler's previously mentioned total misperception of the fighting potential of the Soviets when opening up his second front against them.

Balance of power politicking might be alleged to help create wars in other ways too. An already cited example of this might be the arming of Iraq by the United States and other states to balance Iranian power during the 1980s, to the point where they were faced with a leader who felt strong enough to threaten war with them. In their anxiety to balance Iranian power in the Middle East and the Persian Gulf, the West failed to take adequate account of the aggressive and imperialist nature of the regime which they were arming.

The American 'containment' balance of power policy during the Cold War, by which the USA was prepared covertly or overtly to wage war with states it saw as Soviet clients if they threatened in its eyes to upset the communist/capitalist world balance, is another good example of how balance of power policies can actually lead directly to war.

So, overall, the case for the balance of power in its various forms being greatly successful as a method of preventing war, to say the least, looks extremely shaky. It could be argued that it could only be made on the basis of alternative policies being a complete disaster.

However, is there a case for saying that balance of power policies can be useful preventers of war if they become part of effective tension reduction processes such as arms control? Here the picture is more promising perhaps. If arms races can be contained or even reversed through arms control agreements, which *both* reduce tension through the limiting of weapons stockpiles *and* encourage stability by aiming for *what are perceived to be balanced* reductions or limits, then perhaps that is the best means of preventing war that is available within the problematical world that confronts policy-makers.

However, a glance through the Change Map reveals some serious potential problems. For example, one might consider *political elite perceptions of the desirability of specific goals that may require change* through war – and *opportunity factors* in the form of government personnel changes. When these are taken into account it becomes apparent that with 'balanced' arms control there would still be a gamble involved, because no matter what the reality of a situation, a new government of a particular state, rather less peaceful in intent than its predecessor which had agreed to an arms control treaty, might rightly or wrongly believe that the agreed stable 'balance' is actually in its favour. It might reach such a conclusion because of, for example, what it believes to be the superior effectiveness of one or more of its permitted weapons systems. On the basis of its belief it might conclude that an attack on its apparently weaker fellow treaty signatories would be a worthwhile means of achieving a particular policy goal and start a war. Ultimately, everything would still come down to intent and perception.

Equally, verification measures in arms control need to be very effective in order to ensure that once any arms reduction process gets under way, one party is not simply manufacturing and stockpiling clandestinely replacement weapons to use against other parties to the agreement as soon as their genuine reductions have reached such a level as to make them vulnerable. There is always the risk of someone cheating.

Finally, in Europe at least, there is the option of trying to extend the cooperative framework of the European Union gradually across the continent, tying the states of the East into the integrative process and thereby in time hopefully creating a situation in which war becomes unfeasible across both East and West because the member states are so closely linked that any military conflict would automatically seriously damage the economic interests of the attacker as well as those of the attacked.

However, as is shown in the chapters on Europe, continued progress on integration cannot be guaranteed for a number of reasons. Equally, should the EU acquire too many members, then it could easily become ungovernable as a result of the consequent administrative complexity and start to fall apart. For example, the very different levels of economic development of the various new member states would make it hard for the Union to function effectively as a coherent economic unit. However, senior German and French politicians have on several occasions proposed a way of tackling this second problem by creating a Union of up to three tiers. This would involve a closely integrated core of already economically compatible states, probably around a Franco-German axis, with middle and outer tiers of less integrated and less economically or politically compatible states. The core group would probably remain small enough to enable continued effective decision-making on many key issues and real progress on deepening integration to occur within it, given the absence of the problems of complexity that a larger arrangement would create, while the middle and outer tiers would still be able to benefit from the integrative process without being committed to or involved in all its aspects. They would participate only in decisions relating to the aspects of integration in which they were involved, thereby avoiding an overload of the EU decision-making system. But even in the outer tiers they would still be benefiting from the integrative process and its related peace aims, with the option of moving to the core group if or when they and members of the group thought this to be both desirable and feasible.

If such a continent-wide arrangement could be created, and as pointed out, there are some big uncertainties in this respect, not least the question of whether all of the states in the East would want to join on the terms which ultimately they might be offered, then it would make a potentially enormous contribution to reducing the likelihood of war within Europe.

However, as was emphasised earlier, on the basis of present evidence there do not appear to be any full-blown EU-style political–economic integrative organisations likely to materialise in other areas of the world with long histories of violent conflict, certainly within the short to medium term, so the extent to which the EU model has relevance outside Europe appears to be limited. Nevertheless, this does not mean that aspects of it cannot be applied in an attempt to reduce the tensions that can lead to war within particular regions. For example, it might be perfectly feasible for major states, internal or external to a particular region which it is in their interests to keep peaceful, to promote within it a series of economic trade and/or assistance agreements or arrangements which together give potentially warring states a strong common economic interest in peace.

In Change Map terms, a decision to extend a multi-tiered EU right across the continent of Europe in order to reduce the chances of war within the region would be to deliberately promote further and exploit the process of global interfusion in order to create inter-elite perceptions across East and West to the effect that future European wars could only seriously damage the interests of the aggressors as well as those attacked. The strategy of simply increasing economic cooperation and interlinkages across a region in order to reduce the tensions that can lead to war would be designed to turn peace into a perceived core interest of the governments of potentially conflictual states via a less ambitious promotion of global interfusion processes.

The methods of war prevention evaluated here are only a selection of some of the most prominent possibilities.[14] Each has potential limitations. But this author has found that every war prevention measure additional to those above which he has examined also has its attendant problems. Policymakers interested in avoiding war therefore ultimately must choose the method which they believe to be the most effective in any particular set of circumstances and which they perceive as carrying the lowest risk of failure. There is no irrefutable evidence to prove that one particular method is going to succeed above all others in, for example, preventing a future war between India and Pakistan. It is important to emphasise, however, that a belief in the appropriateness of any route towards war prevention must be based upon as thorough a process of research both of its merits relative to possible alternatives, and of the apparent needs of particular situations, as is practicable within the decision-time available. If this is done, then despite the fact that the method chosen may still turn out to be inappropriate when it is tried, at least the chances of it being successful theoretically will have been enhanced greatly. In a world in which there is no certainty of perfect judgement in any political matter, that is no inconsiderable achievement.

If, in a context where general and comprehensive disarmament looks to be the remotest of possibilities, it is still possible to negotiate and maintain a perceived balance of power globally, or in one or more heavily armed regions, which satisfies the main participating parties and which simultaneously involves a programme of balanced reductions in both armaments and tensions, then one suspects that this will be a means of war prevention that relevant policy-makers intent on trying to guarantee peace by the most immediately practical available route will aim at. It seems, for example, to have been the means of securing peace that Gorbachev's Soviet Union believed to be superior to all other available alternatives at the time and which seems still to be appropriate to its Russian successor state and the USA. There is always the risk of someone cheating on the arms control side of the equation in this kind of exercise, or misperceiving 'the balance' of power, but on the other hand, if the gamble comes off and such measures work, then their tension reduction function should be a powerful war preventer. Where circumstances permit, they can also be added to, by, for example, introducing valuable economic cooperation agreements into regional or global power balances which are designed to try and give the participating parties a vested material interest in peace.

As an application of the Change Map emphasises, the extent to which such a peace-orientated strategy can succeed will be determined by the intervention of such variables as opportunity factors, in the form of changes in government personnel for instance (thinking back to the example cited previously in this respect), ideologies (in particular the rise or reawakening of ambitious nationalisms), elite perceptions of such things as interests and relative power (thinking back again to the above-mentioned example), or fortune.

In the context specifically of Europe, some would argue that an extension of the EU right across the continent in the manner suggested earlier would be the best war prevention strategy for that region.

But it should be remembered that in some regions and circumstances, enmities and ambitions might be on such a scale that tension-reducing measures of any kind prove impossible. In such situations it may well be that simple but credible deterrence, whether it be through conventional or nuclear means, is the only practical war prevention strategy, no matter what its accompanying risks and uncertainties. This is the policy which some argued should have been implemented by NATO against Serbia when the Balkan wars started to look likely.

Finally, it can be noted that outside of the large-scale solutions such as the above there are a number of relatively small measures which could be taken to reduce the number of wars among the world's lesser powers. For example, arms-manufacturing states such as the USA, Britain, France, Germany, Italy, Russia and Israel could agree not to supply, directly or indirectly, leaders of states in areas of actual or potential instability with enough weapons or weapons-manufacturing machinery to allow them to feel confident enough to attack their neighbours (although, as previous discussions of the balance of power have shown, such good intentions can easily be subverted by misperceptions of regional 'balances'). Saddam Hussein is an obvious case in point. States such as the USA could also refrain from intervening in areas such as Latin America or Asia in order to fan wars that would *either not occur or rapidly would fizzle out* without their involvement (as opposed to wars that *could* burn on for years *without* great-power intervention, as in the case of the former Yugoslavia, where convincing arguments might be made in favour of great-power action). The American assistance to the Contras in Nicaragua during the 1980s was a case in point. While the end of the Cold War has reduced the likely incidence of such interventions, it has not in itself ruled out the possibility of great-power meddling in order to fan or encourage wars. The Croatian attack on the Krajinan Serbs in August 1995, for example, was rumoured to have been supported by the United States through secret arms supplies, the provision of military advisers and tacit diplomatic encouragement[15] (although the USA at the time was said to be justifying the Croat attack in terms of its relief of the pressure on Bihac and its potential for tilting the balance against the Bosnian Serbs, thereby hopefully *shortening* the wars in the former Yugoslavia). However, reference to the Change Map reminds the analyst of the importance of interests. In short, the likelihood of such measures being implemented is dependent, for example, upon how the governing elites of the arms-producing states define their economic or global political interests at any moment in time – sometimes in the recent past it has seemed that they have been quite happy to risk or even intentionally help cause a war between or within other states where they have believed this to be to their benefit. The American involvement in Nicaragua has already been mentioned.

So, in conclusion, what this and the previous chapter have done has been to show something of the enormous range of potential causes of war that exists and, via appropriate selective applications of the Change Map, the complexities that can confront those wishing to prevent or simply reduce the incidence of war. What they have done also has been to show that while war prevention may often be difficult, this does not mean it is impossible. Individual wars *can* be prevented provided that the requisite balance of such things as power, opportunity factors and imperatives is in place and provided peace is (or, via diplomacy or other means, comes to be) perceived to be in the interests of the key governmental elites involved in any international security equation. The skill of the peacemaker is in being able to discern the opportunities and limitations of any situation and to correctly estimate ways in which it might be possible to tip the balance of relevant variables in the direction of peace. One essential guiding fact which an application of the Change Map sets out before such people is that the extent to which war can be prevented among potentially conflictual parties will be dependent upon the extent to which they or others as peace-promoters can introduce restraining imperatives into a situation and/or create common interests among the potential belligerents in the maintenance of peace. While this 'carrot and stick' idea is hardly new in international relations, it remains as important now as it has always been.

This serves to emphasise the importance of diplomacy in any peace equation. It is a crucial channel through which images – whether they be of imperatives such as credible deterrence, previously unperceived interests in peace, or simple but vital trust – can be created and reinforced. Its importance in deterrence, for example, could be argued to have been demonstrated by the Glaspie incident prior to the 1991 Gulf War and the failure of British diplomacy prior to the 1982 Falklands/Malvinas war. In the first case, the US government, via its ambassador to Iraq, was accused of giving Saddam Hussein the impression that the United States was not prepared to take any strong measures against him if he invaded Kuwait, and in the second case, the British were accused of giving the Argentines the impression that the Falkland Islands were not seen as being an issue which they would go to war over. Failures in diplomacy in these cases, in combination with other factors, were accused of being a direct cause of the wars that followed. In the British case, such failure rendered their long-practised conventional deterrence strategy in the area completely ineffective, and in the Glaspie case also, the Iraqis believed there was nothing to deter them from military action in the attitude of the US government. On the other hand, had diplomatic channels been used to create strong deterrent images in both cases, probably backed up by highly visible military displays of intent, then both Saddam Hussein and the Argentine junta at the very least would have been given strong cause for thought before proceeding with their invasions.

Diplomacy is crucial also in the successful promotion of such tension-reducing measures as arms control negotiations. The first nuclear arms control agreement between the USA and the then USSR, the SALT I agreement of 1972, for example, was facilitated greatly by a wide range of trust-building diplomatic processes, including contacts through third parties, formal and informal direct negotiations between military, technical and political experts and direct negotiations at the highest level of state. Equally, diplomacy has been crucial at every stage of the development of the intra-European cooperation-promoting body, the European Union. The success of the negotiations to establish the first European Community, the ECSC, for example, ultimately was crucially dependent on the intervention of American diplomacy. Most recently, Gorbachev's personal diplomacy, which included taking his new image of a friendly Soviet government directly to the American people, was of considerable importance in helping to bring down the Cold War barriers between the USA and the erstwhile USSR.

In short, where the opportunity for peace exists, the success or failure of any peace-promoting strategy often will be critically dependent upon the quality of the diplomacy that implements it. It is possible to have a strong desire to promote peace and to undermine it completely through incompetent diplomacy. Skilful diplomacy, on the other hand, can play a crucial role in facilitating war prevention measures.

Ultimately, however, an awful lot is dependent upon those who wish for peace, at both elite and popular levels, being both far-sighted and courageous enough to stand up for it, both in the case of their own states and that of others. If governments or individual arms of government are left to their own devices, for example, they can all too easily pursue simple economically or politically motivated external policies that ignore the requirements for peace in the regions at which they are directed. But the problems of judgement that confront those wanting to prevent war can be enormous. For example, one of the often stated ironies that afflicts international politics is that in order to preserve the wider peace, it may sometimes be necessary to go to war to try and extinguish conflicts that may spread if left unattended. No one interested in promoting peace should ever embark upon the task with the illusion that their work will be easy. But the slaughter that has occurred in both Rwanda and the former Yugoslavia during the 1990s demonstrates graphically just how vital it is that someone should make the effort.

The next chapter will examine in more detail the possible roles which the UN can play in peace-keeping among other things and will look also at the role that can be played by international law in the protection of innocent human lives.

Chapter 12

The problem of 'murderous' and 'aggressive' regimes –

the role of international law and the United Nations

by Steven Wheatley

with Peter J. Anderson

Introduction

Considerable power lies in the hands of most governments within the territories which they rule, subject only to the limitations which global interfusion, the political systems within which they operate, their consciences and international law may place upon them. Many of the avoidable problems in the world may be laid at the feet of governments, and in particular a small number of 'rogue' regimes who exhibit apparent contempt for the rules of the international community. Examples of rogue behaviour may be found in the 'aggressive' policies of Serbia and Iraq during the early 1990s, by which these states utilised military means outside their own borders to achieve political ends, or in the internally repressive policies of what became known as the 'murderous' regimes of Burma, Iraq and Indonesia during the early 1990s, which led many to feel that the governments in question held the lives and well-being of their own people in contempt. This chapter will examine the extent to which international law and the United Nations are able – and might become more able – to control the practices of such regimes, focusing in particular upon recent developments in the post-Cold War era. The Change Map will be brought into the discussion as appropriate.

How has international law developed as a means of controlling the actions of governments?

International law, like all legal systems, is at its most basic a system of rules. All societies develop rules to regulate the behaviour of their members. The society of states is no different in this respect. International law does differ, however, in that there is no international government, no central elite laying down rules to be followed and providing for punishment for those who break the rules.

So, how are these rules of international law arrived at? They are essentially created by one of two processes, first, the negotiation of international treaties, by which states agree by way of a contract that a certain set of rules will regulate their relations, and second, the evolution of customary international law. Custom is a pattern of behaviour which states engage in because they believe themselves to be legally obliged to do so on the basis of the established practices of the international community. For example, it is a recognised rule of customary international law that states should not use military force against the territory of another. Evidence of this rule is found in the fact that an overwhelming majority do not engage in aggressive acts, and the reaction of third states to such aggression which is invariably negative. By definition, custom is a pattern of behaviour which develops over time.[1]

The first function of any legal system is to promote peace and harmony amongst its members. Only when this is achieved can more sophisticated rules be agreed upon. The development of international law has been driven to a significant degree by states attempting to establish an international order in which they could peacefully coexist, particularly in the postwar, United Nations era.

The earliest limitations on the right of states to resort to force were based upon the 'just war' theories, which held, for example, that war could only be waged if all other means of resolving a disagreement had been tried and had failed, and that it must only be employed in pursuit of a 'right intention'. The period up until the seventeenth century was dominated by 'just' wars, fought allegedly on the basis of such principles, until the Peace of Westphalia in 1648. This marked the conclusion of the Thirty Years War and the end of papal supremacy over Christian nations and ushered in a period when the notion of state sovereignty and independence began to predominate over the rules of international law. At its extreme, this concept of sovereignty gave states the power to wage war without restriction in pursuit of national self-interest. The sheer destructiveness and massive loss of life involved in the pursuit of war has led states, during the twentieth century, to vigorously renew their efforts to devise an international legal system in which they could coexist peacefully. The League of Nations placed procedural steps in the way of states resorting to war, whilst the Pact of Paris, of 1928, demanded that states abandon the right to wage war as an instrument of national policy. The failure of these attempts was evident in the coming of the Second World War.

What changes did the United Nations system bring?

The United Nations, established in 1945, radically developed on the principles which had been laid down in the Covenant of the League of Nations. The primary purpose of the United Nations, as set out in its Charter, is to

> maintain international peace and security, and to that end to take effective collective measures for the prevention and removal of threats to the peace, and for the suppression of acts of aggression or other breaches of the peace, and to bring about by peaceful means, and in conformity with the principle of justice and international law, adjustments or settlement of international disputes or situations which might lead to a breach of the peace. (Article 1)

The main prohibition on aggressive force is contained within Article 2(4), which provides that force shall neither be threatened nor used 'against the territorial integrity or political independence of any state or in any manner inconsistent with the purposes of the United Nations'. The reference to force rather than war is intended to prohibit all armed conflicts rather than merely those technically considered wars by the international community. Under international law 'force' includes aggressions defined by the UN General Assembly as invasions or attacks by the armed forces of one state on the territory of another state, any military occupation, however temporary, bombardment, the blockading of the ports of a coastal state, and the sending of armed bands by or on behalf of a state to carry out acts of armed force against another state which are of such gravity as to qualify as an 'aggression'. The General Assembly further declared that an act of aggression 'constitutes a crime against the peace for which there is responsibility under international law' (General Assembly Resolution on the Definition of Aggression [1974] GA Res 3314). All of the above acts clearly would be caught by most definitions of military force, but lesser acts also have been considered a violation of Article 2(4). The extent of the prohibition on the use of the military can be seen in the Corfu Channel Case (1949) ICJ Rep 4, where the International Court of Justice found that a mine-sweeping operation by British warships in Albanian territorial waters was a violation of Article 2(4). In pronouncing on the case the International Court asserted that 'the alleged right of intervention [was] the manifestation of a policy of force, such as has, in the past, given rise to the most serious abuses . . . [and] would be reserved for the most powerful state'.

Claims of exceptions to the blanket prohibition in Article 2(4), for example in the context of rescue missions (Entebbe, 1976, Tehran, 1989), have met with little international support. Equally, a number of superpower interventions have been regarded as having been contrary to international law. Soviet interventions in Hungary, 1956, Czechoslovakia, 1968, Afghanistan, 1979 and United States military action in the Dominican Republic in 1965 all provide graphic examples of military incursions by superpowers into the affairs of smaller states within their spheres of influence. These interventions may be seen as demonstrating the maxim 'might is right', and were often followed by attempts to justify them. In the case of Czechoslovakia Brezhnev, the then Soviet leader, declared that a socialist state enjoyed sovereign rights of independence subject to the proviso that it could not divert from 'the true path of socialism'. Similarly the United States alluded to the doctrine of limited sovereignty in its intervention in the Dominican Republic, when President Johnson noted that the USA could not allow another socialist state (after Cuba) to establish itself in the Western hemisphere. Both these claims are clearly invalid and no evidence exists for the acceptance of such rights under international law.

Even with the legal prohibition on the use of force states require the right to defend themselves once attacked by an aggressive neighbour. This right is now contained in Article 51, which provides that, 'Nothing in the present Charter shall impair the inherent right of the individual or collective self-defence if an armed attack occurs until the Security Council has taken the necessary measures to maintain international peace and security.' If the Charter is read carefully it would appear to give Article 51 only a temporary role and to determine that the preeminent responsibility for dealing with aggressive acts lies with the Security Council.

It is interesting to see how states have interpreted the Article in practice. The 1982 Falkland Islands incident where, following the Argentine invasion of the British-claimed islands, the United Kingdom despatched a large naval task force to the South Atlantic, may be taken as an example in this regard. The Security Council called on the two parties to find a peaceful and diplomatic solution to the territorial dispute (SCRes 502). The Argentines believed this resolution meant that the issue was now the exclusive concern of the Security Council, and that the British could not act alone under the provisions of Article 51. The British government did not accept this view and argued that the right of self-defence under Article 51 would only be lost where the Council had taken *effective* action, that is repelled the aggression, which SCRes 502 clearly had not done. Similar arguments were heard in relation to the allied action in liberating Kuwait from the Iraqi intervention. The allies believed that until Iraq was removed from Kuwait, neither Kuwaiti rights under Article 51, nor the rights of collective self-defence of the United States and other intervening forces were lost to the Security Council, where the Soviet veto could prevent the authorisation of military enforcement measures.

The right of self-defence can also be described as an *inherent* right, existing independently from Article 51, and on this basis it has been argued that the Security Council arms embargo on the former Yugoslav republic of Bosnia is unlawful as it denies Bosnia its inherent right to defend itself.

The UN Charter, like many legal documents, is open to different interpretations, as the discussion above illustrates. Another demonstration of this fact can be seen with regard to the notion of anticipatory self-defence. It has been argued by many international lawyers that the right of self-defence, contained within Article 51, is limited to circumstances where an armed attack has occurred already (see, for example, M. Akehurst, *A Modern Introduction to International Law*, London, HarperCollins, 1991, p. 262). This limitation is designed to avoid, among other things, spurious claims of self-defence being used to mask aggression. Not all international lawyers accept this interpretation of Article 51, however, and it has been suggested by some states that such a restriction is in any case unreasonable and one that bears little relevance to the needs of the real world of contemporary international politics. Given the speed of modern military assault, particularly in the nuclear age, then if the state waits until an attack is under way, it may not get the opportunity to utilise the right of self-defence, and it is interesting that, in 1967, the United Nations refused to condemn Israel for utilising anticipatory self-defence (i.e. attacking first those whom it believed to be about to attack it) following the blockade of the Israeli port of Eilat, the conclusion of a military pact between Egypt and Jordan, the eviction of a United Nations peace-keeping force and the mobilisation of Egyptian troops. Following on from all of the above, it is useful to look in a little more detail at the Security Council and, in particular, the question of what has been its past role in preventing aggression and what is its current role.

The Council is composed of fifteen members, five of whom, at the moment, are permanent, the USA, the UK, Russia, China and France, and ten elected periodically by the General Assembly. The five permanent members all possess the power of veto, that is, no resolution may pass if one of the five votes against. The Council's real powers are to be found under Chapter VII of the UN Charter, which gives it the ability to demand the implementation of economic sanctions or military force where it determines there to be a 'threat to, or breach of, international peace and security'. Originally it was intended that the Council would have a standing military force at its disposal but disputes within the permanent five prevented this happening. Thus the Security Council has relied upon the authorising of states to use force on its behalf. In the case of Korea in 1950, the UN was able to authorise states to come to the defence of South Korea following the attack from the North. The absence of the Soviet Union from the Security Council meant that no veto was exercised and the United States was able to bend the Council to its will. However, following that action, the operation of the veto by the two ideologically opposed global superpowers for many years largely prevented the Council from effectively undertaking its role. Stalemate occurred on many issues, and the Cold War was fought out to varying degrees around the globe.[2]

The successful nature of the UN-sanctioned operation to free Kuwait in 1991, which benefited from a new cooperative relationship between the erstwhile Soviet Union and the USA, inevitably caused people to start asking if this was a fresh beginning for the Security Council. Certainly, in theory at least, the ending of the Cold War has given the UN the opportunity to fulfil its intended role which it demonstrated in its response to the Iraqi invasion of Kuwait. Here, an anti-Iraq coalition was able to hold together under the banner of the United Nations, declaring that aggressive acts should not bring rewards to those who engage in them. The invasion by Iraq was followed by a declaration by the Council that the aggression threatened international peace and security, and when demands for a withdrawal were not met, mandatory sanctions were imposed which effectively isolated Iraq from the rest of the world. Again the Iraqi forces refused to withdraw and resolution 678 followed, authorising states to use 'all necessary means to uphold and implement Security Council resolution 660 [demanding a withdrawal from Kuwait]'. This was the green light for the commencement of Operation Desert Storm, which culminated in the forced withdrawal of the Iraqi military forces.

However, as has been seen already in the previous chapter, such relatively effective action is not necessarily the new norm for the Council. It has, amongst other initiatives following on from the 'high point' reached during the Gulf War, authorised the use of force to restore democratic government in Haiti and has also authorised limited military action against the aggressive policies of the Bosnian Serbs in the former Yugoslavia, and some military operations have indeed been conducted on its behalf. But prior to the massive UN/NATO air strikes of late August and September 1995 the UN and NATO forces were little more than spectators at the slaughter of thousands during the Balkan wars.

In Change Map terms, the new situation in which the West and the erstwhile Soviet Union, followed by its Russian successor on the Council, have been prepared wherever possible to cooperate rather than obstruct each other's attempts to initiate UN interventions has come about to a substantial degree because of the opportunity factor of the rapid decline and ultimate collapse of the USSR. This has produced relative ideological compatibility between the United States, Britain and France on the one hand and Russia, as the inheritor of the Soviet Union's Security Council seat, on the other. This, together with the disappearance of most of the Cold War tensions and the fact that all Security Council members, even China, now have a stake in the successful operation of the global capitalist economy, has produced a much greater compatibility of interests within the Council than has existed at any time during its previous history.

However, while US President George Bush was quick to talk of a 'New World Order' in which the UN would play a leading role after the Gulf War, a cursory perusal of the Change Map suggests, as experience in the Balkans has proved so far, that there are still substantial actual and potential limitations upon the Council's effectiveness. There is, for example, still a significant ideological gulf between the declaredly Marxist People's Republic of China and the other members, and one would expect that that in itself would produce greatly different stances on issues involving potential Council interventions where Marxist values clash seriously with capitalist ones. Equally, perceived pressures on individual Council member governing elites from BTC elites or, where relevant, their electorates, might cause them to veto or obstruct UN intervention in particular issues. In the years immediately prior to the 1991 Gulf War, for example, it is known that powerful business interests in the USA had been exerting considerable pressure on the American government and Congress in favour of a tolerant approach towards Iraq, despite Saddam Hussein's massive use of lethal chemical weapons against Kurdish civilians.[3] As far as the electorates of democratic states are concerned, one would anticipate that their voting power will make governing elites generally at the very least cautious about sanctioning interventions which might involve their own forces in actions which ultimately could damage them at the polls. Such damage could be the result of an inability to meet domestic policy pledges as a result of the high costs of a particular intervention, or of becoming ensnared in a situation where effective action is difficult and television news services are presented only with the negative images of a series of frustrations and humiliations and an unwelcome stream of body bags being returned home. The United States, for example, still remembers its disastrous part in the 1983 Western intervention in the Lebanon when 241 marines were killed at one go by a suicide bomber. The French also lost 58 soldiers on the same day.[4] It was the fear that such disasters may have been repeated that cautioned the Western powers about becoming directly embroiled *on the ground* in the Balkan wars after they had missed the opportunity for what may well have been relatively low-cost, effective preventative intervention just prior to, and indeed, shortly after, their outbreak, and it is in the former Yugoslavia where the continuing limitations on the UN's effectiveness have been illustrated most graphically. Had Bosnia, like Kuwait, been sitting on a wealth of oil reserves, of course, then one suspects that the West would have overcome its fears . . .

Cultural, economic, political or ethnic ties can also create important specific interests for Council members in areas in which an intervention is proposed, and potentially can cause affected members to be cautious about such interventions or even to veto them. During the early part of 1994, for example, the Russian attitude towards NATO intervention in Bosnia on behalf of the UN was complicated greatly by historical ties with the Serbs and by the fact that, traditionally, Eastern Europe had been seen as within the erstwhile Soviet Union's sphere of influence, even though Yugoslavia had pursued an independent line under Tito and his successors.[5]

On top of all of this, opportunity factors, such as changes of government within members of the Council, can have a significant impact on its effectiveness. An incoming government in the United States, for example, might have little interest in foreign affairs and be intent on directing all of its efforts towards the success of its domestic policies, unless American interests overseas are so seriously and directly threatened that it becomes impossible not to intervene in the relevant part of the globe. Such an attitude might be the result of the pressures which the new governing elite perceives from a domestic popular opinion clamouring for more or less exclusive attention to its economic and social problems and for foreigners to be left to sort out their own messes. To a degree the Clinton administration in the USA has been accused of operating in such a manner as the above, with its keenness to avoid committing combat troops overseas unless internal pressures or external circumstances made this inevitable. Where such attitudes become entrenched within a member as significant as the United States, it may well be that the Council is able to act effectively only where commonly perceived imperatives present themselves.

How has international law attempted to ensure the effective protection of human rights?

Traditionally, international law did not concern itself with the rights of individuals. International law was the law which applied as between states. Again, the United Nations ushered in a new era in this regard, declaring one of its purposes to be the promotion of respect for human rights and fundamental freedoms. The protection of human rights guaranteed under the Charter has largely been taken under the wing of the Human Rights Commission, which has drafted the more important human rights treaties, and also has played an important role in highlighting and criticising human rights abuses.

There are certain human rights obligations which are deemed to be common to all states, such as the prohibitions against genocide, racial discrimination and violations of the right to life. Breach of one of these rights may bring condemnation from an organ of the United Nations, be that the Security Council, General Assembly or Human Rights Commission. Where a state has agreed to undertake certain obligations with respect to human rights under a treaty, failure to do so will be deemed a breach of international law.

Over the period of the Charter a number of universal, bilateral, regional and multilateral treaties have developed in the field of human rights. They cover what have traditionally been described as the three generations of human rights: civil and political; economic, social and cultural; and third generation rights.[6] These human rights treaties, in general, apply one or more of the following three methods of implementation: a system of state reports, state-on-state complaints and individual petitions. States traditionally have been reluctant to agree to the granting of 'excessive' implementation mechanisms under the treaties, and often the agreed mechanism will be the one which is felt to be the least contentious, and which will be likely to cause the least embarrassment. Nevertheless, it is fair to say that these treaties have been crucial to the development of a greater respect for human rights by the majority of states over the period of the Charter.

At this point it is important to reemphasise an important difference between national legal systems and international law. In any national system, violation of a particular law will involve the courts, possibly the police, and a sanction may be imposed for violating that law. There is no international police force or international court with the power to make judgements which must be obeyed. So, what pressures are there to ensure compliance with an international obligation? First, it must be noted that international legal obligations are observed by and large, and that serious breaches are rare. But what is there to prevent a government of a state from violating its international obligations if it so wishes? Given the nature of international law, it might appear that ultimately a state may violate its international legal obligations with seeming impunity.

Where a state refuses to comply with a specific human rights obligation created by a treaty to which it is a signatory, the correct recourse for states which wish to rectify this situation is through the mechanisms provided for by the convention. Where this proves inadequate states may respond accordingly. Their response may take the form of some act (e.g. non-compliance with a treaty or other obligation) that if committed would be an international wrong, were it not for the prior international wrong, that is, the non-compliance with the international convention. In relation to violations of general international law, a state may be entitled to 'intervene' in the situation, where it can show itself to be directly affected or acting on behalf of the international community. This intervention may include political pressure or economic coercion, as in the US economic response to the suppression of the Solidarity movement in Poland. Further, humanitarian assistance may be granted to the affected population, particularly in times of conflict. Military intervention may now be deemed to be appropriate in the most serious cases of human rights abuses and humanitarian suffering, although, as will be seen shortly, this used not to be the case. Where intervention is deemed to be appropriate, it must be necessary and proportionate. Ultimately, most legal systems will rely on force and coercion to enforce their rules. Is this appropriate for the international community? Should it be appropriate? Military intervention creates many ethical and legal questions. If an army invades another country does it not violate the rights of the people its invasion is designed to protect? Who is to judge what degree of abuse of human rights will trigger this so-called right of 'humanitarian intervention'? For our purposes the question is simply; is it legal under international law?

To what extent does international law allow the use of military force to protect human rights?

Whatever importance international law has placed on the protection of human rights there existed a general consensus, during much of the period of the Charter's existence, that military force should not be used by outside powers to protect them. Certainly during the Cold War era, with its incumbent geopolitical tensions, it was the attitude of most states that military force was not appropriate to end even the most massive violations of human rights. Vietnam's 1978 invasion of Cambodia to terminate the period in office of the murderous regime of Pol Pot, during which one in eight of the country's eight million people had died, was condemned by the international community and resulted in Vietnam's isolation for the period of the occupation. Similarly, General Assembly resolutions implicitly condemned India for its intervention in Pakistan in 1971, which followed widespread human rights abuses by the Pakistani army against the people of East Pakistan, and resulted in the establishment of the state of Bangladesh.

The basis of this international inactivity was the doctrine of non-intervention. A guiding principle of the postwar development of international law, the doctrine was used by states to prevent the effective implementation and enforcement of the developing human rights provisions. The doctrine demands that states refrain in their actions from dictatorial interference in the affairs of another state. Governments were able to argue even that any criticism of their human rights records was an interference in their internal affairs and thus not legitimate under international law. However, a correct reading of the rule of non-intervention is that criticism of a state's poor human rights record may be bad diplomatic manners, but it does not violate any rule of international law.

Recent events in Iraq, Liberia, Somalia, the former Yugoslavia, Haiti and Rwanda indicate an increasing acceptance of the view that force should now be used to ensure the protection of fundamental human rights where this seems appropriate.

The Security Council, which has the primary responsibility in this area, may employ its wide powers under Chapter VII of the UN Charter to use military force to protect human rights. Security Council resolutions authorising the use of force in Somalia and Bosnia to facilitate the effective supply of humanitarian aid demonstrate a new recognition by the international community of the practical assistance required to prevent large-scale human tragedy in times of conflict, and a new willingness by the Security Council to authorise such action.

What action can regional bodies undertake?

Where the Security Council is unwilling or unable to act, the international community has recognised the competence of regional bodies or a group of states to undertake military action in support of human rights. This was seen in the protection of the Iraqi Kurdish and Shi'ite populations following the ending of the Gulf War. The successful US-led allied campaign to remove Iraqi forces from Kuwait was followed by uprisings against the regime of Saddam Hussein, to which the Iraqis responded with a brutal suppression of the civilian population. The suffering of the Kurdish minority was well-documented in the world media, but calls by the Security Council for Iraq to cease the oppression were ignored by Saddam Hussein. It became increasingly clear that Iraq was immune to the pressures of world public opinion and that only the use of military force could ensure the protection of the Kurdish civilian population. Allied forces present in the area as a regional military actor moved into northern Iraq to establish safe-havens for the Kurds, which were later taken over by the United Nations.

Another intervention to prevent massive violations of human rights, the result of internal strife, occurred in Liberia. By July 1990, the insurrection against the regime of President Doe appeared close to the point of success. The rebel army of Charles Taylor, the National Patriotic Front of Liberia (NPFL) and the splinter group led by Prince Johnson, had advanced on the capital, Monrovia, with little opposition. The killings which had taken place had largely been committed against civilians, most notably the massacre of five hundred in a church compound in Monrovia by government soldiers. The sheer terror felt by the civilian population led the great majority of Liberians either to flee the country or to be displaced within Liberia. Seeing the deterioration of the situation, with substantial human rights violations, and the breakdown of any semblance of civil order, the United Nations and the Organisation of African Unity agreed that the conflict was a regional problem to be solved by the states of West Africa. The Economic Community of West African States (ECOWAS), in its response to the crisis, persuaded the tottering Doe regime to accept a peace proposal for a cease-fire and the deployment of a regional peace-keeping force together with a political solution based on a government of national unity. It was then announced that a peace-keeping force would enter the country. The response of the Security Council was to implicitly condone the actions of the ECOWAS force, by determining that 'the deterioration of the situation in Liberia constitutes a threat to international peace and security, particularly in West Africa as a whole' and to condemn attacks on ECOWAS troops. The Council then used its powers under Chapter VII to impose a mandatory embargo on all arms supplies to Liberia, other than those for the sole use of ECOWAS forces.

Security Council approval for such regional action provides a vital legitimating function, whether that approval be explicit, as in the case of the Security Council's approval of the role of the Conference on Security and Co-operation in Europe in the former Yugoslavia, or implicit, as in Liberia.

Conclusion

As the international community proceeds uneasily into its so-called 'New World Order', governments are tending to be more homogeneous. Most now enjoy mixed economies, engage to one extent or another in free trade, and there is an increasing move towards democratisation. With notable areas of exception, the world is for the moment at least a less tense place, with the ending or at least downgrading of a number of long-standing conflicts (the ending of the Cold War, the cease-fire in Northern Ireland, the achievement of peace in South Africa and Mozambique, for example) and the individual can feel more secure within it (although the comments made at the beginning of the previous chapter need to be borne in mind here). The problems as such at the moment mainly are created by the 'rogue' element, those governments who do not respect international law, either because of their aggressive policies outside their borders, or because of their 'murderous' activities within. In theory, the United Nations, through the Security Council, appears now more able to fulfil its given role, by which aggressive acts can result in effective action to remedy the situation and punishment of the wrongdoer. But as has been shown already through an application of the Change Map, there are still potentially considerable limitations on the UN's effectiveness in this regard.

The latter conclusion applies to attempts to curb the actions of inwardly murderous regimes as well as outwardly aggressive ones. Nevertheless, the picture is not as disappointing as it first might seem. For example, however inadequate the provisions for its implementation may seem, it must be noted that, in the past forty years, there has developed a relatively successful system for the protection of the human rights of the individual. In the 1960s and 1970s the number of states regularly engaged in human rights abuses was large. Today the serious abuses are well-documented but more limited in number. The present system prefers to 'encourage' states to adopt international standards in the treatment of their own people rather than to use sanctions or force, although, as has been shown, force may now be selected as an option.

Despite the above-mentioned improvement, there remains the problem of 'rogue' regimes engaged in serious abuses of the human rights of their peoples. There is little comfort for Kurds, Somalis or Liberians in the knowledge that the protection of and respect for human rights globally is improving if they are suffering greatly at the hands of their governments or those in power in situations where the gun and warlords rule. Only direct action when all else has failed can ensure that massive humanitarian tragedies do not occur. This action should ideally be taken through the United Nations, on behalf of the international community, or where the UN is unable to act, for whatever reason, then regional agencies acting under Chapter VIII of the Charter, or individual states acting collectively, should undertake the operation.

However, an application of the Change Map reveals again the same serious potential limitations upon the effectiveness as 'interveners' of both the UN and regional agencies as were outlined earlier in the chapter when examining the question of the Security Council's 'new beginning'. These were perhaps most graphically illustrated in Rwanda in 1994, where the Security Council, with the partial exception of the French (at the time of writing, in August 1995, the French government's role in Rwanda during the 1994 genocide is the subject of a number of claims and counter-claims) did virtually nothing to intervene and prevent the mass slaughter of the Tutsi civilian population by Hutu death squads.[7] The potential domestic political costs of such an intervention for those carrying it out, as suggested by the then recent somewhat messy US–UN action in strife-torn Somalia, together with its likely economic cost at a time when Western and Russian governments were trying to keep military expenditure down, and the lack of any substantial interests in the state concerned on the part of most Security Council members, meant that there was no enthusiasm for direct involvement while the war was being fought except in the French case. The usefulness of the French intervention was itself partially undermined by the fact that they were forced to go in alone to create safe areas in a state where they were distrusted by the Tutsi rebels because of their past involvement with the Hutu majority. Again, therefore, it is apparent that the effectiveness or even the possibility of Security Council intervention can only have a chance of being guaranteed where common imperatives are at stake. Where the democratic members of the Council are concerned, one might argue that a substantial part of the responsibility for creating such imperatives lies with the electorates of those members.

While the above conclusions might sound more than a little pessimistic concerning the effectiveness of the UN as a protector of humanity from internally or externally directed state violence, it should be remembered that the UN is an evolving, not a static, institution. In the wake of Rwanda there are discussions taking place to try and persuade some states which maintain rapid reaction forces of their own to put these at the disposal of the Security Council in similar future emergencies. In addition, it is often forgotten that the fact that the UN intervened with limited military force in Bosnia, for example, and ultimately helped save lives through its involvement, is a considerable improvement on the situation that prevailed prior to its existence, when the people of Sarajevo, for example, would probably have been left entirely to fend for themselves. Should governments in the future increasingly come to feel that their electorates expect them to turn the UN into a more effective force for peace and human rights preservation, then the embryonic UN policeman may yet be given a more commanding truncheon, and global respect for international law and human rights may increase as a consequence. But, as stated previously, before this happens the Security Council members have to perceive that imperatives, or at the very least, important electoral or other interests, are at stake.

The future –
can it be anticipated and changed?

> Margot appeared in the kitchen doorway. . . . 'Father has received a call-
> up notice from the SS,' she whispered . . . I was stunned . . . everyone
> knows what that means. Visions of concentration camps and lonely cells
> raced through my head. How could we let Father go to such a fate?[1]

After his liberation from a Nazi concentration camp, Otto Frank dedicated
the rest of his life to spreading the symbolic message of his daughter Anne's
diary, from which the above quotation is taken, in the hope that the tragedy
of her death and that of the millions of others who perished as a result of
'ethnic cleansing' during the Second World War might never be repeated.
Yet, in the foreword to the current edition of that same diary, Rabbi
Hugo Gryn writes, 'racists rampage again in Europe, "ethnic cleansing" is
talked about and practised, and in a host of violent conflicts God's image is
desecrated and the memory and sacrifice of Anne Frank and her generation
are betrayed'.[2]

The slaughter and atrocities that recently have stained the reputation of
peoples in territories as diverse as those of the former Yugoslavia and
Rwanda are in both cases rooted in previous ethnic conflicts. Aside from
the issue of how poorly the international community, such as it is,
responded initially to the mass murder and torture that was occurring in
the wars in Rwanda and the former Yugoslavia, is the question of why
was it not all foreseen. Why were steps not taken – by those states with the
necessary power and supposed commitment to humane values – to prevent
past pogroms recurring in the future?

It is the future and the extent to which it can be anticipated and changed
in the context of international politics that will be the primary focus of this
chapter.

The fact that there are serious problems that make prediction difficult
has been mentioned already in relevant parts of the book. When discussing

the prospects for the European Union it was made clear that such problems did not necessarily make the anticipation of the future an impossible task. One method of reducing them was explained and examples provided of how it might be used. Given that this is a method that can be applied to trends and issues around the globe, there are obviously questions to be answered as to why often it is *not* used to look at the way in which particular hatreds, movements, power balances or state ambitions might develop. Such questions are important because its non-use in specific instances might help explain why some of the appalling tragedies that have cursed the twentieth century have been allowed to happen without many of those in political power anticipating them until it has been too late to take effective action. The next section will tackle the questions involved. But even if, as that section will re-emphasise, it is possible to anticipate future dangers to some extent, there is still the need to try and change the course of political developments in order to avert them. Therefore, an attempt will be made also to identify what is most fundamental in determining the extent to which governments with the necessary power to affect global and/or regional developments are prepared to countenance or themselves promote such attempted change.

However, while governments are important in many change 'equations', it has been emphasised throughout the book so far that there is a wide range of additional factors that can be involved. Change frequently is not something that can happen simply because a particular government's politicians (or, for that matter, powerful pressure groups) wish it to do so. This is due to the complexity of the policy environment and the many change-relevant factors within it that often face those wishing to bring about change. In addition, therefore, some of the permutations of such factors that can come into play that have been outlined in previous chapters, together with their implications for the ease or otherwise of achieving change, will be re-examined. The question will then be addressed once more as to whether or not it is possible to create a future for the world that is more humane and peaceful than its past – one in which, for example, dangers within particular regions of the type of genocide that has occurred during the 1990s in Rwanda and the former Yugoslavia can be both anticipated and averted – despite all the complications that can be involved in trying to change the course of political events that have not yet occurred.

Anticipating the future

It used to be an old media maxim that a week is a long time in politics. Certainly, there have been strong biases amongst some against trying to think too far into the future as far as international affairs are concerned. The British Foreign Office, for example, used to be famous for undermining the forward planning units which politicians set up within it by such unsubtle stratagems as locating them in inferior and distant outposts of its empire of offices, where they could be easily isolated and quietly forgotten.[3] Equally, however, there have been those who have gone to great lengths to try and anticipate the future, people such as Paul Kennedy with his *Preparing for the Twenty-First Century* (London, HarperCollins, 1993) or Lester Thurow with his more narrowly focused *Head to Head: The Coming Economic Battle Among Japan, Europe and America* (London, Nicholas Brealey Publishing, 1992). What can be said with reasonable confidence is that as far as political futures are concerned, the only certainty is that much will remain uncertain.

The reason for this, as pointed out previously, is that political science has made only limited progress in the business of prediction and existing evidence suggests that this situation is unlikely to change.[4] The question arises therefore as to how can the future be anticipated and planned for with any degree of effectiveness at all.

Part of the answer to this fundamentally important question was provided in Chapter 9, where it was emphasised that what policy-makers can do is to draw up likely scenarios relating to particular global or regional issues and to try and anticipate what might happen within them. As a result, if one or more such scenarios becomes a reality, then the government or governments concerned should be able to react in a much more rapid and coherent manner than would otherwise be possible. It was pointed out that even if only part of a scenario is realised, as is frequently the case, to have thought that part out in advance means that the policy-makers concerned should be in a much better position to try and formulate effective policy than would otherwise be the case. It was then shown how this can be done with regard to the possible future development of a number of foreign policy issues relating to the European Union. Whether governments individually, or together within international organisations, decide to engage in such scenario construction with regard to possible future issues and dangers is dependent upon whether or not they are *concerned* about the development of those issues. For example, despite the continuing prevalence of global poverty, those governments in both the developed and the less developed world which are most able to help have so far not chosen to respond to the situation on anything like the scale that is needed to deal with it. One might assume, therefore, that unless they are effectively pressurised in the manner suggested in Chapter 7, they will not greatly bother themselves to construct scenarios of what might be done to alleviate continuing mass starvation should this indeed prove to be a feature of the twenty-first century.

With regard to possible future wars that might directly affect the core interests of particular states, however, it is much more likely that scenario-building will occur. During the Cold War, for example, both the Americans and the Soviets had highly developed scenarios in place to help them deal with particular conflict situations should they arise.[5] It has been observed frequently that the problem for the peoples of Rwanda and the former Yugoslavia was that prior to the outbreak of their wars, the major powers did not perceive core interests as being at stake in any conflicts that might occur within them. This in turn meant little in the way of scenario-building and, consequently, even less in the way of ideas of how to react effectively to the Balkan crisis, for example, when it started to become critical during the early 1990s. By 1995, however, scenario construction relating to the situation in the former Yugoslavia had become a preoccupation within the news media at least. Just before the Croatian attack on Krajina in August 1995, for example, *The Economist* set down some concise thoughts on the likelihood of that attack and of other related Croatian moves occurring. The following is an extract:

'Croatia's president, Franjo Tudjman, has mobilised 160,000 troops who could attack Krajina in a pincer movement; about 50,000 Croatian Serb soldiers are braced to defend the statelet, which broke from Croatia four years ago. The two sides were to talk peace in Geneva on August 3rd, but the United Nations was gloomy about the prospects of either accepting a compromise that would allow the Krajina Serbs autonomy within Croatia, and stave off the threatened Croat assault. The West is urging restraint on Mr Tudjman, but his recent attack on the Bosnian Serbs met, if not a green light, an amber one from an outside world glad to see someone else save Bihac.

What are Mr Tudjman's long term plans? He does not want Serbs in Bihac, because they would make it harder for him to recapture Krajina, his immediate priority. But does he really want to strengthen Bosnia's Muslims, with whom his dependents, the Bosnian Croats, are linked in an uneasy federation? He might, if he envisages the federation as a buffer under his tutelage between Croatia and Serbia – rather as Syria treats Lebanon as a client and a buffer between itself and Israel. But Mr Tudjman may hanker for something more: a carve-up of Bosnia between a greater Croatia and a greater Serbia. This was a scheme that he and Slobodan Milosevic, the president of Serbia, mooted in 1991.

Whether Mr Tudjman attacks Krajina may depend on whether he believes he could do so without provoking Mr Milosevic to join the fray. The Serbian president's intentions remain as obscure as those of Mr Tudjman. He is, at present, the very model of statesmanlike moderation.'[6]

What became apparent soon after the attack on Krajina had occurred was that the 'amber light' that the United States had given Croatia had been based on some vigorous scenario construction of its own. It was telling Britain, France and Germany that it had foreseen within Croatia's action the prospect of at the very least relieving the previously relentless pressure of the Bosnian Serbs on Bosnian government-held territory, and at most, the possibility of so changing the strategic situation in the Balkans that an over-all peace deal might be facilitated. Criticism of the Clinton administration's Bosnian policy within Congress, among other things, had by 1995 made the situation in the former Yugoslavia a sufficiently strong interest for the US government for it to spend serious time building scenarios around it and looking at their implications.

So, to sum up, scenario construction, while hardly a foolproof means of dealing with the uncertainties of the future, at least offers the prospect of a more effective response to those uncertainties than would be possible in its absence. However, in the most powerful states, the degree to which it occurs will be dependent upon the extent to which governments and other inter-national actors consider or are persuaded or forced to perceive particular future possibilities to be significant interests. It is worth remembering also that in the smaller or poorer states, the degree to which it can occur may well be constrained heavily by budgetary or expertise limitations.

Finally, to bring in a point that will be developed more fully at the end of the chapter, it should be remembered that groups other than governments can be influential in trying to initiate change and their effectiveness also theoretically should be enhanced if they engage in a process of relevant scenario-building.

Scenario construction can of course be used as part of the process of risk estimation. Risk calculation is something to which attention has been given in a variety of academic disciplines, and a number of different methods of attempting it have been evolved within the latter relating to everything from derivatives markets to surgical procedures.[7] Thinking back to the beginning of the chapter, it is essential to note that the processes used for estimating the risks to specified core interests of policy-makers posed by particular future possibilities *are crucial in determining the extent to which governments will try and change the course of future political developments in order to avert those possibilities.* (The core interests themselves are the most fundamental determining factor of course.) They are important simply because they play a crucial role in shaping the key variable of policy-makers' *perceptions* of such risks. Different processes can produce different risk pictures. The degree to which something that may be described as a future danger to humankind or sections of humankind is responded to by governments therefore is often going to be significantly dependent upon such processes.

There are two possible strategies for risk calculation which usefully can be outlined here, purely to demonstrate the substantial differences of approach that can exist, and to show some of the consequences of this. However their purely illustrative nature must be emphasised, given that there is no 'standardised' method of calculating risks that is used across the state system.

First, in the manner of a judge and jury, one can simply look at the balance of evidence for and against a risk revealed by a particular scenario being highly likely, quite likely, merely possible, or highly unlikely to occur. There is no guaranteed method for approximating accuracy in this regard and any estimate that is made on the basis of such evidence will be highly subjective, given the absence of any means of achieving objectivity within policy science at the moment.[8] All that can be done is to base such estimations on the most thorough research and analysis of the available evidence for and against particular likelihoods that circumstances and resources permit, taking care in so doing to establish appropriate parameters for comparative purposes and to make all relevant assumptions explicit.

A second strategy would take this kind of exercise a stage further and acknowledge those factors in such estimations which are believed likely to prove the least reliable, together with any factors which are simply too complex or intangible to build into the calculation. This would be particularly crucial when dealing with those possible serious consequences of, for example, a failure to secure a continuation of the START nuclear arms reduction process which would *seem* initially to be the least likely. This is because in emphasising just how vulnerable to misperceptions and chance probability estimations can be, such a procedure reminds analysts that it is quite possible for them to have 'got things wrong' and that major errors can all too feasibly turn a scenario of the least likely serious consequences into an actual event or series of events.

Where those serious potential consequences are of the *utmost* severity in terms of their impact upon the interests of states, policy-makers and their peoples, then because past experience (together with the arguments above) suggests that it is all too easy to produce predictions which contain significant unreliable elements,[9] *ideally* prudent policy-makers operating within the realist perspective on international relations would ignore any prediction which estimates the chances of those consequences occurring to be low. They would construct their plans on the assumption that they are a real possibility. This is for the simple reason that their very severity, together with history's unfortunate habit of turning some of the most strongly believed probability calculations on their heads,[10] means that it is not wise to take a chance and then find out that one has got things wrong.

The latter procedure can provide a much more comprehensive picture of possible risks that need to be taken seriously than the first, more limited type of risk estimation outlined above and therefore would be likely to cause those governments using it to make more attempts to change the policy environment to avert perceived risks than those using the first method. For example, using the more comprehensive strategy, it could be argued that those scenarios of the possible adverse consequences of failing to achieve further significant European integration which seem to have a low likelihood of being realised from the perspective of the present, but which might be reasonably assumed to be intolerable within the value systems of most EU citizens should they become reality (such as a future war between two or more of the larger current EU member states – a possibility that was used by the French government within the context of this method of risk calculation during its deliberations over the Treaty on European Union), should be treated by member state governments as of equal significance to the most likely scenarios in considering the need or otherwise for further European integration. This is because of their grossly unacceptable nature and history's previously mentioned unfortunate habit of upsetting carefully constructed predictions of what is and what is not likely within the future. If the first strategy was used, however, such scenarios quite probably would be regarded as too unimportant to merit any further attention on the basis of their 'unlikeliness' and it is very possible that no attempt to change the policy environment to guard specifically against them being realised would be made.

Other factors which might affect governments' preparedness to countenance or promote change to avert specific future possibilities and dangers can be identified simply by running through the Change Map checklist and include, obviously, not only governments' definitions of their own interests but also the wide range of political pressures that previous chapters have identified as being likely to affect their perceptions of what is and what is not in their interest. These can include representations from BTC elites, administrative elites and public opinion for example. Whether such pressure will be for or against change will be dependent upon how informed those exerting it are about the future possibilities concerned and how they define their own core interests.

But even if governments decide that they do wish to respond effectively to any anticipated risks by changing the policy environment in ways that will avert them, this can be an extremely difficult business, and as was pointed out at the beginning of this chapter, governments are hardly the sole factors of relevance in 'change equations'. The application of the Change Map throughout the book has emphasised two things from the point of view of those who would want to change or protect from change particular aspects of the international system – whether they be governments, business corporations, individuals or whatever. First, it has shown something of the enormous complexity that often surrounds questions of global and regional change, both with regard to the number and different permutations of Change Map factors that can be involved, and, implicitly, with regard to the close, policy-complicating interlinkages that can exist between different issue areas. Second, it has shown also how change generally is a result of the interaction of several factors rather than of any one factor. The full extent to which this is the case is demonstrated below in order to re-emphasise just how complex a business any attempt at global or regional change can be. The implications of all of this for those who might wish to create what they believe to be a 'safer' world, whether they be governments, groups or individuals, will be examined in the conclusion.

Interaction and global change

Most fundamentally, in the preceding chapters it was shown in several places how change is affected not just by interactions between the various elites *within* states, and between them and the wider populations, but between the same groups *between* states. This was emphasised most strongly with regard to the GATT negotiations at the beginning and was demonstrated again in the chapter on the environment, for example, with regard to the THORP problem in the UK and the nuclear problems of Ukraine.

The theme of interaction was a particular concern of the chapter on the United States and of the two chapters on the future of the European Union. For example, in the chapter on the USA it was shown how American policy on Iraq prior to the outbreak of the Gulf War was determined by interest-driven competition between BTC elites, political elites and administrative elites within the USA's political system. In examining the factors that encouraged continued progress on European integration during the early years of the community idea, the importance of the interaction between relevant opportunity factors, fortune, ideology, interests and elite perceptions of the desirability of change was emphasised. When discussing the reasons for the continued interest of French and German governments in European integration in recent times, the importance of the interaction between interests, fortune and elite perceptions of the desirability of change was stressed. In looking at the circumstances in which the single market might have a negative impact on the integration process, the potential interaction between a relevant opportunity factor, popular perceptions of the desirability of change and ideology was demonstrated.

It is the end of the first European chapter, however, which perhaps most fully demonstrates the scale on which interactions can occur. There, it is pointed out that how much additional integration is possible in the future is dependent potentially upon interactions between, for example, relevant ideologies, interests, imperatives, power factors, fortune, a variety of opportunity factors, and the perceptions of the desirability or otherwise of goals which may change the course of the integrative process which are held at both elite and popular levels across the member states.

In the chapter on the environment, by means of the THORP example, it was shown how environmental questions can involve a complicated interplay between various elite and popular perceptions of the desirability of change, interests and ideologies across several states. In particular it was demonstrated how many environmental issues can only be resolved adequately via imperatives as a result of the variety of perceptions, interests and ideologies which are involved across a large number of state actors. It was illustrated also in discussing the ideas for reform of Al Gore how opportunity factors can create imperatives where none existed previously.

Imperatives were shown to be a key factor in bringing about global change with regard to a number of issues. But what must be realised is that their existence often is reliant upon the prior and continuing interaction of several other Change Map factors. For example, their presence and importance has to be perceived by policy-making groups before they can have an impact on decision-making. Equally, whether one government is able to make a particular course of action into an imperative for another is dependent frequently on the power which it has at its disposal.

It was emphasised that imperatives are not so crucial to the process of change that it is entirely unable to occur without them. For example, at the end of her book, *The Politics of International Economic Relations*, (London, Routledge, 1992) Joan Edelman Spero concludes that there is unlikely to be any significant improvement of the economic lot of people in the less developed world. She argues that this is because the states involved will continue to lack the muscle to make the large-scale global economic reforms necessary to change a substantial redistribution of the world's wealth into an imperative (while not used directly, this term is implied) for the developed states.[11] In the section on global poverty within this study, however, one particular route was shown by which it might be possible to make significant reform a substantial enough interest for real progress to occur, even though an imperative as such would probably not be involved. Equally, it was shown in the chapters on war how the interaction between a variety of opportunity factors, together with elite and electoral perceptions of interests, has made it possible to achieve real progress on nuclear arms control. The important role of interactions between such factors as interests, opportunity factors, ideologies, various elite perceptions and so on in achieving progress on European integration also has been emphasised both in this chapter and in earlier sections of the book. So the overall conclusion would seem to be that imperatives are highly desirable if effective global change is to be achieved, but not absolutely essential in every case.

This discussion in itself highlights dramatically the complexities that can be involved in any attempt to achieve change within the international system, whether the actor involved is a government or an alternative elite group or whatever, but the analysis below shows those complexities to be even greater when issue linkages are taken into account.

Linkages between issues

Before any real changes can be made within the arena of global politics the type of complexity set out above first has to be dealt with. The second factor which implicitly the Change Map has shown to be important for those planning to make or block future changes to aspects of the international system takes the form of linkages between issues. These can complicate yet further the whole change business. Several that can be found within the book are summarised below. Their importance for the process of trying to change the course of political developments in order to avert future dangers is then demonstrated briefly.

First, the linkage between war and global poverty might be noted. In the chapters on poverty, for example, it was emphasised how great had been the cost of wars in Africa and Asia in particular where there had been superpower involvement in one guise or another. Such wars and their after-maths had severely set back the economies of states such as Mozambique, as well as causing additional problems of famine and deprivation for other lands that were already heavily burdened. It was pointed out also how entirely home-grown wars in the less developed world can have an equally destructive economic impact on impoverished states and their people.

On the other hand, in the chapters on Europe it was shown how closely the questions of war and integration have been linked. For example, it was demonstrated how the memories of the huge destructive cost of the Second World War and anxiety to prevent another one played a crucial role in encouraging the establishment of the first European communities. It was shown also how such anxiety has continued to play a role in the integrative process in recent years and how it has helped to facilitate the construction of the present European Union.

It was noted additionally, in the chapter on murderous and aggressive regimes, that the destructiveness and massive loss of life in wars in the twentieth century played a crucial part in prompting a number of states to establish the United Nations and to renew vigorously their efforts to devise an international legal system in which they could coexist peacefully.

In the chapter on the environment it was shown how many environmental issues are closely intertwined with economic developmental issues, and how this interlinkage complicates enormously the environmental debate.

In several of the early chapters it was shown how the process of global interfusion was serving to bring both environmental and poverty issues to the attention of a global audience. In one case, television pictures beamed back to the United States had enabled American viewers to see directly the linkage between the war being fought in Somalia and famine among the local population and in consequence to press their government to intervene to try and relieve the suffering that was being beamed directly into their homes.

Global interfusion was seen also to be playing a role in the European integration process by, for example, bringing Western European economies ever closer together as a result of the operations of multinational business corporations. This example encapsulated neatly the intimate linkage that can exist between many economic and political issues, given that it was later shown how degrees of political integration can follow on directly from economic integration.

What all of this means is that in order to bring about effective change with regard to one issue area[12] in world politics often it is necessary to try and bring about change in another as well. If one wishes to try and tackle the problem of poverty in the less developed parts of the world, for example, it is not enough to deal with the economic questions. Attempts have to be made to try and eliminate or at least reduce the incidence of war in many of the states involved in order to try and remove the enormously debilitating human and economic costs which military conflict brings. Equally, in order to try and achieve the full cooperation of the less developed states in any significant efforts to bring about global environmental reform, it will probably be necessary for the developed states to have to accept at least some of the linkages with the need for global economic reform which the less developed states see as being important. Furthermore, given continuing memories of the costs of previous wars among older members of Western European political elites, it could be argued that those who would wish to unravel the European integrative process would have to come up with a convincing alternative means of helping to keep Western Europe peaceful and cooperative to the EU if they wished to maximise their chances of success.

On a rather more positive note, however, what the above examples illustrate also is how linkages between issues can be exploited to *advance* desired global or regional changes. As has been pointed out previously, those who have been most in favour of European integration, for example, have been able to make considerable use of the negative popular and elite memories of past wars in that region in order to push the integrative process forwards.

These are just a few examples of the ways in which linkages between issue areas can be important in any attempt to introduce far-reaching global changes in an effective manner.

Conclusion

Overall, what the above material and this book in general have done has been to show something of the enormous complexity of global change processes in order, among other things, that the difficulties of producing a 'better future' should not be underestimated. But, more positively, what the book has done also – in the chapters on global poverty for example – has been to show that even where that complexity makes change most difficult to achieve, it does not necessarily make it impossible. This chapter has shown how change can be achieved even in the absence of imperatives, as well as how the complexities of such factors as issue linkages may be actually exploited in order to advance the prospects for change. Additionally, it has shown that, despite the many difficulties that impede the business of prediction and planning effectively in order to try and change or preserve aspects of the existing international system in such a way that it might become 'safer' for humanity in the future, devices such as scenario construction and risk calculation are available to help overcome at least some of the problems.

Furthermore, while space limitations have meant that governments have figured large within this final chapter at the expense of other groups, it has been emphasised that they are only one part of the 'change equation', and as has been shown in the chapters on the environment and global poverty, for example, it should be remembered that individuals, pressure groups and, on occasion, even wider public opinion, can be influential also in initiating change. This is important because it means that even when governments decide that they will do nothing to avert a likely future danger to one or more sections of humanity because their self-defined core interests are not threatened, there is still the opportunity for others – well-organised pressure groups for example – to try and manoeuvre them into a position in which they are forced to change their interest definition and act. To be able to do this however, as pointed out earlier, such groups will need to do a certain amount of scenario construction for themselves, and to have access to enough relevant information to be able to do this effectively. Their ultimate success or failure will of course be dependent crucially upon the amount of leverage which they are able to deploy.

In short, the future of the world may be uncertain, but for those who hold visions of positive reform, it is not entirely without hope. Two of the many qualities for which the young Anne Frank became most renowned after her brutal death were her courage and hope for the future in the middle of an appalling and complicated present. Arguably, at a time when barbarism, racial hatred and mass murder committed in the name of nationalism have reappeared again on a frightening scale within the so-called civilised world, it is the duty of all students of politics committed to the future of humanity to make her hope their own – and to do whatever they can to realise it. The study of international relations is at its most useful when it not only increases understanding of the complex global society that confronts us, but helps us also generate ideas on how to try and change for the better aspects of that society that are an affront to the respect for human rights and life that is at the core of the United Nations in its supposed role as guardian of the international conscience.

Appendix

The wider purposes of the Change Map

The main intention in this book has been to address an undergraduate audience. The aim has been to present a method of analysing international politics that will introduce them to the dynamics of global change in a form that will be comprehensible and stimulating. The question-led structure, woven as it has been around several of the key issues at the heart of contemporary global politics, has been designed primarily to facilitate this objective. This, necessarily, has involved some sacrifice of entirely Change Map-focused analysis in order to provide room for the background detail and examination of preliminary issues and questions necessary to make such a structure fulfil its intended purpose.

Despite all of this, it is hoped that the book will have something of interest and use to say to more experienced students and researchers of international relations as well. While the 'sacrifice' referred to above has not permitted the kind of Change Map-driven, comprehensive, in-depth case study analyses that would be most satisfying to experienced students, it has nevertheless allowed sufficient demonstration of the framework's flexibility, ease of empirical application and utility as a teaching device to justify the book's intention of addressing usefully such a dual audience. Furthermore, the book has laid out sufficient structural detail of the framework and employed enough suitably qualified empirical examples to provide analysts with adequate information to apply the framework themselves empirically if they so wish, or to develop it further. It would be useful here to summarise the overall range of potential purposes of the Change Map from the point of view both of experienced analysts and those who might wish to use it as an aid in trying to achieve change. Accordingly it can be noted that a number of things have become apparent explicitly or implicitly as the book has progressed. First, on the basis of the limited, illustrative rather than definitive, case study material utilised here, it would seem that the map is of considerable use as a checklist. In this respect it is very simple to use. When confronted with an example of global change which they wish to understand in a comprehensive manner, analysts can use the map as a structuring device for their research and see how many of its components are applicable in the matter under investigation. This helps ensure that lines of research that might simply be ignored or forgotten about are taken fully into account. If they feel that there are some important potential factors which the map does not include they can simply add these on to increase its effectiveness.

Second, it is often the case that researchers do not have the time and/or resources to look comprehensively at the causes of every instance of global change which they might be interested in. In providing a checklist the map offers them a ready-made comprehensive range of potentially relevant factors from which they can select those which might seem likely to be the most appropriate and productive concepts to employ with regard to the matter under investigation. They would do this presumably on the basis of their prior information concerning the latter. Such a selective strategy, even in the hands of highly skilled analysts, may well be less accurate and less insightful in its interpretation of the instance of change under investigation than a more comprehensive one, but it does offer a means of logically structuring a selective analysis in cases where research time is short, one which hopefully will increase the chances of researchers choosing the most appropriate 'tools for the job' from a sufficiently wide choice of relevant possibilities – and, importantly, from a checklist which reminds them effectively in readily comprehensible diagram form of the possible *interlinkages* between relevant variables.

But the map is of use not just with regard to change that has occurred already. It can be used to help try and establish the factors which would be necessary for change to occur in particular instances in the future and to help those who might wish themselves to try and facilitate change to identify some of the most profitable means by which they might attempt this.

With regard to the first of these additional possible uses, it was shown in the section on the environment how difficult and complex many of the obstacles in the way of significant environmental reform are and what kind of broad requirements reformers will need to meet if they are to act effectively against these. Equally the chapters on war showed some of the factors which have in the past facilitated, and might yet in the future facilitate, a reduction in the incidence of war between states, together with the limitations that potentially can hamper the effective utilisation of these. In the section on global poverty, some of the factors which potentially might facilitate a significant alleviation of the plight of the world's poor were identified in an appropriately qualified manner.

Where the second of these additional possible uses is concerned, it was shown again in the chapters on global poverty how one approach towards trying to bring about change might be constructed. Other routes were discussed, for example, in the chapters on the environment. As far as those wishing to use the Change Map to assist their own efforts in bringing about change are concerned, the appropriate strategy is for them to analyse a particular issue by using the map to help identify the key obstacles to change, and then to decide which of those factors they might be able to directly or indirectly influence. Having done this, their next task will be to decide how best to do this. Overall, their chances of success will be dependent upon their skill as political analysts and practitioners together with the resources of power and influence which they are able to make use of. The Change Map can do no more than assist them in the quality of the analysis that defines their course of action. Limited as this function may be, however, it is undoubtedly an important one. Again, if necessary, they might wish to add on to the map factors which they feel it leaves out and which need to be taken into account.

The final use to which the map might be put is explained at the end of the global poverty section. In short, it has considerable potential as a 'thought generator' – underlying it is an intention to provide a framework which can help to generate as many new avenues of well-structured thought on global issues and the possibility for change as is possible.

It has not been possible to demonstrate in full detail the map's usefulness in all of the above regards within the necessary limitations of this study. Nevertheless, it is argued that there is enough material within the book to at the very least show its strong *potential* usefulness in each case and to thereby justify interested analysts testing it for themselves to see if the reality matches the promise as far as their own particular research requirements are concerned. What has been shown very clearly is that the map in its entirety is a useful aid to understanding change in global politics, even if its precise utility with regard to each relevant dimension of such change must await the opportunity for a more detailed investigation.

Glossary

Explanations of terms and bodies not listed below can generally be accessed easily via the index. Concepts such as power and supranationality, for example, are defined within the main body of the text and the index lists the page numbers on which the definitions can be found.

ACP states (African, Caribbean and Pacific states)
In an EU context this is a body of over forty developing states which participate in a special relationship with the European Union which is supposed to provide them with valuable assistance in their efforts to achieve economic development. The relationship has been formalised through the Lomé Conventions (see below).

CAFOD (Catholic Overseas Development Agency)
This is the official overseas development agency of the Roman Catholic Church in England and Wales. Its projects are intended to help people to help themselves. CAFOD's stated aims are to benefit people regardless of race, creed or ideology, and to be concerned with the causes as well as the results of hunger. It is one part of a worldwide network of Catholic development agencies.

CAP (Common Agricultural Policy)
This is the oldest common policy of the European Union, being originally established within the EEC. Its general objectives were set down in the Treaty of Rome. In short, it was intended that the CAP would aim to ensure that farmers would receive a fair standard of living, that agricultural markets would be stabilised, that food supplies would be guaranteed, that consumer food prices would be reasonable, and that agricultural productivity would be increased. The policy became highly controversial due to what many people within the EU saw as an over-concern with farming interests at the expense of the consumers, and a large amount of financial waste. A

number of measures have been introduced in recent years to reduce CAP expenditure. CAP has been seen as significant because, despite its many problems, it was the first demonstration of the fact that major policies could be integrated at the European level. As such it has been seen as one of the vital seeds from which subsequent European integration has grown.

ECOWAS (The Economic Community of West African States)

This was set up by sixteen West African states in 1975 with the aim of promoting cooperative projects in education, agriculture and communications and of increasing trade between the various members. Its prospects have been somewhat dampened by developments in Nigeria within recent years among other things. ECOWAS also incorporated a defence dimension in 1981. It has tried to stabilise the situation in Liberia and sent a peace-keeping force into that country in the early 1990s for this purpose.

ECSC (The European Coal and Steel Community)

This was the first of the European communities that would eventually develop into the present European Union. While its scope was limited, in so far as its main concern was the development of a common market for coal and steel, it was important because it established the basic institutional structure that was taken and developed by later communities and contained a prominent supranational (*see* Index) element. Its perceived success was important in helping persuade its members to later expand the scope of European integration. It began operating in 1952.

EEC (European Economic Community)

Along with the setting up of EURATOM, the formation of the EEC was the next major step in the progress of European integration following the introduction of the ECSC. The Rome Treaty by which it was established set the aim of achieving an ever closer union among Europe's citizens by means of a common market, which would promote the free movement of capital, goods, people and services, common policies covering such important activities as agriculture, and a customs union. The EEC began operating in 1958 and its apparent success soon persuaded the initially highly sceptical British Conservative government of the day that they needed to apply for membership.

EMS (European Monetary System)

This began operating in March 1979. Among its main underlying aims have been the desire to control inflation and to increase business and investors' confidence through stable exchange rates. In order to achieve these things the aim has been to maintain a system of fixed (within a band of strictly limited permitted variations) but adjustable exchange rates among its members. Simply because the German economy is the largest within the EU and the German currency the strongest, the Deutsche Mark has dominated the system. Not all EU states have been able or willing to meet the rigorous requirements of full EMS membership, but it still remains one of the key linchpins upon which future prospects for EMU rest.

EMU (Economic and monetary union)

This is a three stage process, set out within the Treaty on European Union, for the achievement of a single currency, a European Central Bank and detailed coordination of EU member states' economic policies. The final stage of the process is designed to come into operation by 1999 at the latest. Strict criteria are laid down in the Treaty which states must meet if they are to be able to participate in EMU. It is not yet clear how many states will be in a position to join such a union by the end of the twentieth century, but it is anticipated that several will not be. The issue is likely to be further complicated if or when some of the economically weaker Eastern European states are allowed to join the EU.

Exchange rates

The exchange rate of a currency is its price in terms of other currencies. When governments or central banks leave market forces to determine exchange rates they are said to 'float'. When the same bodies intervene to maintain exchange rates within agreed limits they are said to be fixed.

Four Tigers

These are usually taken to be the newly emergent economies of Singapore, Hong Kong, Taiwan, and South Korea. Each is characterised by high growth and private investment rates and, by the standards of the developed world, relatively low public spending. Some in the developed world, such as right-wing British Conservatives, believe that they at least partially offer a model which industrialised states can learn from. Critics of this view suggest that they are merely at a stage of growth which all successful industrial societies go through and that they will start to adopt Western style welfare systems and public spending levels as their wealth increases, thus slowing their economic growth down to levels that are more comparable to the older industrial societies.

GATT (General Agreement on Tariffs and Trade)

This is both a treaty and a process, the underlying principles of which were first drawn up in 1947. Basically, GATT derives from the belief that global free trade is the best way of achieving economic growth for everyone and sets out to remove barriers to trade through multilateral trade negotiations, the most recent manifestation of which took the form of 'the Uruguay Round'. GATT negotiations frequently are complicated by several factors: strong domestic interest groups within some states which demand protection from outside competitors; a less than full acceptance of all the ideological underpinnings of GATT's free trade prescriptions on the part of a number of participating governments; and rivalries between some powerful states and international organisations, as in the case of the USA and the EU. During the period of its existence GATT has facilitated a dramatic reduction in the average industrial tariff within the global economy.

GNP (Gross national product)

The value in monetary terms of a state's total output of goods and services over any given year. While a number of the world's states are economic giants in GNP terms, some, such as Bangladesh, are burdened with a GNP that is smaller than the turnover of many multinational business corporations.

G7 (Group of Seven)

This is a body which is intended to facilitate closer coordination of international monetary management and of domestic economic policies, and to promote healthy growth with low inflation. Domestic and inter-state difficulties among its members have limited its effectiveness to varying degrees. Its members are the United States, Germany, Japan, Britain, Italy, France and Canada.

IMF (International Monetary Fund)

This is an agency of the United Nations, originally set up effectively under American economic leadership in the early post-Second World War period. It is intended to facilitate the achievement of global monetary stability and to help member states that have trouble in funding balance of payments difficulties. Its original purpose was complementary to GATT in so far as the stabilisation of exchange rates was intended to encourage global trade. Initially focusing its efforts on developed states, from the 1970s onwards it was forced to start looking increasingly at the problems of the less developed states. It has been accused of applying conditions to any assistance which it provided to several LDCs which were so severe that they damaged the interests of the poorest people within their economies.

INF (Intermediate Nuclear Forces agreement)

The Intermediate Nuclear Forces agreement of 1987 provided for the elimination of large parts of the nuclear armoury of the two then superpowers that had been deployed in Europe specifically for use in a European war. Throughout much of the Cold War the Americans had not been prepared to agree to such a weapon destruction treaty without the right to send inspection teams to the relevant Soviet missile sites and places of missile destruction to check that the agreement was being honoured. Previously the Soviets had refused to grant the US such a right because, allegedly, of the opportunities for spying which it would offer. When they changed their policy on this and went forward to the INF agreement, they opened the way for much bigger cuts in the nuclear armouries of the two sides.

LDCs (Less developed countries/states)

Alternatively referred to as the developing states, broadly speaking LDCs are those states which have not yet acquired rates of economic growth and living standards which are comparable to those enjoyed by people in the advanced industrial world (the USA, Japan and the EU, for example) or the intermediate world (Russia or Poland, for example). They vary enormously in their levels of economic development, some having strong industrial components within their economies (India, for example) and some being mainly agrarian and very poor (such as Burkino Faso).

League of Nations

This was the precursor to the United Nations. Established after the First World War in 1919, it was concerned with the promotion of international peace and security. Towards this end it set out to prevent international disputes and to settle as rapidly as possible any that did arise and to promote disarmament. It was fatally weakened by the fact that the USA never joined and that Germany, Japan and Italy had all withdrawn by 1936. As a result it was ineffective in the face of the final build-up to the Second World War.

Lomé Convention

The first Lomé Convention was agreed between over forty ACP states (see above) and the then European Community in the mid 1970s. It gave the ACP states preferential access to EC markets, an increased level of aid funding of $1,600 million and established the Stabex scheme. The latter was a compensatory finance scheme which set up a fund from which compensation was to be paid to those ACP states who were parties to the convention when the market price for a list of twelve important commodities fell below a specified level. As such it was designed to help stabilise the export earnings of the states involved. There have been four conventions so far. While they have been of undoubted assistance to the poorer states they have been criticised for mobilising only a small percentage of the European Union's wealth in the service of ACP states' development. During the period of the conventions' existence the economies of most of the recipient states have become worse off due to a variety of factors, increasing the feeling on the part of ACP governments that they should receive more assistance.

MAD (Mutually Assured Destruction)

By the early 1960s, with the significant erosion of US strategic superiority over the Soviet Union, the Cold War had become dominated by the notion of deterrence within the context of MAD. MAD required both super-powers to maintain second strike capabilities, by which they would be able to launch a devastating retaliatory attack on an aggressor even after they had suffered a massive nuclear bombardment. By these means, both sides would be assured of unacceptable levels of damage being inflicted on themselves should either start a nuclear war with the other. MAD greatly accelerated the arms race because it caused each superpower to become paranoiac about the danger of the other developing weapons which might neutralise the value of its second strike capability and therefore to feel it necessary to ensure that it always had available the latest and most effective nuclear weapons within its arsenal.

Marshall Plan

This was the European Recovery Program, announced by George Marshall, the then US Secretary of State, in 1947. This provided substantial economic assistance to those European states which chose to participate and was of significant importance in helping them recover from the costly destruction of World War Two. The Soviet Union refused the offer of Marshall aid on behalf of itself and the Eastern European states which it now dominated. It is generally agreed that it did this because it feared that the exposure of the full extent of its economic weaknesses, which would result from the opening of its economy to American scrutiny under the scheme, would damage it in its strategic relationship with the West. A variety of motives have been ascribed to the USA's decision to provide the funding. These range from the desire to remove the conditions of poverty in post-war Europe (which it feared would provide a breeding ground for the spread of communism), to a wish to reconstruct European markets for the benefit of its own exporters, and the ambition to help reorder European relations in such a way that future wars might be less likely. To this latter end the European states were required to participate in a cooperative effort to administer the aid.

NAFTA (The North American Free Trade Agreement)

In 1991 the leaders of Canada, Mexico and the United States began negotiations to conclude a NAFTA agreement which was intended to create a free trade area of 360 million people, with a year by year output of over six trillion dollars. The agreement came to fruition in 1993. Proponents argued that it would boost the wealth of all the participants via the logic of free trade economics; while opponents argued against it on a variety of grounds. Some in Canada, for example, felt that it would lead to increased US dominance of the Canadian economy, while some in the US feared that it would cause the loss of American jobs to low wage Mexico.

NATO (North Atlantic Treaty Organisation)

Set up in 1949, NATO was originally a Western military alliance designed to protect its members against the possibility of Soviet aggression. Its most powerful member is the United States and it includes also the four largest states in the EU. With the end of the Cold War the organisation floundered for some time while trying to evolve an effective new role in the much-changed international environment. It began to reinvigorate itself, however, with the restoration of determined American leadership in August/ September 1995, and the decision to use a multinational NATO force to help implement the peace agreement for Bosnia. Eastern European states have wanted to join NATO for some time, but Russia has made it increasingly clear that it would regard their membership as unacceptable.

NIEO (New International Economic Order)

See OPEC, UNCTAD and Index.

Non-tariff barriers

These are measures designed to protect a state's domestic industries by restricting imports by means other than formal taxes. They include such things as unnecessary product design regulations, which foreign producers find it difficult to comply with, and national and local government procurement policies, which state that domestic producers will always be given first preference when purchases are made by public bodies.

OECD (Organisation for Economic Cooperation and Development)

This is the successor to the OEEC, the Organisation for European Economic Cooperation, which was set up to meet the American require-ment for European cooperation in the administration of Marshall aid (see above). Over the years the OEEC helped revive European economies by such means as quota reductions and credit creation. In 1960, with the task of reconstruction in Western Europe substantially complete, it was replaced by the OECD which extended its focus to the needs of the less developed states. The USA, Japan and Canada are full members of the OECD in addition to the European membership. There are mixed views on how far it has been of assistance to developing economies, with the already small aid budgets of many OECD member states being vulnerable to the whims of enthusiastic cost cutters, as the Republican Congress during the second half of the Clinton administration demonstrated pointedly.

OPEC (Organisation of Petroleum Exporting Countries)

Originally established in 1960, OPEC's primary purpose is to protect the interests of its members by such means as the fixing of prices and the production quantities of crude oil. Its members are drawn from around the globe and include several of the key states in the Middle East and the Persian Gulf, including Saudi Arabia and Iran. OPEC discovered its potential economic muscle during the 1970s when it greatly raised the price of oil, thereby increasing significantly the wealth of its members. However the consequence of this move was to push the global economy into recession and it became apparent that oil prices could not be greatly raised without damaging the entire world economy. The poorest states were particularly badly hit. They had originally hoped that OPEC would use its oil power to force a renegotiation of global economic arrangements in favour of a New International Economic Order (NIEO), in which the richer states would be forced to redistribute a significant amount of their wealth for the purpose of aiding the developing world. However, while OPEC states themselves began to provide some compensatory aid to poorer states, the fact that oil rapidly was demonstrated to be a double edged sword which could hurt the poor even more than the rich, together with political differences among OPEC members, meant that this hope was not fulfilled.

OXFAM (Oxford Committee for Famine Relief)

Originally set up in Britain in 1942 to help the starving within Greece, its remit is now one of global development assistance with the aim of helping people in the less developed states to help themselves. It has played a key role in the United Kingdom in trying to increase public awareness of the plight of the world's poor.

SALT I (Strategic Arms Limitation Treaty I)

The first of two agreements (1972 and 1979) whose most significant purpose was to limit the number of intercontinental nuclear weapons in the armouries of the two superpowers and thereby to stabilise the arms race and the strategic relationship between them.

START (Strategic Arms Reduction Talks)

The START process was originally begun by the USA and the USSR in 1982 and has continued, since the demise of the USSR, between the USA and the inheritors of the Soviet nuclear arsenal. It is the first to have actually succeeded in implementing reductions in the strategic armouries of the parties (i.e. those weapons which would be used in any nuclear attack on the home territories of the main parties, Russia and the USA). Facilitated by the earlier success of the INF agreement (see above) and the ending of the Cold War, the START process has in the 1990s yielded agreements to reduce dramatically the nuclear arsenals of Russia and the United States by the early part of the next century. While the nature of the weapons to be eliminated should lessen the chances of a future nuclear war in the eyes of some, others have observed that both sides will still retain formidable nuclear capabilities at the end of the process.

UNCED (United Nations Conference on Environment and Development)

Held in Rio de Janeiro in 1992, UNCED, otherwise known as the Earth Summit, was attended by 35,000 people and 106 heads of government and state. While many were disappointed that it produced little in the way of effective measures to remedy world environmental problems, others have deemed it a success for greatly raising both the profile of those problems on the global political agenda and public awareness of their existence.

UNCTAD (United Nations Conference on Trade and Development)

First convened in 1962, UNCTAD evolved as a UN forum for trying to reorder international economic relations in a way that the poorer states believed would be fairer to themselves. For much of the 1970s UNCTAD was preoccupied with demands for a New International Economic Order (see OPEC above). However, the failed promise of OPEC oil power as a means of exerting leverage in favour of the LDCs case, together with political and economic differences among the poorer states, their general lack of any effective means to pressure the richer states, and the inward-looking focus which recession promoted in the West, meant that very little was achieved in this regard. Most of the poorer states' aims advanced within UNCTAD remain unachieved in 1995.

WEU (Western European Union)

The WEU, which came into existence in 1954, evolved militarily as a European ingredient within NATO. Since the end of the Cold War it has become increasingly to be seen by Europeanists as a means of developing a future EU common defence policy. A declaration attached to the Maastricht Treaty stated the EU's intention to build it up gradually as the Union's defence arm. There is a continuing debate as to how this is to be done, focused most strongly around the extent to which the WEU should be built up as a European Union pillar of NATO or, alternatively, developed as something capable of acting more independently of NATO. In 1995 its members were Britain, Germany, Italy, France, Spain, Belgium, Holland,

Luxembourg, Portugal, and Greece. The question of the WEU's future is complicated by the presence of neutral states within the EU.

World Bank

Established along with the GATT and the IMF (see above) during the early post-Second World War period, and initially known as the International Bank for Reconstruction and Development, the World Bank was originally designed as part of the overall framework to help with the reconstruction of Europe. When this task had been largely completed, the Bank began to redirect its attention more to the wider world and questions of economic development. Its most significant move in this direction was the establishment of the International Development Agency in 1960, which was mandated to make interest-free loans to LDCs. These were to be financed mainly by Western governments and were used predominantly for infrastructure projects. The initially modest scale of its activities was increased significantly during the 1970s, but ultimately the amount of money which is available is limited by the generosity and political complexion of contributor governments. American policy is always particularly important in this regard. The World Bank in 1995 started to address significantly the question of how to assist the vital role of women in development and began to make small loans available to poor women in LDCs.

Notes

1 A game beyond chess: explaining the Global Change Map

1. Elites are variously defined within the literature. Gabriel Almond, for example, described them as governmental and non-governmental leadership groups which carry on the specific work of policy formulation and policy advocacy (see C.F. Alger, 'Foreign Policies of US Publics', in R. Little and M. Smith (eds), *Perspectives on World Politics*, London, Routledge, 1991, pp. 199–206). The precise understanding of the term to be used in this study will be explained shortly. It draws heavily on Almond's work.

2. The notion of perception has been used in a variety of useful ways within the international relations literature. See, for example, how the notions of elite images and attitudinal prisms are used in M. Brecher, B. Steinberg and J. Stein, 'A Framework for Research on Foreign Policy Behaviour', *Journal of Conflict Resolution*, 1969, vol. XIII, pp. 75–101. For a more expansive discussion of the significance of perception see R. Jervis, *Perception and Misperception in International Relations*, Princeton, NJ, Princeton University Press, 1976.

3. Almond and others have split the population of states into two groups – the 'general' public and the 'attentive' public. While the former is only occasionally interested in foreign affairs, and serves usually only to set the broad boundaries of acceptability within which policy-makers may operate, the attentive public is informed and interested in foreign policy matters and forms the audience for ongoing elite debates (see C.F. Alger, 'Foreign Policies of US Publics', pp. 199–200). This distinction is implicit here.

4. See, for example, J.E. Spero, *The Politics of International Economic Relations*, London, Routledge, 1992, pp. 244–5.

5. See, for example, P. Pringle, 'How Bush got to the brink', *Independent on Sunday* (Supplement), 2 December 1990.

6. See G.T. Allison, *Essence of Decision*, Boston, Mass., Little, Brown, 1971, and G.T. Allison and M.H. Halperin, 'Bureaucratic Politics: A Paradigm

and some Policy Implications', *World Politics*, 1971–2, vol. 24, (supplement), pp. 40–79.

7. Again, this is covered in the two Allison items listed above. For more sceptical views of the importance of administrative elite players in the policy-making process see S.D. Krasner, 'Are Bureaucracies Important (or Allison Wonderland)?', *Foreign Policy*, Summer 1972, vol. 7, pp. 159–79, and L. Freedman, 'Logic, Politics and Foreign Policy Processes', *International Affairs*, 1976, vol. 52, pp. 434–49.

8. See, for example, W. Wallace, *The Foreign Policy Process in Britain*, London, RIIA/George Allen & Unwin, 1977.

9. P. Anderson, 'British European Policy, 1957–58', unpublished MSc thesis, University of Southampton, 1977.

10. For a detailed discussion of transnationalism see R.O. Keohane and J.S. Nye, *Transnational Relations and World Politics*, Cambridge, Mass., Harvard University Press, 1976, and R. Little and M. Smith (eds), *Perspectives on World Politics*.

11. See, for example, J. Frankel, *The National Interest*, London, Macmillan, 1970; G.T. Allison, *Essence of Decision*; R. Little and M. Smith (eds), *Perspectives on World Politics*, Parts I and II; R. Gilpin, 'Three Ideologies of Political Economy', in K.W. Stiles and T. Akaha (eds), *International Political Economy*, New York, HarperCollins, 1991, p. 3; K. Mannheim, *Ideology–Utopia*, London, Routledge, 1991; R. Goodman and K. Refsing, *Ideology and Practice in Modern Japan*, London, Routledge, 1992.

12. See, for example, R.A. Scalapino, *The Foreign Policy of Modern Japan*, Berkeley, University of California Press, 1979.

13. See, for example, P. Bachrach and M. Baratz, 'Decisions and Non-Decisions: An Analytical Framework', *American Political Science Review*, 1963, vol. 57, pp. 632–42; P. Bachrach and M. Baratz, 'Two Faces of Power', *American Political Science Review*, December 1962, pp. 947–52; H.J. Morgenthau, *Politics Among Nations*, New York, Alfred A. Knopf, 1967; R. Little and M. Smith (eds), *Perspectives on World Politics*; K.J. Holsti, *International Politics*, London, Prentice-Hall International, 1974.

14. R. Little and M. Smith (eds), *Perspectives on World Politics*, p.34.

15. H.J. Morgenthau, *Politics Among Nations*.

16. This is defined purely for the purposes of this discussion as those economic ideologies with free-market economics at their core, even though many of them may provide for varying degrees of interventionism.

17. See, for example, A.G. McGrew and P.G. Lewis (eds), *Global Politics*, Cambridge, Polity Press, 1992, pp. 253 and 258–59.

18. Such factors as massive financial assistance from the USA under the Marshall Aid scheme, a device for helping reconstruct and stabilise Western Europe after the Second World War, were also enormously helpful.

19. H. Macmillan, *At the End of the Day*, London, Macmillan, 1973.

20. A.G. McGrew and P.G. Lewis (eds), *Global Politics*, and P. Hirst, 'Globalisation is fashionable but is it a myth?', *Guardian*, 22 March, 1993.

21. P. Hirst, 'Globalisation is fashionable but is it a myth?'

22. See Chapter 5 on the environment.

23. Although it is not certain that all of the industrialising states will agree to

change their relevant practices. Some of the poorer ones may feel that their economic and environmental position is already so bad that there is little damage that climactic problems could do that has not been done to them already by other means.

24. A. Gore, *Earth in the Balance*, London, Earthscan, 1992.
25. See, for example, A. Bullock, *Hitler: A Study in Tyranny*, Harmondsworth, Penguin, 1973, for a discussion of the factors around Hitler which facilitated the pursuit of German expansion prior to the Second World War.
26. See, for example, J.E. Spero, *The Politics of International Economic Relations*, pp. 4–5. Mercantilism held that power and wealth were intimately related to the possession of precious metals, such as gold and silver. In consequence, governments structured their international trade in a manner which they hoped would allow them to maintain a favourable balance of trade and thereby accumulate such metals. This involved, among other things, regimes of export subsidies, tariffs and quotas on imports and, where feasible, the acquisition of colonies.

2 The American pivot

1. The My Lai massacre involved the systematic murder of around 500 women, children and old men by American forces under the command of Lieutenant William Calley. For a concise account see M. Walzer, *Just and Unjust Wars*, New York, Basic Books, 1992, pp. 309–13.
2. See, for example, P. Kennedy, *The Rise and Fall of the Great Powers*, London, Fontana, 1989.
3. See, for example, S. Strange, 'The Future of the American Empire', in R. Little and M. Smith (eds), *Perspectives on World Politics*, London, Routledge, 1991, pp. 434–43.
4. At the time of writing in 1995, for example, the USA was facing strong public criticism from the Kremlin over its advocacy of air strikes on the Bosnian Serbs, and was unable to persuade the British and French of the desirability of its preferences on the question of arms supplies to the Bosnian combatants.
5. P. Pringle, 'How Bush Got to the Brink', *Independent on Sunday* (Supplement), 2 December 1990.
6. J. Carlin, 'Big bucks keep US politicians lined up in pro-Israel camp', *Independent on Sunday*, 21 May 1995, p. 15.
7. R. Maidment and A. McGrew, *The American Political Process*, London, Sage/Open University, 1991, pp. 155–9.
8. R. Maidment and A. McGrew, *The American Political Process*, p. 159.
9. R. Maidment and A. McGrew, *The American Political Process*, pp. 168–9.
10. Please see the further reading examples at the end of the chapter.
11. J .Carlin, 'Big bucks keep US politicians lined up in pro-Israel camp'.
12. For a discussion of the rational actor paradigm see, for example, G.T. Allison, *Essence of Decision*, Boston, Mass., Little, Brown, 1971.

3 Can the state survive? The threat from economic global interfusion

1. There are a variety of different ways in which the state has been defined by analysts. Some for example, point to the importance of considering the purposes of states as well as their physical bases and institutions (B. Buzan, 'The Idea of the State and National Security', in M. Smith and R. Little (eds), *Perspectives on World Politics*, London, Routledge, 1991, pp. 36–46

2. State capitalism here is defined as the control of economic production that is centred in a communist party apparatus that effectively runs the state.

3. W.S. Jones, *The Logic of International Relations*, New York, HarperCollins, 1991, p. 448.

4. 'The dark side of the boom', *The Economist*, 5 August 1995, p. 21.

5. Such burdens here are deemed to be irremovable in terms of practicality – governments are unlikely to want to do something in most cases that would result in them being voted out of office.

6. W.S. Jones, *The Logic of International Relations*, p. 457.

7. W. Hutton, 'Freedom to ignore our best interests', *Guardian*, 20 April 1995, p. 10.

8. The version that was advocated by Ronald Reagan and Margaret Thatcher when they were leaders of their respective states is a case in point.

9. As in the case of the Single European Act, which will be explained in the chapters on the future of European integration.

10. C.W. Kegley and E.R. Wittkopf, *World Politics*, New York, St Martin's Press, 1993, pp. 194–6.

11. 'The world turned upside down', an article contained in 'A Survey of Multinationals', p. 6 in *The Economist*, 24 June 1995.

12. S. Caulkin, 'British firms resurrected by courtesy of Japan', *Finance Guardian*, 8 May 1993.

13. See, for example, J.E. Spero, *The Politics of International Economic Relations*, London, Routledge, 1992, pp. 244–5.

14. B. Morris, 'Wrestling with the octopus', *Independent on Sunday* (Business supplement), 12 April 1992, p. 4.

15. Although EU policy on multinationals has been and remains ambiguous. See for example V. Lintner and S. Mazey, *The European Community: Economic and Political Aspects*, London, McGraw-Hill, 1991, pp. 128–45.

16. V. Keegan, 'Thank heaven for foreign investment', *Guardian*, 7 August 1995, p. 13.

17. P. Kennedy, *Preparing for the Twenty-First Century*, London, HarperCollins, 1993, p. 55.

18. See, for example, P. Kennedy, *Preparing for the Twenty-First Century*, p. 57.

19. Such a viewpoint tends to use the example of the United States' preferential treatment of Japan after the Second World War and to cite the economic benefits that apparently flowed from this.

4 The second challenge: the threats to the state from scientific, technological and cultural aspects of global interfusion

1. See, for example, the chapters on the environment in this study and A. Gore, *Earth in the Balance*, London, Earthscan, 1992.
2. P. Kennedy, *Preparing for the Twenty-First Century*, London, HarperCollins, 1993, pp. 82–94.
3. *Newsnight*, BBC Television, 31 July 1995.
4. Toby Young, *Newsnight*, BBC Television, 31 July 1995.
5. A.G. McGrew and P. Lewis *et al.*, *Global Politics*, Cambridge, Polity Press, 1992, pp. 253–68.
6. See, for example, C.W. Kegley and E.R. Wittkopf, *World Politics*, New York, St Martin's Press, 1993, pp. 154–87, and W.S. Jones, *The Logic of International Relations*, New York, HarperCollins, 1991, pp. 541–93.

5 Global environmental problems

1. W. Hutton, 'Heated debate on road to Rio', *Guardian*, 18 May 1992.
2. J. Whitelegg, 'Dirty from the cradle to the grave', *Guardian* (Europe section), 30 July 1993.
3. *The Economist, Book of Vital World Statistics*, London, Hutchinson, 1991, p. 111.
4. *The Economist, Book of Vital World Statistics*, p. 111.
5. Oxfam/ *Guardian*, *Earth*, London, Guardian Publications, 1992.
6. J. Porritt, *Save the Earth*, London, Dorling Kindersley, 1992, p. 109.
7. J. Whitelegg, 'Dirty from the cradle to the grave'.
8. See for example, P. Kennedy, *Preparing for the Twenty-First Century*, London, HarperCollins, 1993, pp. 106–21, and J. Porritt, *Save the Earth*, pp. 95–101.
9. P. Kennedy, *Preparing for the Twenty-First Century*, p.108, and J. Porritt, *Save the Earth*, p. 97.
10. In J. Porritt, *Save the Earth*, p. 97.
11. M. Allaby, *Green Facts*, London, Hamlyn, 1990, pp. 127–8.
12. J. May, 'From Alpha to Omega: a Disaster Log, 1972–92', *Independent on Sunday* (Supplement), 31 May 1992, and Oxfam/ *Guardian*, *Earth*, p. 27.
13. G. Lean, S. Crawshaw and L. Doyle, 'Europe rises in protest at Shell dumping', *Independent on Sunday*, 18 June 1995, p. 1.
14. M. Allaby, *Green Facts*, pp. 38–9 and 152–3.
15. A. Gore, *Earth in the Balance*, London, Earthscan, 1992, p. 305.
16. A. Gore, *Earth in the Balance*, pp. 305–60.
17. For a detailed discussion of technical solutions to global warming see, for example, M. Grubb *et al.*, *Energy Policies and the Greenhouse Effect, Volume Two: Country Studies and Technical Options*, Aldershot, Dartmouth, 1992.
18. P. Kennedy, *Preparing for the Twenty-First Century*, pp. 120–1.
19. A. Gore, *Earth in the Balance*, pp. 301–5.
20. P. Kennedy, *Preparing for the Twenty-First Century*, pp. 120–1.

21. A. Gore, *Earth in the Balance*, pp. 304–5.
22. A. Gore, *Earth in the Balance*, p. 360.
23. M. Imber, 'Too many cooks? The Post-Rio Reform of the United Nations,' *International Affairs*, 1993, vol. 69, pp. 66–7.
24. M. Imber, 'Too many cooks?', p. 67.

6 The political economy of death: what causes global poverty?

1. J. Bennett, *The Hunger Machine*, Cambridge, Polity Press, 1987, p. 12.
2. N. Twose, *Cultivating Hunger*, Oxford, Oxfam, 1985, p. 36.
3. K. Nielsen, 'Global Justice, Capitalism and the Third World', in R. Attfield and B. Wilkins (eds), *International Justice and the Third World*, London, Routledge, 1992, pp. 17–18.
4. A. Belsey, 'World Poverty, Justice and Equality', in R. Attfield and B. Wilkins (eds), *International Justice and the Third World*, p. 36.
5. N. Dower, 'Sustainability and the Right to Development', in R. Attfield and B. Wilkins (eds), *International Justice and the Third World*, p. 94.
6. J. Porritt, *Save the World*, London, Dorling Kindersley, 1992. For an interesting radical discussion of the whole development question see R.B. Norgaard, *Development Betrayed*, London, Routledge, 1994.
7. J. Spero, *The Politics of International Economic Relations*, London, Routledge, 1992, pp. 4–5.
8. A concise, introductory elaboration of these structuralist arguments is presented in N. Twose, *Cultivating Hunger*.
9. CAFOD, *Review of the Year, 1991*, London, CAFOD, 1992, p. 29.
10. There is quite a detailed examination of some of the problems with Leninist theory in K. Waltz, *Theory of International Politics*, New York, Addison-Wesley, 1979.
11. K. Waltz, *Theory of International Politics*.
12. R. Gilpin, 'Three Ideologies of Political Economy', in R. Little and M. Smith (eds), *Perspectives on World Politics*, London, Routledge, 1991, pp. 426–9.
13. CAFOD, *Review of the Year, 1991*, p. 17.
14. See, for example, J. Bennett, *The Hunger Machine*, Cambridge, Polity Press, 1987, ch. 3.

7 An end to global poverty?

1. W. Brandt, *North/South: A Programme for Survival*, London, Pan Books, 1980, and W. Brandt, *Common Crisis: Co-operation for World Recovery*, London, Pan Books, 1983.
2. See, for example, André Gunder Frank, 'North–South and East–West Keynesian Paradoxes in the Brandt Report', *Third World Quarterly*, October 1980, vol. 11, pp. 669–80.

3. See, for example, L. Anell and B. Nygren, *The Developing Countries and the World Economic Order*, London, Methuen, 1980.
4. GJW Government Relations/Peter Stephenson, *Handbook of World Development*, Harlow, Longman, 1981, p. 6.
5. J.E. Spero, *The Politics of International Economic Relations*, London, Routledge, 1992, pp. 147–57.
6. J.E. Spero, *The Politics of International Economic Relations*, pp. 147–57.
7. For example, this was a view which a BBC team preparing a documentary on ordinary people's attitudes to the notion of structural adjustment during the mid-1970s found to be powerfully articulated by some Preston mill workers whom they interviewed.
8. J.K. Galbraith, *The Culture of Contentment*, London, Sinclair Stevenson, 1992 – the implications of pp. 162–3 are relevant in this regard.
9. For a discussion of the importance of this kind of cooperation in aid strategies see, for example, J. Bennett, *The Hunger Machine*, Cambridge, Polity Press, 1987, ch. 3.
10. The Brandt Reports had the misfortune of coming out just as the global political economic balance was in the process of shifting decisively against many Keynesian-derived ideas, most particularly through the election of Ronald Reagan to the US presidency and Margaret Thatcher as Prime Minister of Britain.
11. R.C. Zaehner (ed.), *The Hutchinson Encyclopedia of Living Faiths*, Oxford, Helicon, 1993, p. 175
12. St Paul, Second Letter to the Corinthians, *Holy Bible* (2 Corinthians 8: 13–15), New International Version, London, Hodder & Stoughton, 1986, p. 1163. This ethos is confirmed in the Acts of the Apostles, p. 1096.
13. See, for example, J.E. Spero, *The Politics of International Economic Relations*, pp. 219–21.
14. In particular, readers might try starting at the 'opposite end' to this analysis, by asking to what extent is it culture-bound and consequently not sufficiently attentive to the question of what the less developed states can do for themselves.
15. N.L. Fyson, *The Development Puzzle*, London, Hodder & Stoughton, 1984, p. 15.
16. N.L. Fyson, *The Development Puzzle*, p. 15.
17. N.L. Fyson, *The Development Puzzle*, p. 16.
18. N.L. Fyson, *The Development Puzzle*, p. 16.
19. CAFOD, *Review of the Year, 1991*, London, CAFOD, 1992, p. 22.
20. *World Service News*, BBC Radio, 7 August 1995.

8 A second United States? Integration in Western Europe

1. For an introductory discussion of some of the alleged causes of the conflict in the former Yugoslavia see P. Brogan, *World Conflicts*, London, Bloomsbury, 1992.
2. See L. Silber and A. Little, *The Death of Yugoslavia*, London, Penguin/BBC Books, 1995, for one view of the causes of the break-up of Yugoslavia, and

R. Sakwa, *Russian Politics and Society*, London, Routledge, 1993, for a discussion of the causes of the break-up of the Soviet Union.

3. See, for example, V. Rich, 'Why Belarus Matters', *World Today*, March 1994, vol. 50, pp. 43–4.

4. D. Dinan, *Ever Closer Union?*, London, Macmillan, 1994, p. 361.

5. See N. Nugent, *The Government and Politics of the European Union*, London, Macmillan, 1994, for further summary details of these powers.

6. See N. Nugent, *The Government and Politics of the European Union*, for further summary details of the powers of the Court of Justice since Maastricht.

7. W. Claes, 'Europe as an unfinished symphony', *World Today*, March 1994, vol. 50, p. 49.

8. 'A light is dimmed', *The Economist*, 19 January 1991, p. 60.

9. D. Dinan, *Ever Closer Union?*, pp. 136–40.

10. S. George, *Politics and Policy in the European Community*, Oxford, Oxford University Press, 1992, pp. 161–2, and J. Lodge (ed.), *The European Community and the Challenge of the Future*, London, Pinter, 1993, pp. 51–2.

11. One of the main reasons for this has been the widespread domestic perception that the more than fifty domestic governments that have briefly held power since the end of the Second World War have been less than satisfactory in their performance.

12. See, for example, E. Haas, *The Uniting of Europe*, Stanford, California, Stanford University Press, 1968, and L.N. Lindberg, *The Political Dynamics of European Economic Integration*, Stanford, California, Stanford University Press, 1963. For a useful modern introductory critique of neofunctionalism see S. George, *Politics and Policy in the European Community*.

13. In particular, prominent figures such as the two key British EC figures in the second half of the 1980s, Prime Minister Thatcher and Commissioner Cockfield. See also S. George, *Politics and Policy in the European Community*.

14. For example, the discouragement to industrial investment caused by Mafia activity and political corruption in southern Italy, or the poor ability of some traditional British firms concentrated in the northern part of the country to adjust to economic change.

15. Although some analysts see robotisation as a long-term rather than a medium-term process. Kennedy, for example, argues that it might take a generation or more before the robotics revolution makes its full impact. (See P. Kennedy, *Preparing for the Twenty-First Century*, London, Harper-Collins, 1993, p. 94.)

16. See N. Nugent, *The Government and Politics of the European Community*, London, Macmillan, 1993, pp. 251–3.

17. This has been one of the lines of argument advanced by the Euro-sceptics in the British parliament for example.

9   The future of European integration

1. While Bill Clinton later toned down his partial reorientation of American interests when speaking to Western European audiences, it was a very

noticeable theme of his discussions with the Pacific states during the early part of his presidency.

2. See, for example, C.W. Kegley and E.R. Wittkopf, *World Politics: Trend and Transformation*, New York, St Martin's Press, 1993, pp. 186–7.
3. For a discussion of these issues from a different perspective see J. Shea, 'Security: the Future', in J. Lodge (ed.), *The European Community and the Challenge of the Future*, London, Pinter Publishers, 1993.
4. S. George, *Politics and Policy in the European Community*, Oxford, Oxford University Press, 1992, p. 162.
5. For an overview of the CAP see N. Nugent, *The Government and Politics of the European Union*, London, Macmillan, 1994, ch. 13, and S. George, *Politics and Policy in the European Community*, ch. 8.
6. See H. Armstrong, 'Community Regional Policy', in J. Lodge (ed.), *The European Community and the Challenge of the Future*, pp. 131–5.
7. V. Lintner and S. Mazey, *The European Community: Economic and Political Aspects*, London, McGraw-Hill, 1991, p. 176.
8. V. Lintner and S. Mazey, *The European Community: Economic and Political Aspects*, p. 178.
9. Recent British Conservative governments frequently have had this charge laid against them for example.
10. See, for example, A. Hewitt, 'Development Assistance Policy and the ACP', in J. Lodge (ed.), *The European Community and the Challenge of the Future*, pp. 300–11.
11. W. Brandt, *North/South: A Programme for Survival*, London, Pan Books, 1980, and W. Brandt, *Common Crisis: North–South Co-operation for World Recovery*, London, Pan Books, 1983.
12. As pointed out in S. George, *Politics and Policy in the European Community*, p. 162, there is a very clear perspective on the single market among key business groups. See also the Single Market supplements produced by *The Economist* in June 1989 and June 1990.
13. D. Dinan, *Ever Closer Union?*, London, Macmillan, 1994.
14. Any greatly expanded international role for Germany's armed forces is likely to be constrained by both German domestic public opinion and the grievances felt against the Nazi-led armies of the past that exist still within several states.
15. Japan's ability to play any significant international role militarily is likely to continue to be constrained by factors similar to those applying to Germany for the immediate future.

10 Global rivalries and the causes of war

1. M. Renner, 'Preparing for Peace', in L.R. Brown *et al.*, *State of the World 1993*, London, Earthscan, 1993.
2. For a useful selection of alternative definitions of war see L. Freedman (ed.), *War*, Oxford, Oxford University Press, 1994, pp. 69–70.
3. K. Waltz, *Man, the State and War*, New York, Columbia University Press, 1959. See Chapters II and III for example.

4. T. Hobbes, *Leviathan*, Harmondsworth, Penguin, 1982.
5. H. Williams, M. Wright, and T. Evans, *International Relations and Political Theory*, Buckingham, Open University Press, 1993, p. 100.
6. J.B. Elshtain, 'Reflections on War and Political Discourse: Realism, Just War, and Feminism in a Nuclear Age', in R. Little and M. Smith (eds), *Perspectives on World Politics*, London, Routledge, 1991, p. 462.
7. J.B. Elshtain, 'Reflections on War and Political Discourse', p. 463.
8. J.B.Elshtain, 'Reflections on War and Political Discourse', p. 463.
9. K. Waltz, *Man, the State and War*, p. 28.
10. K. Waltz, *Man, the State and War*, p. 40.
11. K. Waltz, *Man, the State and War*, p. 41.
12. K. Waltz, *Man, the State and War*, p. 238.
13. For an interesting analysis of the possible causes of the Second World War see, for example, A.J.P. Taylor, *The Origins of the Second World War*, Harmondsworth, Penguin, 1964.
14. See, for example, A. Bullock, *Hitler: A Study in Tyranny*, Harmondsworth, Penguin, 1973.
15. See V.I. Lenin, *Imperialism, the Highest Stage of Capitalism, Collected Works, Vol. 22*, Moscow, Progress Publishers, 1964.
16. W.S. Jones, *The Logic of International Relations*, New York, HarperCollins, 1991, pp. 642–3
17. For an introductory discussion of some of the alleged wider causes of the wars in the former Yugoslavia see P. Brogan, *World Conflicts*, London, Bloomsbury, 1992, pp. 422–32.
18. For introductory discussions of the causes of the Falklands/Malvinas War see P. Calvocoressi, *World Politics Since 1945*, Harlow, Longman, 1991, and P. Brogan, *World Conflicts*, London, Bloomsbury, 1992, pp. 437–40.
19. Baron Franks, *Falkland Islands Review: Report of a Committee of Privy Counsellors*, London, Cmnd 8787, 1983. Due to certain subtle nuances within it, the Franks Report needs to be read in its entirety before a judgement on the precise meaning of any part of its contents is made.
20. Baron Franks, *Falkland Islands Review*.
21. 'Flowing uphill', *The Economist*, 12–18 August 1995, p. 46.
22. For interesting discussions of the relationship between the balance of power, equilibrium, disequilibrium and war see H.J. Morgenthau, *Politics Among Nations*, New York, Alfred Knopf, 1967, and H. Bull, *The Anarchical Society*, London, Macmillan, 1979.
23. See, for example, P. Brogan, *World Conflicts*.
24. The concept of mirror images is particularly interesting in this regard. See, for example, J.E. Dougherty and R.L. Pfaltzgraff, *Contending Theories of International Relations*, New York, Lippincott/Harper & Row, 1971.
25. See, for example, R. Jervis, *Perception and Misperception in International Politics*, Princeton, NJ, Princeton University Press, 1976.
26. See, for example, Chapter 9 in D. Pick, *War Machine*, London, Yale University Press, 1993.
27. See, for example, G. Blainey, *The Causes of War*, New York, Free Press, 1988.
28. See, for example, A. Bullock, *Hitler: A Study in Tyranny*.
29. H. Thomas, *The Suez Affair*, Harmondsworth, Penguin, 1970.

11 The control of war

1. C.W. Kegley and E.R. Wittkopf, *World Politics: Trend and Transformation*, New York, St Martin's Press, 1993, pp. 442–3.
2. For example, this belief in appropriate uses of force and the threat of force was argued to be one of the main reasons why the Labour Party in Britain fared so badly electorally in the early 1980s when it espoused disarmament at a time when the Cold War was still in place.
3. For an explanation of this idea see Chapter 5 in J. Baylis, K. Booth, J. Garnett and P. Williams, *Contemporary Strategy*, London, Croom Helm, 1975.
4. J. Baylis, K. Booth, J. Garnett and P. Williams, *Contemporary Strategy*.
5. A situation which rendered it particularly weak in Rwanda in 1994 and prevented it from having the strength to protect the Tutsi civilian population from large-scale massacre, a tragedy which prompted UN official Larry Hollingworth to comment, 'It will soon be the fiftieth birthday of the United Nations. Perhaps the international community will buy it a rapid reaction force as a present' (*World in Action*, broadcast in the UK on 15 August 1994).
6. See, for example, G. Blainey, *The Causes of War*, New York, Free Press, 1988.
7. Extract from Carl von Clausewitz, *On War*, in H. Williams, M. Wright and T. Evans, *International Relations and Political Theory*, Buckingham, Open University Press, 1993, p. 150.
8. H. Thomas, *The Suez Affair*, Harmondsworth, Penguin, 1970.
9. For an interesting discussion of some additional considerations involving the notion of rationality see K. Waltz, *Man, the State and War*, New York, Columbia University Press, 1959, pp. 168–71.
10. The Intermediate Nuclear Forces agreement of 1987 was a treaty which provided for the elimination of large parts of the nuclear armoury of the two then superpowers that had been deployed in Europe specifically for use in a European war. Throughout much of the Cold War the Americans had not been prepared to agree to such a weapon destruction treaty without the right to send inspection teams to the relevant Soviet missile sites and places of missile destruction to check that the agreement was being honoured. Previously the Soviets had refused to grant the USA such a right because, allegedly, of the opportunities for spying which it would offer. When they changed their policy on this and went forward to the INF agreement, they opened the way for much bigger cuts in the nuclear armouries of the two sides, most immediately via the Strategic Arms Reduction Treaties (START), which dealt with large numbers of nuclear missiles directly targeted at the homelands of the USA and the former USSR.
11. Former Cold War 'warrior' Margaret Thatcher being one of the most prominent.
12. K. Waltz, 'The Spread of Nuclear Weapons: More May be Better', *Adelphi Paper 171*, London, IISS, 1977.
13. T. Barber, 'How to contain the Asian colossus', *Independent on Sunday*, 9 July 1995, p. 13.

14. See, for example, Michael Renner's ideas on enhancing the role of the United Nations in L.R. Brown *et al.*, *State of the World 1993*, London, Earthscan, 1993.
15. Dan McGuire, *Newsnight*, BBC Television, 8 August 1995.

12 The problem of 'murderous' and 'aggressive' regimes – the role of international law and the United Nations

1. This is a necessarily brief explanation of the nature of customary law. For
   . a fuller discussion see, for example, M. Akehurst, *A Modern Introduction to International Law*, London, HarperCollins, 1991, ch. 3.
2. See, for example, P. Calvocoressi, *World Politics Since 1945*, Harlow, Longman, 1991.
3. P. Pringle, 'How Bush Got to the Brink', *Independent on Sunday* (Supplement), 2 December 1990.
4. See, for example, P. Brogan, *World Conflicts*, London, Bloomsbury, 1992, pp. 340–2.
5. For an introductory discussion of Yugoslavia's place within Eastern Europe after the Second World War see P. Calvocoressi, *World Politics Since 1945*, p. 218 and P. Brogan, *World Conflicts*, pp. 425–32.
6. For a concise discussion of existing human rights provisions, see, for example, M. Akehurst, *A Modern Introduction to International Law*, pp. 76–81.
7. The UN commander in Rwanda at the time of the massacres stated that he believed that a significant number of lives could have been saved had the Security Council given him an effective force (*World in Action*, interview broadcast in UK on 15 August 1994).

Conclusion   The future – can it be anticipated and changed?

1. Anne Frank, *The Diary of a Young Girl*, copypright by Anne Frank-Fonds, Basel, Switzerland.
2. Anne Frank, *The Diary of Anne Frank*, London, Macmillan Children's Books, 1995, pp. ix–x.
3. W. Wallace, *The Foreign Policy Process in Britain*, London, RIIA/George Allen & Unwin, 1977.
4. For one strongly argued viewpoint on the impracticality of trying to achieve a predictive science of policy analysis in the field of international relations see H. Bull, 'International Theory: The Case for a Classical Approach', *World Politics*, vol. XVIII, April 1966 (in supplement).
5. Scenario construction was a particular predilection of Henry Kissinger during the Nixon presidency.
6. 'Turn of the Tide', *The Economist*, 5–11 August 1995, pp. 41–2.
7. The most prominent and most important type of risk calculation that has

been used within international relations, for example, has relied upon the utilisation of models from within the rational actor paradigm for the purpose of the development of nuclear deterrence theory. Those who doubt the comprehensive relevance to nuclear deterrence of the paradigm obviously have regarded reliance on it as being highly dangerous.

8. On the question of objectivity see, for example, P. Anderson, 'The Consolidation of Selected Approaches to the Study of Foreign Policy: A Theoretical and Empirical Analysis', unpublished PhD thesis, University of Southampton, 1987.

9. For a discussion of why certainty is so difficult to achieve in the field of international relations see P. Anderson, 'The Consolidation of Selected Approaches to the Study of Foreign Policy: A Theoretical and Empirical Analysis'.

10. As happened, for example, with Chamberlain's famous misjudgement of Hitler's aims and character when predicting that his Munich agreement would bring 'peace in our time', or with the Bush administration's initial belief that Saddam Hussein's sabre-rattling over Kuwait did not make it very probable that he was considering trying to seize the whole territory, or the British Thatcher government's belief until too late that it was unlikely that the Falklands/Malvinas were in any serious danger of being seized by Argentina during 1982, or Germany's miscalculation of the likely results of an early recognition of Croatia.

11. J.E. Spero, *The Politics of International Economic Relations*, London, Routledge, 1992, p. 355.

12. Issue areas are defined in a number of different ways within the international relations literature. For the purposes of this study they refer to policy areas, such as those relating to poverty questions, war, the environment, or international law, which are distinct enough to form a legitimate subject of focus in their own right. However, such a focus will only be a productive one if the linkages of any one issue area with other issue areas are not overlooked.

Select bibliography

Akehurst, M., 1991, *A Modern Introduction to International Law*, London, HarperCollins.

Allaby, M., 1990, *Green Facts*, London, Hamlyn.

Allison, G.T., 1971, *Essence of Decision*, Boston, Mass., Little, Brown.

Allison, G.T. and Halperin, M.H., 1972, 'Bureaucratic Politics: A Paradigm and some Policy Implications', *World Politics*, 1971–72, vol. 24 (supplement), pp. 40–79.

Anderson, P., 1977, 'British European Policy 1957–58', unpublished MSc thesis, University of Southampton.

Anderson, P., 1987, 'The Consolidation of Selected Approaches to the Study of Foreign Policy: A Theoretical and Empirical Analysis', unpublished PhD thesis, University of Southampton.

Anell, L. and Nygren, B., 1980, *The Developing Countries and the World Economic Order*, London, Methuen.

Attfield, R. and Wilkins, B., 1992, *International Justice and the Third World*, London, Routledge.

Bachrach, P. and Baratz, M., 1962, 'Two Faces of Power', *American Political Science Review*, vol. 56, pp. 947–52.

Bachrach, P. and Baratz, M., 1963, 'Decisions and Non-Decisions: An Analytical Framework', *American Political Science Review*, vol. 57, pp. 632–42.

Barber, J. and Smith, M., 1974, *The Nature of Foreign Policy*, Edinburgh, Holmes McDougall/Open University.

Barber, T., 1995, 'How to contain the Asian colossus', *Independent on Sunday*, 9 July, p. 13.

Baylis, J., Booth, K., Garnett, J. and Williams, P., 1975, *Contemporary Strategy*, London, Croom Helm.

Bennett, J., 1987, *The Hunger Machine*, Cambridge, Polity Press.

Bhagwati, J.N. (ed.), 1977, *The New International Economic Order: the North–South Debate*, Cambridge, Mass., MIT Press.

Blainey, G., 1988, *The Causes of War*, New York, Free Press.

Blake, D.H. and Walters, R.S., 1976, *The Politics of Global Economic Relations*, Englewood Cliffs, NJ, Prentice-Hall.

Brandt, W., 1980, *North/South: A Programme for Survival*, London, Pan Books.

Brandt, W., 1983, *Common Crisis North–South: Co-operation for World Recovery*, London, Pan Books.

Braybrooke, D. and Lindblom, C.E., 1963, *A Strategy of Decision*, New York, Free Press.

Brecher, M., 1973, 'Images, Process and Feedback in Foreign Policy: Israel's Decisions on German Reparations', *American Political Science Review*, vol. 67, pp. 73–102.

Brecher, M., 1974, 'Inputs and Decisions for War and Peace: The Israel Experience', *International Studies Quarterly*, vol. 18, pp. 131–77.

Brecher, M., Steinberg, B. and Stein, J., 1969, 'A Framework for Research on Foreign Policy Behaviour', *Journal of Conflict Resolution*, vol. XIII, pp. 75–101.

Brogan, P., 1992, *World Conflicts*, London, Bloomsbury.

Brown, L.R., Kane, H. and Ayres, E., 1993, *Vital Signs 1993–1994*, London, Earthscan.

Brown, S., 1974, *New Forces in World Politics*, Washington, DC, Brookings Institution.

Bull, H., 1966, 'International Theory: The Case for a Classical Approach', *World Politics*, vol. XVIII, April (in supplement).

Bull, H., 1979, *The Anarchical Society*, London, Macmillan.

Bullock, A., 1973, *Hitler: A Study in Tyranny*, Harmondsworth, Penguin.

Burton, J., 1972, *World Society*, London, Cambridge University Press.

Buzan, B., 1991, *People, States and Fear*, Hemel Hempstead, Harvester Wheatsheaf.

CAFOD, 1992, *Review of the Year, 1991*, London, CAFOD.

Calvocoressi, P., 1992, *World Politics Since 1945*, Harlow, Longman.

Carlin, J., 1995, 'Big bucks keep US politicians lined up in pro-Israel camp', *Independent on Sunday*, 21 May, p. 15.

Caulkin, S., 1993, 'British firms resurrected by courtesy of Japan', *Finance Guardian*, 8 May.

Claes, W., 1994, 'Europe as an unfinished symphony', *World Today*, vol. 50, pp. 45–9.

Claude, I.L., 1962, *Power and International Relations*, New York, Random House.

Clausewitz, Karl von, 1976, *On War*, Princeton, NJ, Princeton University Press.

Cohen, B.J., 1973, *The Question of Imperialism: The Political Economy of Dominance and Dependence*, New York, Basic Books.

DiRenzo, G.J. (ed.), 1974, *Personality and Politics*, Garden City, NY, Doubleday/Anchor.

Dinan, D., 1994, *Ever Closer Union?*, London, Macmillan.

Dougherty, J.E. and Pfaltzgraff, R.L., 1971, *Contending Theories of International Relations*, New York, Lippincott/Harper & Row.

The Economist, 1991, *Book of Vital World Statistics*, London, Hutchinson.

The Economist, 1991, 'A light is dimmed', 19 January, p. 60.

The Economist, 1995, 'The world turned upside down', an article contained in 'A Survey of Multinationals', 24 June, p. 6.

The Economist, 1995, 'The dark side of the boom', 5 August, p. 21.

The Economist, 1995, 'Turn of the Tide', 5–11 August, pp. 41–2.

The Economist, 1995, 'Flowing uphill', 12–18 August, p. 46.

Anne Frank, 1995, *The Diary of a Young Girl*, copyright by Anne Frank-Fonds, Basel, Switzerland.

Anne Frank, 1995, *The Diary of Anne Frank*, London, Macmillan Children's Books.

Frank, André Gunder, 1980, 'North–South and East–West Keynesian Paradoxes in the Brandt Report', *Third World Quarterly*, vol. 11, pp. 669–80.

Frankel, J., 1970, *The National Interest*, London, Macmillan.

Frankel, J., 1971, *The Making of Foreign Policy*, New York, Oxford University Press.

Frankel, J., 1976, *International Relations*, London, Oxford University Press.

Baron Franks, 1983, *Falkland Islands Review: Report of a Committee of Privy Counsellors*, London, Cmnd 8787.

Freedman, L., 1976, 'Logic, Politics and Foreign Policy Processes', *International Affairs*, vol. 52, pp. 434–49.

Freedman, L. (ed.), 1994, *War*, Oxford, Oxford University Press.

Frieden, J.A. and Lake, David A. (eds.), 1991, *International Political Economy: Perspectives on Global Power and Wealth*, London, Unwin Hyman.

Fyson, N.L., 1984, *The Development Puzzle*, London, Hodder & Stoughton.

Galbraith, J.K., 1992, *The Culture of Contentment*, London, Sinclair Stevenson.

George, S., 1992, *Politics and Policy in the European Community*, Oxford, Oxford University Press.

Gilpin, R., 1991, 'Three Ideologies of Political Economy', in Stiles, K. W. and Akaha, T. (eds), *International Political Economy*, New York, HarperCollins, p. 3.

GJW Government Relations/Peter Stephenson, 1981, *Handbook of World Development*, Harlow, Longman.

Goodman, R. and Refsing, K., 1992, *Ideology and Practice in Modern Japan*, London, Routledge.

Gore, A., 1992, *Earth in the Balance*, London, Earthscan.

Grubb, M., *et al.*, 1992, *Energy Policies and the Greenhouse Effect, Volume Two: Country Studies and Technical Options*, Aldershot, Dartmouth.

Haas, E., 1968, *The Uniting of Europe*, Stanford, California, Stanford University Press.

Hammond, P.Y., 1965, 'Foreign Policy Making and Administrative Politics', *World Politics*, October 1964/July 1965, vol. XVII, pp. 656–71.

Hanrieder, W.F., 1971, *Comparative Foreign Policy*, New York, McKay.

Hermann, C.F., 1990, 'Changing Course: When Governments Choose to Redirect Foreign Policy', *International Studies Quarterly*, vol. 34, no. 2, pp. 3–21.

Herz, H., 1959, *International Politics in the Atomic Age*, New York, Columbia University Press.

Hirst, P., 1993, 'Globalisation is fashionable but is it a myth?', *Guardian*, 22 March.

Hobbes, T., 1982, *Leviathan*, Harmondsworth, Penguin.

Holsti, K.J., 1974, *International Politics*, London, Prentice-Hall International.

Holsti, O.R., 1970, 'Individual Differences in Definition of the Situation', *Journal of Conflict Resolution*, vol. 14, pp. 303–10.

Holy Bible, 1986, New International Version, London, Hodder & Stoughton.

Hutton, W., 1992, 'Heated debate on road to Rio', *Guardian*, 18 May.

Hutton, W., 1995, 'Freedom to ignore our best interests', *Guardian*, 20 April, p. 10.

Hutton, W., 1995, *The State We're In*, London, Jonathan Cape.

Imber, M., 1993, 'Too many cooks? The Post-Rio Reform of the United Nations', *International Affairs*, vol. 69, pp. 55–70.

Jervis, R., 1976, *Perception and Misperception in International Relations*, Princeton, NJ, Princeton University Press.

Jones, R., 1970, *Analysing Foreign Policy*, London, Routledge.

Jones, W.S., 1991, *The Logic of International Relations*, New York, HarperCollins.

Kaplan, M.A., 1957, *System and Process in International Politics*, New York, John Wiley & Sons.

Kaplan, M.A., 1968, *New Approaches to International Relations*, New York, St Martin's Press.

Keegan, V., 1995, 'Thank heaven for foreign investment', *Guardian*, 7 August, p. 13.

Kegley, C.W. and Wittkopf, E.R., 1993, *World Politics*, New York, St Martin's Press.

Kennedy, P., 1989, *The Rise and Fall of the Great Powers*, London, Fontana.

Kennedy, P., 1993, *Preparing for the Twenty-First Century*, London, HarperCollins.

Keohane, R.O. and Nye, J.S., 1976, *Transnational Relations and World Politics*, Cambridge, Mass., Harvard University Press.

Knorr, K. and Rosenau, J.N., 1969, *Contending Approaches to International Politics*, Princeton, NJ, Princeton University Press.

Knorr, K. and Verba, S., 1961, *The International System: Theoretical Essays*, Princeton, NJ, Princeton University Press.

Kramer, F.A., 1973, *Perspectives on Public Bureaucracy*, Cambridge, Mass., Winthrop.

Krasner, S.D., 1972, 'Are Bureaucracies Important (or Allison Wonderland)?', *Foreign Policy*, vol. 7, pp. 159–79.

Lean, G., Crawshaw, S. and Doyle, L., 1995, 'Europe rises in protest at Shell dumping', *Independent on Sunday*, 18 June, p. 1.

Lenin, V.I., 1964, *Imperialism: The Highest Stage of Capitalism, Collected Works, Vol. 22*, Moscow, Progress Publishers.

Lindberg, L.N., 1963, *The Political Dynamics of European Economic Integration*, Stanford, California, Stanford University Press.

Lintner, V. and Mazey, S., 1991, *The European Community: Economic and Political Aspects*, London, McGraw-Hill.

Lodge, J. (ed.), 1993, *The European Community and the Challenge of the Future*, London, Pinter.

McGrew, A.G. and Lewis, P.G. *et al.*, 1992, *Global Politics*, Cambridge, Polity Press.

McGrew, A.G. and Wilson, M.J. (eds), 1982, *Decision-Making: Approaches and Analysis*, Manchester, Manchester University Press/Open University.

Macmillan, H., 1973, *At the End of the Day*, London, Macmillan.

Maidment, R. and McGrew, A., 1991, *The American Political Process*, London, Sage/Open University.

Mannheim, K., 1991, *Ideology–Utopia*, London, Routledge.

Mansbach, R.W., Ferguson, Y.H. and Lampart, D.E., 1976, *The Web of World Politics*, Englewood Cliffs, New Jersey, Prentice-Hall.

May, J., 1992, 'From Alpha to Omega: a Disaster Log, 1972–92', *Independent on Sunday* (supplement), 31 May.

Morgenthau, H.J., 1967, *Politics Among Nations*, New York, Alfred A. Knopf.

Morris, B., 1992, 'Wrestling with the octopus', *Independent on Sunday*, (Business supplement), 12 April, p. 4.

Morse, E.L., 1976, *Modernization and the Transformation of International Relations*, New York, Free Press.

Norgaard, R.B., 1994, *Development Betrayed*, London, Routledge.

Nugent, N., 1993, *The Government and Politics of the European Community*, London, Macmillan.

Oxfam/*Guardian*, 1992, *Earth*, London, Guardian Publications.

Patterson, W.C., 1983, *Nuclear Power*, Harmondsworth, Penguin/Pelican.

Perlmutter, A., 1974, 'The Presidential Center and Foreign Policy', *World Politics*, vol. 27, pp. 87–106.

Pick, D., 1993, *War Machine*, London, Yale University Press.

Porritt, J., 1992, *Save the Earth*, London, Dorling Kindersley.

Porter, B., (ed.), 1972, *The Aberystwyth Papers: International Politics 1919–1969*, London, Oxford University Press.

Pringle, P., 1990, 'How Bush Got to the Brink', *Independent on Sunday* (Supplement), 2 December.

Prins, G., 1990, 'Politics and the Environment', *International Affairs*, vol. 66, pp. 711–30.

Renner, M., 1993, 'Preparing for Peace' in Brown, L.R. *et al.*, *State of the World 1993*, London, Earthscan.

Reynolds, C., 1973, *Theory and Explanation in International Politics*, London, Martin Robertson.

Reynolds, P., 1978, *An Introduction to International Relations*, London, Longman.

Reynolds, P., 1979, 'Non-State Actors and International Outcomes', *British Journal of International Studies*, vol. 5, pp. 91–112.

Rich, V., 1994,'Why Belarus Matters', *World Today*, vol. 50, pp. 43–4.

Rosenau, J.N., 1969a, *International Politics and Foreign Policy*, New York, Free Press.

Rosenau, J.N., 1969b, *Linkage Politics: Essays on the Convergence of National and International Systems*, New York, Free Press.

Rosenau, J.N., 1974, *Comparing Foreign Policies*, New York, Sage/Halstead Press.

Rosenau, J.N., 1980, *The Scientific Study of Foreign Policy*, London, Frances Pinter.

Rosenau, J.N., Davies, V. and East, M.A., 1972, *The Analysis of International Politics*, New York, Free Press.

Sakwa, R., 1993, *Russian Politics and Society*, London, Routledge.

Scalapino, R.A., 1979, *The Foreign Policy of Modern Japan*, Berkeley, University of California Press.

Schelling, T., 1977, *Arms and Influence*, New Haven, Conn., Yale University Press.

Silber, L. and Little, A., 1995, *The Death of Yugoslavia*, London, Penguin/BBC Books.

Smith, A., 1993, *Russia and the World Economy*, London, Routledge.

Snyder, R.C., Bruck, H.W. and Sapin, B., 1963, *Foreign Policy Decision-Making*, New York, Free Press of Glencoe.

Spero, J.E., 1992, *The Politics of International Economic Relations*, London, Routledge.

Sterling, R.W., 1974, *Macropolitics – International Relations in a Global Society*, New York, Knopf.

Tanter, R. and Ullman, R.H., 1974, *Theory and Policy in International Relations*, Princeton, NJ, Princeton University Press.

Taylor, A.J.P., 1964, *The Origins of the Second World War*, Harmondsworth, Penguin.

Taylor, T. (ed.), 1978, *Approaches and Theory in International Relations*, London, Longman.

Thomas, H., 1970, *The Suez Affair*, Harmondsworth, Penguin.

Thurow, L., 1992, *Head to Head: The Coming Economic Battle Among Japan, Europe and America*, London, Nicholas Brealey Publishing.

Twose, N., 1985, *Cultivating Hunger*, Oxford, Oxfam.

Wallace, W., 1977, *The Foreign Policy Process in Britain*, London, RIIA/George Allen & Unwin.

Waltz, K.N., 1959, *Man, the State and War*, New York, Columbia University Press.

Waltz, K.N., 1979, *Theory of International Politics*, New York, Addison-Wesley.

Whitelegg, J., 1993, 'Dirty from the cradle to the grave', *Guardian* (Europe section), 30 July.

Wight, M., 1978, *Power Politics*, Leicester, Leicester University Press.

Williams, H., Wright, M. and Evans, T., 1993, *International Relations and Political Theory*, Buckingham, Open University Press.

Zaehner, R.C. (ed.), 1993, *The Hutchinson Encyclopedia of Living Faiths*, Oxford, Helicon.

Index

absolute poverty: definition of 110–11
ACP states, *see* European Union (less developed states) and Glossary
Adams, Gerry 35
Afghanistan: Soviet Union and 13–14, 122
AIDS 77–8, 123
Albania 239
Allaby, Michael 88, 91, 93
Allende, President 7, 61
Allison, G. 8, 40
Archangel 89
Argentina 11: calculations relating to Falklands/Malvinas conflict 207–8, 240
Armenian community in the USA 205
arms control 222–4, 232; definition of 222
arms sales 233
asbestos 83
Athens 86
Aziz, Tariq 158

Baker, James 158
balance of power 200; as a cause of war 208–9; as a preventor of war 224, 226–30, 232
Balkans: the Balkan wars in the former Yugoslavia 149, 196, 205–6, 212, 236, 252, 255; the Balkan wars and Article 51 of the UN Charter 241; the Balkan wars and US involvement 177–8; reasons for Serbian non-intervention during Croatia's attack on the Krajinan Serbs in 1995 225; recognition of Bosnian Republic 41–2;
Baltic States 149

Bangladesh 206, 247
Belarus 89, 149
blocking factors, *see* Change Map Factors
BNFL (British Nuclear Fuels Limited) 90
Bosnia, *see* Balkans and Yugoslavia
Bosnian Serbs, *see* Balkans
Boudicca 201
Brandt Reports 101, 108, 126–7; and European Union 189–90; lessons of 137; and reactions to 131, 137; on women and development 146
Britain: and Article 51 of the UN Charter 240; and attitude on EU common defence policy 179, 180; and the causes of the Falklands/Malvinas conflict 207–8, 235; and causes of relative economic decline 53–4; and Corfu Channel Case 239; cultural factors and economic competitiveness 49; and decision to seek EEC membership 19; and decline in power 22, 219; and failure to control ambitions of Nazi Germany prior to the Second World War 204; and impact of traditional liberalism on 52–4; and impact upon economy of multinational business corporations 64–6; and leaving of EMS 68; and motor vehicle accidents 82; as part of possible European global policeman 194; and pragmatic approach of Foreign Office 9; and regional impact of the EU single market 169, 192; and the 1956 Suez War 210, 219; US–UK defence officials' collaboration 9
van den Broek, Hans 158